Approaches to Teaching Woolf's *To the Lighthouse*

Approaches to Teaching
World Literature

Joseph Gibaldi, series editor

For a complete listing of titles,
see the last pages of this book.

Approaches to Teaching Woolf's *To the Lighthouse*

Edited by

Beth Rigel Daugherty

and

Mary Beth Pringle

The Modern Language Association of America
New York   2001

© 2001 by The Modern Language Association of America
All rights reserved
Printed in the United States of America

For information about obtaining permission to reprint material from
MLA book publications, send your request by mail (see address below),
e-mail (permissions@mla.org), or fax (646 458-0030).

Library of Congress Cataloging-in-Publication Data

Approaches to teaching Woolf's To the lighthouse /
edited by Beth Rigel Daugherty and Mary Beth Pringle.
p. cm. — (Approaches to teaching world literature)
Includes bibliographical references and index.
ISBN 0-87352-765-8 — ISBN 0-87352-766-6 (pbk.)
1. Woolf, Virginia, 1882–1941. To the lighthouse. 2. Woolf, Virginia,
1882–1941—Study and teaching. I. Daugherty, Beth Rigel.
II. Pringle, Mary Beth, 1943– III. Series.
PR6045.O72 T663 2001   823'.912—dc21   00-048022
ISSN 1059-1133

"What Teaching *To the Lighthouse* Taught Me about Reading
Virginia Woolf," by Louise DeSalvo, © 2001 by Louise DeSalvo

Cover illustration for the paperback edition: *To the Lighthouse II*,
by Joanne M. Stichweh, 1984. Used by permission of the artist

Set in Caledonia and Bodoni. Printed on recycled paper

Published by The Modern Language Association of America
26 Broadway, New York, New York 10004-1789
www.mla.org

CONTENTS

Intertextual Approaches

PREFACE TO THE SERIES

In *The Art of Teaching* Gilbert Highet wrote, "Bad teaching wastes a great deal of effort, and spoils many lives which might have been full of energy and happiness." All too many teachers have failed in their work, Highet argued, simply "because they have not thought about it." We hope that the Approaches to Teaching World Literature series, sponsored by the Modern Language Association's Publications Committee, will not only improve the craft—as well as the art—of teaching but also encourage serious and continuing discussion of the aims and methods of teaching literature.

The principal objective of the series is to collect within each volume different points of view on teaching a specific literary work, a literary tradition, or a writer widely taught at the undergraduate level. The preparation of each volume begins with a wide-ranging survey of instructors, thus enabling us to include in the volume the philosophies and approaches, thoughts and methods of scores of experienced teachers. The result is a sourcebook of material, information, and ideas on teaching the subject of the volume to undergraduates.

The series is intended to serve nonspecialists as well as specialists, inexperienced as well as experienced teachers, graduate students who wish to learn effective ways of teaching as well as senior professors who wish to compare their own approaches with the approaches of colleagues in other schools. Of course, no volume in the series can ever substitute for erudition, intelligence, creativity, and sensitivity in teaching. We hope merely that each book will point readers in useful directions; at most each will offer only a first step in the long journey to successful teaching.

Joseph Gibaldi
Series Editor

PREFACE TO THE VOLUME

Polly was a bright, well-read freshman whose strong opinions enlivened discussions all quarter long in the twentieth-century literature class I was teaching. Hardworking and energetic, she read all the assignments and wrote thoughtful papers. Her enthusiasm about literature was so contagious that she often convinced others less enthusiastic to give this or that writer a chance. She loved or at least liked *everything* we read in the class. Everything, that is, except *To the Lighthouse*. Not shy, she pushed me, day after day. "Good writing is supposed to be clear," she'd say. "Difficult is one thing; unclear is another. Some of these sentences are over a page long, and I'm not even sure they're grammatical!" "What's the point? None of this seems to be *saying* anything. Even when I'm not lost, I just don't get it—what is Woolf trying to say?" "Why are we reading this? Nothing hangs together. How can you call this a great novel?" Digging deep into my teaching kit, I used humor, small-group discussions, patience, provocative discussion questions, all sorts of background information, out-and-out argument, and reading advice. Because she was a good student, she stuck with it and eventually admitted she at least understood what Woolf was trying to do. But out in the hall after the final exam, she said, "I still don't get it, Dr. D. Why do you love *To the Lighthouse* so much?" Having already tried to answer that question repeatedly in class, I took another tack. "Polly, promise me something. Late this summer, after a good break, please read *To the Lighthouse* again." Although her face said, "Read it again? Are you kidding?" her mouth said, "OK. I'll try."

The first day of the next school year, she burst into my office, bubbling over at what she had discovered. She couldn't get over how "real" *To the Lighthouse* was, how beautiful, how intricately constructed. "How could I not have seen it?" she asked.

Polly taught Dr. D. three very important lessons. "Why are we reading this?" is a legitimate question, related to theoretical issues about how canons are built but also related to students' lives; the question deserves thoughtful and respectful answers. If good, motivated, well-read students can have trouble reading *To the Lighthouse*, not-so-well-read students can have even greater difficulty. And most important, never *ever* forget the wide gap between reading a book for the first time and reading it for the second. As Woolf says, "the book as a whole is different from the book received currently in separate phrases" ("How Should One" 267).

When we surveyed twentieth-century literature instructors (randomly selected by the MLA) and Virginia Woolf Society members, we discovered that when they must choose only one Woolf text, they often turn to her fifth novel as the one most representative of her genius. The 1989 Harvest-Harcourt paperback edition of *To the Lighthouse* (the edition chosen for this volume) sells over thirty thousand copies a year in the United States, and it is taught occasionally in high school, widely at all levels of the four-year undergraduate curriculum, and frequently at the graduate level. Why? Because, survey respondents reply, it is Woolf's most accessible novel, it grapples with issues students are interested in, "it is brilliant," "it is one of the most beautiful lyrical novels ever written," "it is a quintessential modernist novel," and "it allows one to confront both Woolf's art and her politics."

To the Lighthouse is taught in a wide variety of undergraduate classes. We expected to see it on syllabi for courses on modernism or twentieth-century literature, the novel, women's literature, feminist literary theory, or Woolf, but it also turned up on syllabi for introduction to literature or fiction courses, freshman composition and literature courses, writing courses (rhetoric, for example, or revising or creative), surveys (including those for world literature), general education, humanities, or distribution requirements, and thematic courses such as The Communal Meal in Literature, or Love and Sex in Literature, or Artists, Thinkers, Believers.

Instructors thus teach *To the Lighthouse* to a wide range of undergraduates—advanced majors, beginning majors, nonmajors, and various combinations of those three groups. No matter what type or level of student they teach, however, the majority of the seventy survey respondents said their most challenging teaching task was helping their students read and understand the novel. One instructor said her students found "simply decoding the sentences and pages" difficult, and another noted, "They must learn a new way of reading." Respondents repeatedly asked for practical, eclectic approaches informed by critical theory but not overwhelmed by it. These responses told us that veteran Woolf scholars in graduate seminars with students who are aware of swirling critical currents need very little advice on teaching *To the Lighthouse.* Rather, our primary obligations are to instructors new to teaching, new to translating critical theory into classroom strategy, or new to teaching this novel, as well as to instructors confronting a wide range of undergraduates reading Woolf for the first time. As a result, although all the contributions to this volume grow out of a critical framework and address critical issues, half of them focus first on how to *read* Woolf's *To the Lighthouse.*

Woolf, we believe, would agree with this emphasis. In her 1926 talk to students, "How Should One Read a Book?" she advises them to read "greedily and lavishly," even in the "rubbish-heap." Such wide reading is of first importance, Woolf maintains, and it provides context for the next step in a reader's development, comparing and contrasting texts as a preliminary to evaluating them. Only when students are "laden with questions and suggestions won honestly in the course of [their] own reading" should they turn to the critics (269). Become readers, she suggests, before turning to the critics, and certainly before *becoming* critics.

Like us, Woolf was a teacher. Only from 1905 through 1907, true, but her work at Morley College, where she taught working-class adults English literature, history, and composition, coincided with the publication of her first essays and probably contributed to her lifelong concern and respect for the common reader (Daugherty, "Virginia Woolf"). Because she had seen and experienced both the barriers erected by the lack of an education and the harm "heavily furred and gowned" authorities could do, she insisted that readers, including working-class men, not allow anyone to block their access to literature. Trespass, she said. Literature belongs to no one, certainly not to just one class or the educated; it is everyone's ("How Should One" 258; "Leaning Tower" 181).

In putting together this volume, we and our contributors have operated from the same premise: Woolf belongs to everyone, including undergraduates who perceive her work as difficult. Refusing to listen to the Tansleys who would say, "Students can't read, students can't write," these teachers recommend *To the Lighthouse* and assume students can and will read it, see its relation to their lives, and confront the various questions it raises. Implicit in this attitude is a deep respect for students that parallels Woolf's respect for the reader, a respect that demands active, intelligent reading because it is possible and also gladly answers the question, "How should one read this book?" Implicit as well is an underlying belief about why we teach literature: because literature can help our students live lives "full of energy and happiness" (Highet 6).

We begin by thanking our survey respondents. As editors, we were blessed with dedicated teachers who took the time to answer our questionnaire with care and in voluminous detail; their teaching expertise was palpable. We appreciate, too, our contributors' enthusiastic willingness to share their classrooms and methods with us; they have patiently worked to fit their ideas and skills into this volume's overall framework. We also want to thank Louise De-Salvo for suggesting this project; Patti Rothermich, Mary Ellen Armentrout, and Allen Reichert at Courtright Memorial Library and Mel Ankeny at the Ohio State University Library for their cheerful persistence in the face of numerous puzzles; and Aaron Thompson for his computer expertise. Beth wants to thank Otterbein College and its English department for their support, Mary Beth for her knowledge of and patience in collaboration, and Gary for his creation of her "room." Mary Beth wants to thank Wright State University, her colleagues in the Department of English Language and Literatures, and, in particular, the College of Liberal Arts, for a research grant. She also thanks Beth for the joy of working with her and her family for its ever-generous support.

We thank the Modern Language Association and its Publications Committee for its dedication to this series, Joseph Gibaldi for his patient guidance, Alicia

Mahaney Minsky for her editorial suggestions early on, and Sonia Kane for subsequent assistance. We appreciate Susan Dick's taking the time to read and comment on the "Editions" section, and we want to thank Vicki Austin and Sarah Longstaff of Harcourt for sharing copyright and sales information about *To the Lighthouse* early in this project. Since then, Todd Rupp, a Harcourt sales representative; Diane Gillespie, of Washington State University; Don LePan, of Broadview Press in Canada; and Jeremy Crow, of the Society of Authors, have been instrumental in providing us with accurate information about current copyright laws. We also want to acknowledge the helpful comments of our consultant readers, and to thank the MLA copyeditors who commented on the final manuscript. We are grateful to Lori, Barb, Mildred, Judy, and Lana at Garner's 76 Auto/Truck Stop (now TA Travel Center, Country Pride Restaurant); they provided us with a "room" midway between Columbus and Dayton, supplied us with food and bottomless cups of coffee, and never once suggested, by word or deed, that the two academics completing a book on teaching Woolf's *To the Lighthouse* in the midst of truckers grabbing a bite of lunch might be a little odd. They evidently agree with Woolf, who said that to produce books, writers need space, good food, conversation with one's peers and about one's heritage, and, most important, the knowledge that "our relation is to the world of reality" (*Room* 114). Our deepest gratitude, though, goes to students, those who gave us permission to quote their unpublished writing and those who bring us back to reality by asking the basic and most important questions: "Why read? Why read *this*? OK, but *how*?"

BRD and MBP

Part One

MATERIALS

Introduction

An instructor preparing to teach *To the Lighthouse* faces many external constraints: the academic calendar, a classroom's physical and technological nature, class size, student background, institutional ethos, departmental and institutional expectations for the course, and on and on. Within those constraints, the instructor faces several important choices: Which text of the novel should I use? How much time should I spend on it? What should come before and after it? What kind of assignments should I make and how many? What skills do I want students to learn and practice? Any teaching veteran knows that the pedagogical situation and these practical decisions limit the kind and number of materials used.

Instructors teaching this novel for the first time want, we assume, materials that will enrich their own knowledge and be useful to undergraduates. The sheer amount of material available on Woolf and on *To the Lighthouse*, however, can be daunting—where does one start? Using survey responses, as well as conversations with Woolf scholars and our own teaching experience, we have tried to give instructors a place to start and yet also provide an overview of the numerous materials available.

Editions

In the United States, the first question—Which edition of *To the Lighthouse* should I use?—has been answered for instructors. For many years, the only paperback edition available was the 1955 Harvest edition published by Harcourt. This edition, based on the 1927 first American edition, had the same pagination as the original and had never gone out of print. When Harcourt celebrated Woolf's hundredth birthday in 1982 by publishing a centenary edition of *To the Lighthouse*, the original American text was not changed, but it was reformatted, creating different pagination, and a foreword by Eudora Welty was added. Seven years later, Harcourt replaced its mass-market-sized Harvest paperback edition with a trade paperback reprint of this centenary edition, a change Woolf scholars were neither consulted nor happy about. This *To the Lighthouse* is the only paperback edition available for classroom use in the United States. Originally slated to come out of copyright in 2002, seventy-five years after publication, *To the Lighthouse* is now under copyright in the United States until 2022, in conformity with the Sonny Bono Copyright Extension Act signed into law in October 1998. (Under this act, works with a publication date of 1923 or earlier, such as Woolf's *The Voyage Out* and *Jacob's Room*, are out of copyright and in the public domain; works with a publication date of 1924 or later, such as Woolf's *Mrs. Dalloway* and *To the Lighthouse*, have had copyright protection extended for twenty years and thus remain under copyright until ninety-five years after publication.) For these reasons, we have chosen the 1989 Harvest–Harcourt paperback edition for this volume.

In England, the situation is more complicated, partly because of a brief span of time in which the English edition of Woolf's works went into public domain (1992–95). In 1990, the Hogarth Press issued what they called the definitive edition, and Vintage (UK) brought it out in paperback in 1992, but "definitive" is a misnomer for this novel: no scholar reexamined or edited the text for the Vintage *To the Lighthouse*, although it does include a list of variants between the English and American first editions at the back. A Penguin paperback, based on the first English edition, edited by Stella McNichol and introduced by Hermione Lee, became available in England in 1992, as did an Oxford World's Classics paperback, edited and with an introduction by Margaret Drabble (see J. Marcus, "Embarrassment of Riches," and J. Johnson for more information about the Penguin and Oxford editions). In addition, Routledge issued a paperback for its English Texts series in 1994; based on the first English edition, it is edited, introduced, and commented on by Sandra Kemp. In 1996, however, copyright legislation for the European Community not only extended copyright protection in England from fifty years to seventy years after the death of the author but also brought works that had gone into the public domain under the earlier law back into copyright. In England, then, all Woolf's works are back under copyright through 2011.

In Canada, Woolf's works are now out of copyright since copyright restrictions there do not extend beyond fifty years after the death of the author. Instructors in Canada may choose from among several editions; the major ones are the Penguin, the Oxford, and the Harvest–Harcourt paperback editions. Instructors wanting the text with the least apparatus should choose the Harvest–Harcourt edition since only the Eudora Welty foreword has been added to what readers would have read in 1927. Instructors wanting biographical information, a short introduction to the text, a list of variations between the first English and first American editions, a short, easy-to-read bibliography, and only a few footnotes at the end should choose the Oxford edition. The Penguin edition has the most apparatus, with a much longer introduction, a facsimile of the title page of the first English edition, a bibliography more focused on the novel, and many more footnotes. It, too, has an appendix listing variant readings between the two first editions; even more important to scholars, another appendix lists Stella McNichol's sometimes substantive emendations to the first English edition.

Scholars working with the English and American editions of *To the Lighthouse* have discovered sometimes substantial differences between the two, generating discussion about what the text of *To the Lighthouse* really is. According to Susan Dick, the editor of Blackwell's Shakespeare Head Press edition, deciding the answer to that question in the usual way—choosing between the English and American editions on the basis of Woolf's final intentions—is impossible since Woolf's proofreading process muddied those intentions: Woolf gave her stamp of approval to two different sets of proofs that then became two different first editions published on the same day, 5 May 1927. From the diary and letter evidence Dick traces, Woolf received two sets of galley proofs from the printer, one set destined for Hogarth and English readers, the other for Harcourt and American readers; she seems to have sometimes corrected the two sets of proofs together and other times corrected them separately, completing all revisions for both publishers in about a month. Based on the evidence of the revised proofs for the American edition discovered in the Frances Hooper Collection at Smith College and on the differences between the English and American editions, it appears that Woolf sometimes made exactly the same changes to both sets of proofs. More often, however, she did not. Further complicating the matter, Woolf's American printers sometimes misinterpreted the changes she made on the proofs or made corrections Woolf had not authorized. Thus, when Susan Dick had to choose the copy-text on which to base her edition of *To the Lighthouse*, she chose neither the edition familiar to American readers nor the one familiar to English readers but the one "based on the certainty of [Woolf's] intentions," that is, the proofs Woolf corrected for the first American edition (xxx–xxxvii). Dick reasons that since Woolf's revising process indicates a cavalier attitude about "final" intentions and since no revised proofs for the first English edition have been discovered, the revised proofs we *do* have take precedence (see Briggs, "Editing" 69, for some criticism of this decision, however).

Instructors interested in creating classroom discussions and activities around such textual questions, differences in editions, or Woolf's revising process can consult several sources. The publishing history of *To the Lighthouse* can be traced in B. J. Kirkpatrick and Stuart N. Clarke's exhaustive *A Bibliography of Virginia Woolf*, fourth edition. Woolf's *To the Lighthouse* manuscript is available on microfilm (*The Virginia Woolf Manuscripts: From the Henry W. and Albert A. Berg Collection at the New York Public Library*, reel 7) and in Susan Dick's transcription (To the Lighthouse: *The Original Holograph Draft*). James Haule's transcriptions of Woolf's typescript and Charles Mauron's translation of an early version of "Time Passes," published as "Le temps passe" in the French periodical *Commerce* a year before the novel was published, appear in *Twentieth Century Literature*, and Haule's study of Woolf's revisions, *"To the Lighthouse* and the Great War: The Evidence of Virginia Woolf's Revisions of 'Time Passes,'"* appears in Mark Hussey's *Virginia Woolf and War: Fiction, Reality, and Myth*. United States instructors can examine the English edition of Woolf's novel in the Everyman Library hardcover edition (published in the United States through an arrangement with Harcourt), introduced by Julia Briggs. They can also consult *Major Authors on CD-ROM: Virginia Woolf*, edited by Hussey and available from Primary Source Media or in major university libraries; this resource brings together all Woolf's published works, in both the English and the American editions, many of the manuscripts, and Hussey's

Virginia Woolf A to Z reference work. They can also find a list of variants between the American and English editions in *A Concordance to* To the Lighthouse (Haule and Smith). Susan Dick's Shakespeare Head Press edition of *To the Lighthouse* lists the variants between the two editions, includes a long passage about James's memories of his parents that Woolf cut in the proofs, pieces together what seems to have been Woolf's revising process, and provides a careful rationale for the choice of copy-text, but the edition is available only through Blackwell Publishers in Canada and Great Britain. However, United States readers can find the introduction and rationale to the Shakespeare Head Press edition in volume 3 of *Virginia Woolf: Critical Assessments* (McNees). Finally, those interested in contemporary theoretical discussions of textual criticism should consult Brenda Silver's "Textual Criticism as Feminist Practice; or, Who's Afraid of Virginia Woolf, Part II." Although not specifically about *To the Lighthouse*, this essay discusses what happens to the notion of a stable text and to Woolf's texts in particular once readers become aware of the many drafts and versions of those texts.

Further Reading for Students

By far the most common response to our question, What other reading related to *To the Lighthouse* do you ask students to do? was some version of "I don't." One survey respondent comments, "I want them to confront the texts on their own," and another instructor asserts, "Too much theory kills Virginia Woolf." Another warns against the danger of giving students "the impression that modern, experimental works require weighty elucidative aids—as though the works cannot speak directly for themselves," and several warn against studies that "try to sum up Virginia Woolf's art in terms of her mental health."

When instructors do assign supplemental reading, they prefer to send students first to Woolf's multivolume *Diary* and *Letters* (in both cases, the third volume), where Woolf discusses planning and writing the novel, and then to other primary works by Woolf: "The best way to read Woolf is to read more Woolf." Several instructors recommend *Mrs. Dalloway*, while another suggests *Between the Acts* because of its emphasis on time, history, and the individual. Still others note that Woolf's short stories are good "finger exercises" for reading her novels. Particularly helpful are "Kew Gardens," "The Mark on the Wall," "An Unwritten Novel," "Moments of Being: 'Slater's Pins Have No Points,'" and "The Introduction," all in *The Complete Shorter Fiction of Virginia Woolf*. James Holt McGavran, Jr., suggests that undergraduates read Woolf's nonfiction in conjunction with her fiction (8–9), and many instructors agree. Some use *Three Guineas*, and many use *A Room of One's Own* or "A Sketch of the Past" in *Moments of Being*. Others pair *To the Lighthouse* with individual essays from the four-volume set of *Collected Essays*: "Mr. Bennett and Mrs. Brown" in volume 1, "Modern Fiction," "Evening over Sussex," "The Narrow Bridge of Art," "The Leaning Tower," "The Art of Fiction," "Professions for Women," and "How Should One Read a Book?" in volume 2, and "Thoughts of Peace during an Air Raid" in volume 4. *The Virginia Woolf Reader* brings together a variety of Woolf's fiction and nonfiction for classroom use, including some letters and diary entries, but instructors need to be aware that some of the selections are excerpts.

Instructors occasionally incorporate secondary materials by handing out a selected bibliography, putting materials on reserve, using them in their own minilectures, asking students to report on critical articles, or teaching a particular critical conflict through a small set of representative essays. One instructor has students compare their bibliography of 1960s and 1970s criticism on the novel to her list of 1980s and 1990s criticism to show them how it has changed.

Instructors agree that the early collections of essays centered on *To the Lighthouse*, such as *Twentieth Century Interpretations of* To the Lighthouse (Vogler) and *Virginia Woolf*: To the Lighthouse, A Casebook (Beja), are still useful to students, and they point out that Harold Bloom's casebook, *Virginia Woolf's* To the Lighthouse, includes more recent essays but strips them of their critical apparatus. Other books and essays often mentioned as useful for undergraduates are the biography by Susan Gorsky in the Twayne series, updated in 1989; John Lehmann's *Virginia Woolf and Her World*; Mark Hussey's *Virginia Woolf A to Z*; Dorrit Cohn's "Narrated Monologue"; Thomas Matro's "Only Relations: Vision and Achievement in *To the Lighthouse*"; Jane Lilienfeld's groundbreaking essays on the Ramsays, "'The Deceptiveness of Beauty': Mother Love and Mother Hate in *To the Lighthouse*" and "Where the Spear Plants Grew: The Ramsays' Marriage in *To the Lighthouse*"; Elizabeth Abel's "'Cam the Wicked': Woolf's Portrait of the Artist as Her Father's Daughter"; and Beth Rigel Daugherty's "'There She Sat': The Power of the Feminist Imagination in *To the Lighthouse*."

Finally, instructors indicate that they like to show students how Woolf has influenced contemporary writers. General influence can be seen in Margaret Drabble's "Virginia Woolf: A Personal Debt," Alice Walker's "In Search of Our Mothers' Gardens," and Jeanette Winterson's *Art Objects: Essays on Ecstasy and Effrontery*, to name just a few. Two specific examples of *To the Lighthouse*'s influence can be seen in George Ella Lyon's poem "Lighthouse" and in Thomas Beller's short story "A Different Kind of Imperfection," in which Alexander searches for his father's inner life by examining the man's underlinings in Woolf's novel. Students interested in finding other connections between *To the Lighthouse* and contemporary literature or popular culture should consult the "Passing Glances" section of the International Virginia Woolf Society annual bibliography (see the Web site at www.utoronto .ca/IVWS).

Hours in a Library

Reference Works, Bibliographies, and Resources

Mark Hussey's *Virginia Woolf A to Z* is subtitled *A Comprehensive Reference*, and it is. Alphabetically organized entries, superb cross-referencing, an alphabetical and a topical list of works cited, and a thorough index make this compendium of information about the works, characters, allusions, family, times, and criticism easy to use. Instructors with time to consult only one bibliographic resource should choose this one. Other specialized bibliographies include *Virginia Woolf: An Annotated Bibliography of Criticism, 1915–1974*, by Robin Majumdar; *Virginia Woolf: A Guide to Research*, by Thomas Jackson Rice; the *Modern Fiction Studies* bibliographies in 1956, 1972, and 1992, by Maurice Beebe, Barbara Weiser, and Laura Sue Fuderer, respectively; the *Index to the Virginia Woolf Miscellany, 1973-1998*, by Laura Moss Gottlieb; and the yearly bibliography by the International Virginia Woolf Society (see the society's Web site, given above).

To find current secondary materials on *To the Lighthouse*, instructors should of course consult the annual *MLA Bibliography* and the *Year's Work in English Studies*, but they may also want to look at some publications devoted solely to Woolf criticism: the *Selected Papers* of the Annual Conference on Virginia Woolf; the *Woolf Studies Annual*; and *Virginia Woolf Miscellany*. In addition, special Virginia Woolf issues were published by *Modern Fiction Studies* in 1972 and 1992 (Jones).

Critical Reception

Instructors wanting to trace this novel's reception for themselves should consult *Virginia Woolf: The Critical Heritage* (Majumdar and McLaurin), particularly for its sampling of early reviews, and volume 3 of the four-volume *Virginia Woolf: Critical Assessments* (McNees). Essays on *To the Lighthouse* in early collections of essays on Woolf give the instructor an overview of Woolf criticism at the time. See "Art in *To the Lighthouse*," by Ruby Cohn and "Never Say 'I': *To the Lighthouse* as Vision and Confession," by Ruth Temple, from the early 1970s, for example, and "Private and Public Consciousness in *Mrs. Dalloway* and *To the Lighthouse*," by Tori Haring-Smith, and "Speech Acts in *To the Lighthouse*," by Mary Libertin, from the early 1980s.

Critics providing summaries of the critical reaction to this novel include Suzanne Raitt, who in *Virginia Woolf's* To the Lighthouse (in St. Martin's Critical Studies of Key Texts series) concisely surveys the novel's reception (10–19), and Su Reid, who in *To the Lighthouse* (a volume in the Critics Debate series) surveys and evaluates early reviews; literary histories; New Critical, mythological, and Freudian readings; aesthetic and narrative theories; and feminist and biographical interpretations (9–78). Mark Hussey discusses critical responses to the novel at length in *Virginia Woolf A to Z*, and Jane Goldman selects representative excerpts and essays for a decade-by-decade discussion of critical frameworks in the Icon Critical Guides volume *Virginia Woolf: To the Lighthouse; The Waves*.

This volume's inclusion in the MLA's Approaches to Teaching World Literature series indicates how the overall critical reception of Virginia Woolf has changed, although, as Brenda Silver points out in "Retro-Anger and Baby-Boomer Nostalgia: A Polemical Talk," Woolf's position in the canon is still not secure. During Woolf's lifetime, her reputation shifted several times, from critically noticed (with small sales) to critically praised (with larger sales) to critically attacked (steady sales). Many of her contemporaries identified *To the Lighthouse* as her best novel, and most of their criticism, whether positive or negative, focused on her technique and style. After her death, with F. R. Leavis ruling the British critical scene (Batchelor concisely describes the *Scrutiny* animus against Woolf at that time [23–25]) and the New Critics ruling the American one, Woolf was generally denigrated as an aesthete and her work labeled minor.

Through Leonard Woolf's efforts, her work remained in print, and several studies also kept it in public view in the 1940s and 1950s. The best of these studies are still useful, though dated, such as Bernard Blackstone's *Virginia Woolf: A Commentary* and James Hafley's examination of Henri Bergson's theories about time and their relation to Woolf's prose, in *The Glass Roof: Virginia Woolf as Novelist*. Work done on *To the Lighthouse* at this time, such as Erich Auerbach's famous "The Brown Stocking" or Joseph Blotner's classic "Mythic Patterns in *To the Lighthouse*," focused mainly on formal features of the narrative or on mythic underpinnings.

As Leonard Woolf continued to select, compile, and publish more of Virginia Woolf's work, including *A Writer's Diary* in 1954, the criticism began to take a subtle turn. In Jean Guiguet's *Virginia Woolf and Her Works*, a philosophical study that one survey respondent calls "the single best piece of criticism of Woolf's fiction I've read" and that other respondents cite as still the place to begin any serious study of Woolf, Guiguet keeps Woolf's "life and art connected." Woolf critics have been connecting the personal and the aesthetic ever since, sometimes to attack her reputation but more often to elevate it.

The largest single influence on the critical reception of Woolf in general and *To the Lighthouse* in particular was the willingness of Woolf's literary executors to make her papers available, a willingness that made connecting Woolf's life and art possible—and contested. The family constructed an "official" version of Virginia Woolf, which has occasionally caused tension between executors and scholars (see J. Marcus, "Pathographies"). But Woolf's family also, in contrast to the executors for many other modern writers, made it possible for critics to question that official version: the family collected and published many of her works after her death, made her papers available, and gave scholars permission to publish unpublished work. As a result, as Woolf scholars examine her published work, they can consult manuscripts, diaries, letters, reading notebooks, and many other materials unpublished in her lifetime; what's more, much of this material is now available to a larger audience. The publication of key primary texts—*Collected Essays* (*selected* is a more accurate word), *The Letters of Virginia Woolf*, *The Diary of Virginia Woolf*, *Moments of Being*, *The Complete Shorter Fiction of Virginia Woolf*, four volumes of a projected six in *The Essays of Virginia Woolf* (truly collected), and *A Passionate Apprentice: The Early Journals, 1897–1909*—has had enormous impact on the reception, interpretation, and teaching of Woolf's works.

During the 1950s and 1960s, as many an older feminist critic can attest, few students read Woolf in either undergraduate or graduate classes. From our vantage point, such a dismissal seems part of the general "gendering of modernism" noted by Bonnie Kime Scott. Florence Howe's comparison of Eliot's and Woolf's reputations in "T. S. Eliot, Virginia Woolf, and the Future of 'Tradition'" also notes this bias. All those attitudes changed, however, as feminist scholars converged on Woolf's manuscripts in the Henry W. and Albert A. Berg Collection at the New York Public Library and in the British Library and at Sussex University in England in the 1970s and 1980s, resulting in an explosion of scholarship. (On 12 March 1979, the *New Yorker* even printed a James Stevenson cartoon of a bookshop with only books by and about Woolf in it!) Quentin Bell's biography appeared in 1972; centenaries were celebrated in England and the United States in 1982; manuscript transcriptions were published, including To the Lighthouse: *The Original Holograph Draft* in 1982; special Virginia Woolf issues of journals appeared, including those in the *Bulletin of the New York Public Library* and *Women's Studies* in 1977 (M. Moore) and those in the *Bulletin of Research in the Humanities* and *Twentieth Century Literature* in 1979 (Ruotolo); and the collections and critical studies just kept coming and coming.

Most influential, as repeatedly noted by survey respondents, are the collections edited by Jane Marcus in the 1980s: *New Feminist Essays on Virginia Woolf*, *Virginia Woolf: A Feminist Slant*, and *Virginia Woolf and Bloomsbury: A Centenary Celebration*. Indeed, the influence on Woolf studies of the feminist critics Jane Marcus, Louise DeSalvo (*Virginia Woolf: The Impact of Childhood Sexual Abuse on Her Life and Work*), Jane Lilienfeld, Susan Squier (*Virginia Woolf and London: The Sexual Politics of the City*), and Brenda Silver (*Virginia Woolf's Reading Notebooks*) simply cannot be measured. Their transcriptions, essays, and books have changed Woolf's image from that of the traumatized aesthete focused on subjective experience, the traditional British view, as John Mepham points out (*Criticism* 25), to that of the courageous, socially aware cultural critic.

As the 1980s drew to a close, Toril Moi's challenge to American materialist feminists in *Sexual/Textual Politics* to engage with French feminist theory was taking hold. The resulting juxtapositions of psychoanalytic, narrative, postmodern, and/or postcolonial theory with feminist theory have raised questions about Anglo-American feminism and Woolf's place in it as a foremother. In Woolf studies, this contentious yet fruitful conjunction of feminism and theory can be seen most clearly in Makiko Minow-Pinkney's *Virginia Woolf and the Problem of the Subject*, Rachel Bowlby's *Feminist Destinations and Further Essays on Virginia Woolf*, and Pamela L. Caughie's *Virginia Woolf and Postmodernism: Literature in Quest and Question of Itself*. Woolf studies in the 1990s were marked by close attention to Woolf's attitudes about fascism and empire as well as about ethnicity and class (see, e.g., Emery's "'Robbed of Meaning': The Work at the Center of *To the Lighthouse*"), while interest in gender, narrative, and overall historical and cultural context remains high. For two examples of the latter, see Melba Cuddy-Keane, Natasha Aleksiuto, Kay Li, Morgan Love, Chris Rose, and Andrea Williams in "The Heteroglossia of History, Part One: The Car" and Jane Marcus in "Registering Objections: Grounding Feminist Alibis."

Two sources that put the current diverse and complex reception of Woolf into context are John Mepham's *Criticism in Focus: Virginia Woolf* and Clare Hanson's *Virginia Woolf*. Mepham describes realist, Marxist, psychoanalytic, modernist, feminist, existentialist, and poststructuralist approaches, among others, and Hanson clarifies current divisions among feminist critical positions in her introduction. And finally, Julia Briggs, writing from a British perspective, provides a summary of reactions to Woolf and her work over the decades and on both sides of the Atlantic in "The Story So Far," and Jane Marcus, writing from an American perspective, summarizes recent permutations of the British and American versions of Virginia Woolf in "A Tale of Two Cultures."

Backgrounds and Foregrounds

Assuming, as one survey respondent points out, that "most beginning teachers are under great time constraints and cannot become overnight experts on Woolf or this novel," we have tried to limit our recommendations to a representative and suggestive list rather than an exhaustive and definitive one. (Works mentioned in the previous sections are also recommended, though they are not named again here.) Our categories are also not definitive but, instead, representative of the contexts within which Woolf material can most easily be found. We have arranged the information within these categories so that it ranges from the most general to the most specific: background or contextual works, if any, first; then works on Woolf; and finally, works that foreground *To the Lighthouse*.

Modernism

The classic sourcebook for information on modernism is *The Modern Tradition*, edited by Richard Ellmann and Charles Feidelson; useful background can be found in Robert Hughes's *Shock of the New*, Malcolm Bradbury and James

McFarlane's *Modernism 1890–1930*, and Peter Nicholls's *Modernisms: A Literary Guide*; and nine essays on the topic have been collected by Michael Levenson in *The Cambridge Companion to Modernism*. Committed to looking once again at the question, What is (or was) modernism? are Astradur Eysteinsson's *The Concept of Modernism*, Matei Calinescu's *Five Faces of Modernity: Modernism, Avant-Garde, Decadence, Kitsch, Postmodernism*, and Sanford Schwartz's "The Postmodernity of Modernism." Paul Fussell's *The Great War and Modern Memory* was one of the first studies to capture the horror of World War I and its effect on male writers, and Michael Levenson's *The Genealogy of Modernism: A Study of English Literary Doctrine, 1908–1922* reflects the more traditional view of modernism, with Woolf barely appearing.

Studies that correct this masculine slant and include Woolf are "History as Suppressed Referent in Modernist Fiction" and *Rich and Strange: Gender, History, Modernism*, by Marianne DeKoven; *The Gender of Modernism*, edited by Bonnie Kime Scott; *Rereading Modernism: New Directions in Feminist Criticism*, edited by Lisa Rado; the three-volume *No Man's Land*, by Sandra Gilbert and Susan Gubar; and "The Asylums of Antaeus: Women, War, and Madness," by Jane Marcus. *Virginia Woolf in the Age of Mechanical Reproduction*, a collection of essays edited by Pamela L. Caughie, situates Woolf within a global and technological modernism. For a revisionist study of modernism that includes a chapter on *To the Lighthouse*, see Perry Meisel's *The Myth of the Modern: British Literature and Criticism after 1850*.

Postmodernism

For general studies, see Andreas Huyssen's *After the Great Divide: Modernism, Mass Culture, Postmodernism*; Linda Hutcheon's *A Poetics of Postmodernism: History, Theory, Fiction*; Silvio Gaggi's *Modern/Postmodern: A Study in Twentieth-Century Art and Ideas*; Brian McHale's *Postmodernist Fiction*; Jean-François Lyotard's *The Postmodern Condition*; the collection of essays called *Feminism/Postmodernism*, edited by Linda J. Nicholson; and *Postmodernism and the Re-reading of Modernity*, edited by Francis Barker, Peter Hulme, and Margaret Iverson. For work more directly related to Woolf, see Bonnie Kime Scott's *Refiguring Modernism* (vol. 1: *Women of 1928*; vol. 2: *Postmodern Feminist Readings of Woolf, West, and Barnes*); Patricia Ondek Laurence's poststructuralist study, *The Reading of Silence: Virginia Woolf in the English Tradition*; and Pamela L. Caughie's *Virginia Woolf and Postmodernism*. Geoffrey Hartman examines *To the Lighthouse* from an early deconstructionist perspective in "Virginia's Web," and Gayatri C. Spivak, in "Unmaking and Making in *To the Lighthouse*," J. Hillis Miller, in "Mr. Carmichael and Lily Briscoe: The Rhythm of Creativity in *To the Lighthouse*," and Bill Martin, in "*To the Lighthouse* and the Feminist Path to Postmodernity," all examine Woolf's novel through a postmodern lens. In addition, Patricia Waugh has a chapter on Woolf and one on reading *To the Lighthouse* in her *Practising Postmodernism / Reading Modernism*.

Postcolonialism

For background and a general introduction to the issues associated with post-colonialism, see *The Post-colonial Studies Reader*, edited by Bill Ashcroft, Gareth Griffiths, and Helen Tiffin; their *The Empire Writes Back: Theory and Practice in Post-colonial Literature*; and *Nation and Narration*, edited by Homi K. Bhabha. Kathy Phillips's *Virginia Woolf against Empire* locates an imperial critique throughout Woolf's works, and the exchange between Jane Marcus ("Britannia Rules *The Waves*") and Patrick McGee ("The Politics of Modernist Form; or, Who Rules *The Waves*?") has generated a great deal of discussion about Woolf's anti-imperialism. For an essay on *To the Lighthouse* within this framework, see Janet Winston's "'Something out of Harmony': *To the Lighthouse* and the Subject(s) of Empire," and for an essay that includes *To the Lighthouse* within a larger discussion of the global Virginia Woolf, see Susan Stanford Friedman's "Geopolitical Literacy: Internationalizing Feminism at 'Home'—The Case of Virginia Woolf." See also *Virginia Woolf International* (Chapman), a special issue of the *South Carolina Review*.

Historical and Social Context

For information and sources on Woolf's Victorian background and her relation to it, see Janis Paul's *The Victorian Heritage of Virginia Woolf: The External World in Her Novels*, Katherine Hill's "Virginia Woolf and Leslie Stephen: History and Literary Revolution," Alison Booth's *Greatness Engendered: George Eliot and Virginia Woolf*, and Gillian Beer's *Virginia Woolf: The Common Ground*. For information and sources on Woolf's own social and historical context, see the collection of essays edited by Wayne K. Chapman and Janet M. Manson, *Women in the Milieu of Leonard and Virginia Woolf: Peace, Politics, and Education*. Alex Zwerdling's *Virginia Woolf and the Real World* is often cited by survey respondents for its wealth of contextual background and its particularly good chapter on *To the Lighthouse*, and Michael Tratner's *Modernism and Mass Politics* includes a chapter on working-class women in *To the Lighthouse* and other modern texts. Christina Hauck's "'To Escape the Horror of Family Life': Virginia Woolf and the British Birth Control Debate," Kate Flint's "Virginia Woolf and the General Strike," Mark Hussey's "*To the Lighthouse* and Physics: The Cosmology of David Bohm and Virginia Woolf," and Megumi Kato's "The Politics/Poetics of Motherhood in *To the Lighthouse*" provide other kinds of social context for Woolf's novel.

Feminist or Materialist Perspectives

To develop a sense of early feminist discussions of Woolf's work, instructors should begin with Sandra Gilbert and Susan Gubar's *The Madwoman in the Attic*, Carolyn Heilbrun's *Toward a Recognition of Androgyny*, and Elaine Showalter's *A Literature of Their Own*. For examples of feminism intersecting with theory, see *New French Feminisms: An Anthology*, edited by Elaine

Marks and Isabelle de Courtivron; Patricia Waugh's *Feminine Fictions: Revisiting the Postmodern*; Chris Weedon's *Feminist Practice and Poststructuralist Theory*; and Mary Lydon's *Skirting the Issue: Essays in Literary Theory*.

Books examining Woolf and her work from a feminist perspective include Herbert Marder's *Feminism and Art: A Study of Virginia Woolf*, the earliest such study; Nancy Topping Bazin's influential *Virginia Woolf and the Androgynous Vision*; Ellen Rosenman's *The Invisible Presence: Virginia Woolf and the Mother-Daughter Relationship*; Jane Marcus's *Virginia Woolf and the Languages of Patriarchy*; and Madeline Moore's *The Short Season between Two Silences: The Mystical and the Political in the Novels of Virginia Woolf*.

Many essays have been published about *To the Lighthouse* as a feminist novel. The classics among them are Annis Pratt's "Sexual Imagery in *To the Lighthouse*: A New Feminist Approach," Sally Alexander Brett's "No, Mrs. Ramsay: Feminist Dilemma in *To the Lighthouse*," Margaret Homans's "Postscript: Mothers and Daughters in Virginia Woolf's Victorian Novel," Joan Lidoff's "Virginia Woolf's Feminine Sentence: The Mother-Daughter World of *To the Lighthouse*," Evelyn Haller's "The Anti-Madonna in the Work and Thought of Virginia Woolf," Anne Hoffman's "Demeter and Poseidon: Fusion and Distance in *To the Lighthouse*," Carolyn Heilbrun's "*To the Lighthouse*: The New Story of Mother and Daughter," and Jane Lilienfeld's, "'Like a Lion Seeking Whom He Could Devour': Domestic Violence in *To the Lighthouse*." Some more recent feminist interpretations include Laura Doyle's "'These Emotions of the Body': Intercorporeal Narrative in *To the Lighthouse*" and Susan Bennett Smith's "Reinventing Grief Work: Virginia Woolf's Feminist Representations of Mourning in *Mrs. Dalloway* and *To the Lighthouse*." Maggie Humm examines *To the Lighthouse* from a French feminist point of view in her *Practising Feminist Criticism: An Introduction*, Jane Goldman situates Lily Briscoe's aesthetic practice within a "materialist feminist exploration of colour" in her book *The Feminist Aesthetics of Virginia Woolf: Modernism, Post-impressionism, and the Politics of the Visual* (168), and Lilienfeld interrogates the politics of codependence in *To the Lighthouse* from a feminist stance in her *Reading Alcoholisms: Theorizing Character and Narrative in Selected Novels of Thomas Hardy, James Joyce, and Virginia Woolf*.

Lesbian Theory

For background in lesbian theory, see Blanche Weisen Cook's groundbreaking essay, "'Women Alone Stir My Imagination': Lesbianism and the Cultural Tradition"; *Inside/Out: Lesbian Theories, Gay Theories*, edited by Diana Fuss; *The Lesbian and Gay Studies Reader*, edited by Henry Abelove, Michèle Aina Barale, and David M. Halperin; Judith Butler's *Gender Trouble: Feminism and the Subversion of Identity*; and Judith Roof's *A Lure of Knowledge: Lesbian Sexuality and Theory*. For works on Woolf's relationship with Vita Sackville-West, see Louise DeSalvo's "Lighting the Cave" and Suzanne Raitt's *Vita and Virginia:*

The Work and Friendship of V. Sackville-West and Virginia Woolf. Eileen Barrett provides a concise history of lesbian and gay criticism of Woolf in *Virginia Woolf: Lesbian Readings*, edited with Patricia Cramer, and the volume includes essays by Ruth Vanita and Lise Weil on *To the Lighthouse.* Marianne Hirsch's "The Darkest Plots: Narration and Compulsory Heterosexuality," Diana Swanson's "The Lesbian Feminism of Virginia Woolf's *To the Lighthouse,*" and Deborah Wilson's "Fishing for Woolf's Submerged Lesbian Text" are other lesbian readings of the novel.

Bloomsbury

Background on Bloomsbury's ties to postimpressionist art can be found in parts of *Principia Ethica*, by G. E. Moore; in Clive Bell's *Art*, where the term *significant form* is defined; and in Roger Fry's "An Essay in Aesthetics," in his *Vision and Design.* The classic work on the topic is J. K. Johnstone's *The Bloomsbury Group: A Study of E. M. Forster, Lytton Strachey, Virginia Woolf, and Their Circle.* S. P. Rosenbaum has also studied the group extensively, publishing two collections of the group's work, *The Bloomsbury Group* and *A Bloomsbury Group Reader*, and two histories, *Victorian Bloomsbury* and *Edwardian Bloomsbury*, with a third, *Georgian Bloomsbury*, planned. Patrick Brantlinger, in answering Bloomsbury critics in "'The Bloomsbury Fraction' versus War and Empire," provides a great deal of information about the group as well as about the attacks on it. Other recent studies of Woolf in the context of Bloomsbury include *Multiple Muses: Virginia Woolf and the Other Arts*, edited by Diane Gillespie; *On or about December 1910: Early Bloomsbury and Its Intimate World*, by Peter Stansky; *Women of Bloomsbury: Virginia, Vanessa, and Carrington*, by Mary Ann Caws; and *The Sisters' Arts: The Writing and Painting of Virginia Woolf and Vanessa Bell*, by Gillespie. Finally, Avrom Fleishman examines the Cambridge and Bloomsbury connection in Woolf's novel in "Woolf and McTaggart: An Interrogation of the Metaphysics in *To the Lighthouse.*"

Genre or Form

Two classic studies that put Woolf's narrative experiments into context are E. M. Forster's *Aspects of the Novel* and Robert Humphrey's *Stream of Consciousness in the Modern Novel*, and several instructors mention how helpful Northrop Frye's "Four Forms of Fiction" and Joseph Frank's "Spatial Form in Modern Literature" still are. Genre studies more clearly related to Woolf are Ralph Freedman's *The Lyrical Novel: Studies in Hermann Hesse, André Gide, and Virginia Woolf*; *Forms of Modern British Fiction*, edited by Alan W. Friedman; and Daniel R. Schwarz's *The Transformation of the English Novel, 1890–1930*, which includes a chapter on *Mrs. Dalloway* and *To the Lighthouse.*

In the last chapter of *Modernism and the Fate of Individuality*, Michael Levenson considers *To the Lighthouse* against the backdrop of epic (166–216). Those particularly interested in *To the Lighthouse* as elegy should see Gillian

Beer's "Hume, Stephen, and Elegy in *To the Lighthouse*," Elissa Greenwald's "Casting Off from 'The Castaway': *To the Lighthouse* as Prose Elegy," Peter Knox-Shaw's "*To the Lighthouse*: The Novel as Elegy," Karen Smythe's "Virginia Woolf's Elegiac Enterprise," and Laura Marcus's chapter on *Jacob's Room* and *To the Lighthouse* in her *Virginia Woolf*.

Narrative Theory

Background in narrative theory can be especially helpful for teaching Woolf, and survey respondents often praise Dorrit Cohn's *Transparent Minds: Narrative Modes for Presenting Consciousness in Fiction*. Other books mentioned as useful background are Gérard Genette's *Narrative Discourse: An Essay in Method*, Mieke Bal's *Narratology: Introduction to the Theory of Narrative*, Peter Rabinowitz's *Before Reading: Narrative Conventions and the Politics of Interpretation*, and the collection of essays edited by James Phelan, *Reading Narrative: Form, Ethics, Ideology*. Susan Sniader Lanser's *Fictions of Authority: Women Writers and Narrative Voice*, Rachel DuPlessis's *Writing beyond the Ending: Narrative Strategies of Twentieth-Century Women Writers*, and the collection of essays edited by Kathy Mezei, *Ambiguous Discourse: Feminist Narratology and British Women Writers*, provide such background in terms of women's narrative, and Woolf figures prominently in all three.

For studies of Woolf's narrative often mentioned by survey respondents, see Harvena Richter's *Virginia Woolf: The Inward Voyage*, James Naremore's *The World without a Self: Virginia Woolf and the Novel*, and Maria DiBattista's *Virginia Woolf's Major Novels*; the latter two have separate chapters on *To the Lighthouse*. An influential study of point of view and narration is Mitchell Leaska's *Virginia Woolf's Lighthouse: A Study in Critical Method*. For an essay on narrative in Woolf's novel, see Susan Stanford Friedman's "Lyric Subversion of Narrative in Women's Writing: Virginia Woolf and the Tyranny of Plot." Also helpful are Judith Espinola's "Narrative Discourse in Virginia Woolf's *To the Lighthouse*," Jane Fisher's "'Silent as the Grave': Painting, Narrative, and the Reader in *Night and Day* and *To the Lighthouse*," and Rebecca Saunders's "Language, Subject, Self: Reading the Style of *To the Lighthouse*."

Philosophical Approaches

Along with Jean Guiguet's massive study, already noted, Josephine O'Brien Schaefer's *The Three-Fold Nature of Reality in the Novels of Virginia Woolf* provides a clear introduction to the philosophical issues embedded in Woolf's work. More recently, in *The Singing of the Real World*, Mark Hussey examines Woolf's philosophy, and Lucio Ruotolo, in *The Interrupted Moment*, claims that Woolf's novels reflect a philosophy of anarchy. Essays that focus more specifically on philosophy in *To the Lighthouse* include Deborah Esch's "'Think of a Kitchen Table': Hume, Woolf, and the Tradition of Example," A. C. Hoffman's "Subject and Object and the Nature of Reality: The Dialectic of *To the Lighthouse*," Graham Parkes's "Imagining Reality in *To the Light-house*," Martha A. Nussbaum's "The Window: Knowledge of Other Minds in Virginia Woolf's *To the Lighthouse*," William R. Handley's "The Housemaid and the Kitchen Table: Incorporating the Frame in *To the Lighthouse*," Robert Lumsden's "Virginia Woolf's 'As If' in *To the Lighthouse*: The Modernist Philosophy of Meaning in Absentia," and Eric Levy's "Woolf's Metaphysics of Tragic Vision in *To the Lighthouse*."

Psychological Perspectives

For general background, see Leon Edel, *The Modern Psychological Novel, 1900–1950*. Studies placing Woolf within a psychoanalytic framework are Mark Spilka's *Virginia Woolf's Quarrel with Grieving* and Elizabeth Abel's *Virginia Woolf and the Fictions of Psychoanalysis*, both of which include chapters on *To the Lighthouse*, and James M. Mellard's *Using Lacan, Reading Fiction* includes a chapter on *To the Lighthouse* as well. Essays focused specifically on psychological issues in *To the Lighthouse* are Claire Kahane's "The Nuptials of Metaphor: Self and Other in Virginia Woolf," Mary Jacobus's "'The Third Stroke': Reading Woolf with Freud," Val Gough's "The Mystical Copula: Rewriting the Phallus in *To the Lighthouse*," and Tina Barr's "Divine Politics: Virginia Woolf's Journey toward Eleusis in *To the Lighthouse*," in which Barr juxtaposes Elizabeth Abel's and Julia Kristeva's ideas with Woolf's mythic strategies to read *To the Lighthouse* politically.

Autobiography

Woolf's own statements about transforming her parents, Leslie and Julia Stephen, into Mr. and Mrs. Ramsay and her use of Cornwall for the Hebrides have made the autobiographical nature of her novel a critical commonplace. Survey respondents thus agree that if instructors have time for nothing else, they should browse in the third volumes of Woolf's *Diary* and *Letters* as background for the novel and then read the description in *A Passionate Apprentice* of Woolf's return to Cornwall in 1905. They also repeatedly mention Woolf's unrevised memoir "A Sketch of the Past," in *Moments of Being*, as a necessary supplement to the novel.

Essays that focus on Woolf's relationship with her parents include Jane Marcus's "Virginia Woolf and Her Violin: Mothering, Madness, and Music" and Jane Fisher's "The Seduction of the Father: Virginia Woolf and Leslie Stephen." Sara Ruddick, in "Learning to Live with the Angel in the House," reads Woolf's life through the novel. Articles that focus more on the Ramsays as characters include Glenn Pedersen's "Vision in *To the Lighthouse*" (an essay with the distinction of seeing Mrs. Ramsay not just as problematic but also as villainous), the conversation between Randall Stevenson and Jane Goldman about Mrs. Ramsay's death in the *Yearbook of English Studies*, and Ellen Tremper's "In Her Father's House: *To the Lighthouse* as a Record of Virginia Woolf's Literary Patrimony."

Biography

Most respondents reluctantly recommend Quentin Bell's *Virginia Woolf: A Biography* as a place to start ("fairly basic, if biased," says one). Jane Marcus ("Tintinnabulations") and Ellen Hawkes Rogat outline the most serious objections to the Bell biography, but Bell does provide a great deal of information in a readable chronology. If instructors have time for only one biography, however, we recommend Hermione Lee's *Virginia Woolf* because of its comprehensive approach, balance, and down-to-earth tone. Veteran Woolf instructors have other favorite biographies, but note that all are in some way partial. Winifred Holtby, writing the first Woolf biography in 1932, places Woolf's work in relation to the cinema and the feminism of the time; Roger Poole uses a phenomenological approach; Phyllis Rose, Lyndall Gordon, and John Mepham all focus on Woolf as a writer; Louise DeSalvo and Thomas Caramagno both write about Woolf's mental and physical health, with DeSalvo focusing on the effect of abuse and Caramagno focusing on manic-depression; Jane Dunn and Panthea Reid both focus on Woolf's relationship with her sister, Vanessa Bell, but Reid also demonstrates Woolf's connection to Roger Fry's theories about art; and Jean Moorcroft Wilson focuses on Woolf's geographical landscapes, particularly London.

Other material by and about family members is useful in conjunction with *To the Lighthouse*. For example, for writing done by Woolf's parents, see Leslie Stephen's *Mausoleum Book*, which reveals his obsessional relationship with Julia Stephen, along with his *Hours in a Library*; see also *Julia Duckworth Stephen: Stories for Children and Essays for Adults*, edited by Diane F. Gillespie and Elizabeth Steele. Noel Annan's biography of Woolf's father, *Leslie Stephen: The Godless Victorian*, and John Bicknell's "Mr. Ramsay Was Young Once" provide more information about the real man behind Mr. Ramsay, and Diane F. Gillespie's "The Elusive Julia Steven" and Martine Stemerick's "Virginia Woolf and Julia Stephen: The Distaff Side of History" do the same for the real woman behind Mrs. Ramsay.

Joan Russell Noble's *Recollections of Virginia Woolf by Her Contemporaries* and J. H. Stape's *Virginia Woolf: Interviews and Recollections* enlarge the picture of Woolf, revealing a multifaceted person—laughing, working, curious, naughty, bread-making. For the publishing Woolf, see J. H. Willis, Jr.'s *Leonard and Virginia Woolf as Publishers: The Hogarth Press, 1917–1941*; in addition, the fourth volume of Leonard Woolf's autobiography, *Downhill All the Way* sheds light on *To the Lighthouse*'s relation to Hogarth Press.

Comparative or Intertextual Approaches

Beverly Ann Schlack's *Continuing Presences: Virginia Woolf's Use of Literary Allusion* presents Woolf's work as part of an intertextual web. Other studies that read Woolf with and through other authors are Daniel Albright's *Personality and Impersonality: Lawrence, Woolf, and Mann*; Perry Meisel's *The Absent Father: Virginia Woolf and Walter Pater*; Robert Kiely's *Beyond Egotism: The Fiction of*

James Joyce, Virginia Woolf, and D. H. Lawrence ("good context," says one respondent); Richard Pearce's *The Politics of Narration: James Joyce, William Faulkner, and Virginia Woolf* (with Woolf as the most radical); Karen Kaivola's *All Contraries Confounded: The Lyrical Fiction of Virginia Woolf, Djuna Barnes, and Marguerite Duras* (with Woolf as the most conservative); Anne Hermann's *The Dialogic and Difference: "An/Other Woman" in Virginia Woolf and Christa Wolf*; Rachel DuPlessis's essay "Woolfenstein;" Ruth Saxton and Jean Tobin's collection of essays *Woolf and Lessing: Breaking the Mold;* Helen Wussow's *The Nightmare of History: The Fictions of Virginia Woolf and D. H. Lawrence*; and Suzan Harrison's *Eudora Welty and Virginia Woolf: Gender, Genre, and Influence.*

Jane Lilienfeld's "Flesh and Blood and Love and Words: Lily Briscoe, Stephen Dedalus, and the Aesthetics of Emotional Quest" compares the family dynamics of *To the Lighthouse* with those of Joyce's *A Portrait of the Artist as a Young Man*, and Leslie Kathleen Hankins has two studies of the intersection of film and fiction in Woolf's work, "'Across the Screen of My Brain': Virginia Woolf's 'The Cinema' and Film Forums of the Twenties" and "A Splice of Reel Life in Virginia Woolf's 'Time Passes': Censorship, Cinema and 'the Usual Battlefield of Emotions.'" Evelyne Ender reads Charlotte Brontë and Virginia Woolf together in "Feminist Criticism in a Double Mirror," Angela Smith compares Katherine Mansfield and Woolf in "Thresholds in 'Prelude' and *To the Lighthouse*," and Barbara Christian and Paula Bennett read Woolf and Toni Morrison together in, respectively, "Layered Rhythms" and "The Mother's Part: Incest and Maternal Deprivation in Woolf and Morrison."

Teaching Aids

Essays

We found only a few essays on teaching Woolf. James Holt McGavran, Jr., presents several suggestions in "Teaching Virginia Woolf in the University: A First Dose for Unwilling Undergraduates," Marcia McClintock Folsom explores strategies for helping undergraduates confront Woolf's world in "Gallant Red Brick and Plain China: Teaching *A Room of One's Own*," and Beth Rigel Daugherty suggests a pedagogical rationale for pairing Woolf's texts with multicultural ones in "Teaching *Mrs. Dalloway* and *Praisesong for the Widow* as a Pair." Mary Aswell Doll quotes many of her students in *To the Lighthouse and Back: Writings on Teaching and Living*, and a lively roundtable discussion about teaching *To the Lighthouse* was held at the First Annual Conference on Virginia Woolf (Hussey and Neverow-Turk 203–07). Essays with clear potential for classroom use are Sandra Donaldson's "Where Does Q Leave Mr. Ramsay?" and Jane Marcus's "Still Practice, A/Wrested Alphabet: Toward a Feminist Aesthetic" and "Other People's I's (Eyes): The Reader, Gender, and Recursive Reading in *To the Lighthouse* and *The Waves.*"

Films

Though Woolf scholars often express disappointment about screen treatments of Woolf's life and work, many instructors use the 1990 PBS version of *A Room of One's Own* featuring Eileen Atkins with *To the Lighthouse*, but without Alastair Cooke's misleading introduction. Viewers at two Woolf conferences also reacted favorably to John Fuegi and Jo Francis's documentary, *The War Within: A Portrait of Virginia Woolf*. Joseph Christopher Schaub's *Waves of Pure Lemon* is a moving documentary about Muriel Heineman's memories of reading *To the Lighthouse* as a teenager. The film *Virginia Woolf*, in the Modern World: Ten Great Writers Series concentrates on *Mrs. Dalloway* but includes commentary from the English critics Anthony Burgess, V. S. Pritchett, Frank Kermode, and Hermione Lee. Peter Hort wrote, produced, and directed *Virginia Woolf: Novelist, 1882–1941* for the Famous Authors series, and in 1993 another series, Superstar Teachers, produced twelve lessons entitled *The Twentieth Century: Modernism and Existentialism*, including lesson 7, *Woolf's To the Lighthouse*, taught by Victor Brombert.

Controversy surrounds the 1983 "made for BBC" film version of *To the Lighthouse*. On the one hand, a few instructors find the film valuable for classroom use, commenting that the film does a "good job of showing how interior the novel is" and that its "immediacy and sensory vividness" can make Woolf's storytelling "more accessible and palpable" to resistant students. One instructor allows students to watch the film only after they have read the novel, and then they must compare the two. On the other hand, a second instructor describes it as "terrible in spite of good actors," while a third reports that students become "angry because it departs so far from the text." Many others are adamant in their advice not to use it: "Whatever you do, don't use the god-awful BBC version of *To the Lighthouse*! It betrays the material, adding things like a wrestling match, and generally ruins the book."

See the audiovisual section of this volume's works-cited list for more information about the films discussed here.

Audiotapes

Instructors are more favorably inclined toward audiotapes, feeling that they give students a valuable sense of Woolf's skills as a writer. A tape frequently mentioned is Celia Johnson's 1958 reading on Caedmon of *Mrs. Dalloway* (selections) and *To the Lighthouse* ("Time Passes"). Spending approximately twenty minutes on "Time Passes," Johnson "gives voice to Mrs. McNab and thus reveals to students the important role that character plays," according to one respondent. An unabridged version of *To the Lighthouse*, read by Wanda McCaddon, is available from Books on Tape, and an abridged version, read by Eileen Atkins, is available from Penguin Audiobooks. Julie Rivkin and Christine Froula discuss Woolf in relation to women and art, with excerpts from *To the Lighthouse* and *A Room of One's Own*, on a 1989 tape called *Virginia Woolf* in the Introduction to Modern English and American Literature series. In a three-tape set called *Moments of Being*, Peggy Ashcroft reads selections from Woolf's autobiographical essays on five sides; side 6, "A Portrait of Virginia Woolf," includes the voices of Leonard Woolf, Vanessa Bell, and several other Bloomsbury figures and a fragment of "Craftsmanship," a broadcast of Woolf reading from her essay of that name, the only surviving recording of her voice. Also available is a six-cassette set called *Virginia Woolf: A Portrait in Sound*. Read by Irene Worth, this set includes material from the diaries, letters, essays (including "Modern Fiction"), and stories, and from "A Sketch of the Past." We also can't forget the Indigo Girls, Emily Saliers and Amy Ray, who have a song entitled "Virginia Woolf " on their *Rites of Passage* CD and who often use allusions to Woolf in their songs.

See the audiovisual section of this volume's works-cited list for more information about these recordings.

Other Aids

One survey respondent, Evelyn Harris Haller, uses Julia Margaret Cameron's photographs of Julia Stephen (in Cameron), Leslie Stephen's animal sketches (in J. D. Stephen), and a catalog of Barbara Hepworth's Cornwall sculptures (in Gale and Stephens) to help her students "read" Woolf's context; she also has them explore Leslie Stephen and Sidney Lee's *Dictionary of National Biography*, Stephen's mammoth A to Z project.

Many instructors provide undergraduates with visual context to help them understand *To the Lighthouse*: slides of impressionist paintings, with particular emphasis on work done by women artists such as Mary Cassatt; pictures of Vanessa Bell's dust jackets, particularly the one for *To the Lighthouse*; and pictures or slides of Woolf's family and biographical sites, such as the photographs of the Stephen family at St. Ives, the Godrevy lighthouse, Cornwall, and Talland House, along with photographs of London, the Sussex Downs, Monk's House, and the Charleston farmhouse. The best sources for such photographs are the Quentin Bell, Hermione Lee, and Noel Annan biographies, the *Charleston Magazine,* Diane Gillespie's *The Sisters' Arts*, Gillian Naylor's *Bloomsbury*, Ottoline Morrell's *Lady Ottoline's Album*, and Daphne Du Maurier's *Vanishing Cornwall: The Spirit and History of Cornwall*. For a different kind of context, instructors and students may want to try out Miranda Carter's recipe for *boeuf en daube*, as featured in the *Charleston Magazine*.

On the Internet, the Voice of the Shuttle (www.vos.ucsb.edu/shuttle/english/htm) provides excellent links to sites on modernism and individual authors. The International Virginia Woolf Society Web site (www.utoronto.ca/IVWS) makes available the society's annual bibliography of Woolf studies, up-to-date information about the annual conference on Virginia Woolf, information about the society's MLA sessions, and links to other sites and publications. The Virginia Woolf Web (www.orlando.jp.org/VWW/vwbib.html) provides links to modernism and feminism sites, a seminar on Virginia Woolf, Bloomsbury sites, the *To the Lighthouse* Hypertext Project, and much more, including information on books, films, and souvenirs. (Other generally less useful Woolf Web sites can be located with standard Internet search engines, but we should caution instructors that sites appear and disappear and addresses change frequently on the Web.) The VWOOLF discussion list is available by sending the message Subscribe VWOOLF Firstname Lastname to <listproc@lists.acs.ohio-state.edu>, and the ModBrits discussion (focusing on modern British and Irish literature from 1895 to 1955) can be joined by sending the message Subscribe ModBrits Firstname Lastname to <ListServ@ListServ.Kent.edu>.

Finally, some instructors use campus computer networks to enlarge on classroom discussion of *To the Lighthouse*. Students are required to comment on the novel a specified number of times and to respond to their classmates' comments. This strategy continues conversations begun in the classroom, sometimes raises new questions, and empowers those who might be uncomfortable speaking up in class. Other instructors and students create Virginia Woolf or *To the Lighthouse* Web sites, and these can be found by using any of the standard Internet search engines.

Part Two

APPROACHES

Introduction

Although this volume cannot provide instructors with either "fifty pairs of eyes to see [*To the Lighthouse*] with" (198)[1] or all the critical perspectives currently in favor, it does bring together twenty-one essays that represent a range of pedagogical styles and critical approaches. Taken together, these essays cover all the novel's major characters and parts, provide instructors with strategies for helping undergraduates in their initial struggle to understand a difficult text, and give suggestions for moving those students into more complex and theoretical issues.

Respondents to our survey of instructors who teach *To the Lighthouse* also have many practical suggestions for helping students become more actively involved in Woolf's text. Some instructors, for example, assign specific textual tasks. Mark Muggli asks his students to "mark in the novel's margin whether a sentence or paragraph shows the visible world (vw) or the internal world of a particular character (character's initials)." Harvena Richter asked her intermediate creative writing students to find the poetry embedded in Woolf's prose and actually write it down in poetic lines, and Mary Ann Caws asks her students to consider why Woolf interrupts her prose so often with poetry. Katherine Hill-Miller relies on her students' journal entries about family tensions and generational conflicts to open discussion of just those issues in *To the Lighthouse*. Several instructors use the board creatively. For example, Sandra Donaldson helps her students get control of the novel by jotting down the pairs they see—of characters and events—and then suggests how similar their reading response is to Mr. Ramsay's use of logic to "read" his world. Thomas Matro writes down the oppositions the novel creates and his undergraduates find—male/female, logic/intuition, reality/appearance, knowledge/love, life/art, and so on—and then focuses discussion on the ways the novel calls all such dichotomies into question.

Other instructors use methods from speech and drama. Thomas Beattie has his students stage a debate on the Ramsays: "It helps students see the claims of each, creates some reservations about Mrs. Ramsay, and sets us up for the synthesis that I believe is achieved in *To the Lighthouse*." To prepare, each student must come to class with "three reasons for saying Woolf validates Mrs. Ramsay and her position in 'The Window' and three for saying it is Mr. Ramsay who is favored." Don Rice has groups of students research particular characters, and once each group reports, the class stages the dinner party scene. Several instructors, striving to communicate a "living" text, ask students to come to class as characters and speak for those characters in the first person, act out in class how particular characters feel, dramatize the opening scene to illustrate the difference between actual dialogue and stream of consciousness, or perform readers' theater.

Instructors also extract certain parts of the novel to illustrate key points. Linda Ware reads the Grimms' "The Fisherman's Wife" and asks her students to think about the tale in relation to Mrs. Ramsay. Panthea Reid recites William Cowper's "The Castaway" out loud because it reveals so much about Mr. Ramsay, and other instructors locate the entire text of Charles Elton's "Luriana Lurilee" in *Another World Than This* or on the Virginia Woolf Web. Still others read Alfred Tennyson's "The Charge of the Light Brigade" (see Barzilai) or distribute the whole Shakespearean sonnet that Mrs. Ramsay reads (no. 98). Some ask students to find out more about Walter Scott's *The Antiquary* (see Cohan).

To help students see Woolf's work even more clearly, instructors often use comparison. Sally Jacobsen emphasizes Woolf's comedy of manners when she compares the dinner party scene in *To the Lighthouse* to the drawing room humor in Jane Austen and Molière; Mary Beth Pringle uses Mary Catherine Bateson's *Composing a Life* as a "map" for reading *To the Lighthouse*; and Beth Rigel Daugherty's students write about their memories of summer, parents, and places, read E. B. White's "Once More to the Lake," and listen to passages from the 1905 Cornwall diary in *A Passionate Apprentice*, all as a preface to discussions about how memory works in *To the Lighthouse*. Instructors also set up intertextual conversations between *To the Lighthouse* and another text, some of which we list here: Shakespeare's *A Winter's Tale*, William Kennedy's *Ironweed*, Tillie Olsen's "I Stand Here Ironing," W. B. Yeats's *The Tower*, Thomas Wolfe's *Look Homeward, Angel*, Marilynne Robinson's *Housekeeping*, Kamala Markandya's *Nectar in a Sieve*, Rita Mae Brown's *Rubyfruit Jungle*, Jane Austen's *Pride and Prejudice*, Buchi Emecheta's *Joys of Motherhood*, D. H. Lawrence's *The Rainbow*, Edith Wharton's *The Age of Innocence*, Doris Lessing's *The Golden Notebook*, Maxine Hong Kingston's *The Woman Warrior*, Alice Walker's *The Color Purple*, and Hanif Kureishi's *The Buddha of Suburbia*.

Finally, instructors use multiple critical perspectives as a pedagogical tool, saying that even a surface understanding of several ways of looking at a text frees undergraduates to form their own interpretations. Roberta White's students, for example, examine the opening scene—James sitting on the floor and cutting out catalog pictures—from six critical perspectives: biographical, reader-response, psychoanalytic, feminist, historical or Marxist, and aesthetic.

The essays gathered here represent many different critical perspectives but also tell us, once again, that both the best teaching and the best criticism first simplify and then complicate a text. Complex texts challenge students, of course, but they challenge teachers, too: to come up with creative approaches, to translate beloved critical theories into pedagogical tools rather than topics for discussion, to call on resources different from those used to marshal points in an essay. Contributors to this volume, for example, were aware of the ironies inherent in their essay assignment—writing about *an* approach to teaching a novel whose crucial message lies in James's perception that "nothing was simply one thing" (186), recording spoken and written responses to a novel that is about the responses humans have below the surface, and creating a linear product about the provisional, ongoing, often downright messy process of teaching—but they pressed on nonetheless, attempting to capture classroom, context, complexity, criticism, and classes in a few pages of clear prose. The resulting essays, the contributors would be the first to tell you, represent class snapshots—one moment in time, framed, everyone dressed up in his or her best, behaving pretty well. Knowing that teaching is always more complicated than a pedagogical essay can convey, knowing that one's context—institution, course, and students—dictates what is practical, the essayists gathered here assume that instructors will extract from, add to, adapt, and even transform what they have described. The value of this volume, then, lies in the diversity of approaches presented, discourses heard, and pedagogies used. If such diversity encourages novices and experts alike to look again at *To the Lighthouse* and their teaching of it, we will have succeeded.

We have based the organization of this volume on a sequence that instructors often use to introduce students to new material. Grounded in our sense that students must understand the novel before putting it into a critical framework, the volume focuses first on how to read *To the Lighthouse* and then on critical approaches to it. Within this overall sequential structure, contributors range from traditional to postmodern, from teacher-directed to student-centered, and from conversational to theoretical; some aim to make students comfortable with what they perceive as a chaotic style, whereas others aim to make students uncomfortable with their preconceived opinions. The contributors teach students at all levels in various kinds of institutions in different regions of North America. But mainly they illustrate, as one reader told us, "how individual teaching really is."

We have divided the first half of the essays, collected under the heading "How Should One Read *To the Lighthouse*?" into four subsections. The first, "Period Reading Practices," illustrates how instructors might work with students to place Woolf's novel within its literary period. Janis Paul uses a genre approach to focus on the tension between Victorian tradition and modern rebellion in *To the Lighthouse*; in so doing, she reassures the students in her introductory literature and survey classes that Woolf's novel retains many features of traditional novels even as she helps them see its revolutionary contributions to the genre. Mark Hussey, however, uses Woolf's essays about modern fiction and the psychology, philosophy, and science of the day to place *To the Lighthouse* squarely in the modernist tradition, and he shows how the novel itself serves as a guide to reading modern literature. Pamela Caughie illustrates what a pedagogy based on postmodern assumptions would look like by focusing on the way Mrs. McNab exposes the exclusions in Woolf's modernist narrative. Caughie's suggestion that any attempt to reduce this novel to a dominant theme will involve the exclusion of other readings also indirectly theorizes this volume's juxtaposition of different points of view; by continually countering one reading with another, this collection leads us to think more self-consciously about the strategies and assumptions underlying what we do in the classroom.

In the next section, "Close Textual Analysis," contributors show how they help students read the novel well and derive meaning from it. Eileen Barrett models for her lower-middle-class students in her modern British fiction course how to follow the language of an individual image such as fabric, to think about a text's fabrication, and to trace an image pattern; Mary Pinkerton hands the students in her modern British novel and twentieth-century women writers courses some tools from narrative theory to help them ward off the impulse to interpret too quickly; and Patricia Laurence helps her immigrant students hear both the polyphonic voices in *To the Lighthouse* that indicate difference and the up-and-down rhythms that suggest commonality, thus showing how Woolf captures the paradox of human existence: we are both not alike and alike.

Then in "Successful Classroom Strategies," Annis Pratt and Laura Davis encourage students to love *To the Lighthouse*; they remind us how joyful teaching and learning can be when the strategies work! Pratt, after a disastrous first experience teaching Woolf, developed a set of strategies to help the students in her major authors course get over their fear of Virginia Woolf and learn to take risks and think for themselves. Davis describes in detail *one* invaluable technique—selective indexing—that helps her two-year-college students find their own interpretations and write effective essays about *To the Lighthouse*.

Finally, in "Contemporary Lenses," contributors show how instructors might introduce their students to contemporary concerns about the role literature plays. Toni McNaron, Louise DeSalvo, and Jeanette McVicker all explore what *To the Lighthouse* looks like from the margins. What happens, McNaron asks in her undergraduate seminar on Virginia Woolf's major novels, when you look for and value likeness instead of difference? when you move away from heterosexist assumptions about how the world works? In Louise DeSalvo's course on Virginia Woolf's novels, a student's questions send teacher and students on a search for all the novel's working-class characters. Woolf's portrayal of those characters and her comments about working-class people in her manuscript, diary, and letters lead to more questions, particularly about the relation between attitudes expressed in life and those expressed in literature. In a world literature course serving as a humanities elective for the general education curriculum, Jeanette McVicker unsettles her middle-class sophomores' comfortable assumptions about the world as they begin to see how imperialism infuses not only the England of the Ramsays and *To the Lighthouse* but also their own United States; how does Woolf, and how can they, sustain a critique of such a pervasive force?

The first set of essays, then, presents approaches within four possible stages in a student's early reading process: placing a novel within its literary period, learning how to read it closely and well, interpreting it, and discovering what questions it asks. In the second set of essays, reading remains a background concern, with our categories suggesting the progress Woolf's reader makes in her essay "How Should One Read a Book?" That is, after reading *To the Lighthouse*, readers become curious about Woolf's life, want to know more about her times, and begin to compare her novel with other writers' works. Thus, the critical approaches foregrounded here are organized into three main categories—autobiographical, contextual, and intertextual.

Given Woolf's statements about using her parents (Leslie and Julia Stephen) in her novel and the benefits of doing so, several instructors put autobiography front and center as a literary genre. Thus the essays in this section make more explicit the connections between a writer's life and work and those between the work and readers' lives. They also implicitly ask the age-old questions about the relation between fact and fiction, truth and art, life and literature. Nancy Topping Bazin, wanting the conservative students in her women writers class to understand the relevance of a feminist critical approach to literature, encourages them to look at the questions about living, particularly those about work and family, that the novel poses. Thinking about the questions they themselves have about such issues, studying those questions as they appear in Woolf's diaries and letters and in the context of women's history, and paying attention to how those questions play out in the novel, Bazin's students begin to see the usefulness of feminist criticism. Because Gerald Cobb has noticed how often English majors and honors students describe the Ramsays as dysfunctional, he provides them with a sociological and psychological framework through which they can read Woolf's autobiographical accounts of her family life and *To the Lighthouse*. Marcia McClintock Folsom asks the adult students in her evening seminar to overtly consider the autobiographical project and the different forms it takes in memoir and fiction; she places *To the Lighthouse* on a reading list with mainly American autobiographies and family chronicles, many of them multicultural. Folsom and her students explore how life becomes literature and then weaves its way back into life again. In the course of their journey, many discover differences related to nationality and culture but also some surprising similarities.

The essays in "Contextual Approaches" ask students to see art as something besides a formal object; art exists, these essays insist, in a web of aesthetic, economic, social, and historical forces. These approaches, reacting against formalist and structuralist ones, show how cultural context enriches or changes *To the Lighthouse*. The first two approaches ask students to consider the material culture of Woolf's world. Susan Yunis uses an art survey, viewings of Romantic, impressionist, and postimpressionist paintings, and Bloomsbury sources to show the undergraduates in her Forster and Woolf seminar that Woolf's novel exists within a context of changing perceptions about how to "make" art. Edward Bishop focuses on the actual production of a text—the ink, print, paper, cover, advertising—and uses Pierre Bourdieu's ideas about the text's cultural or literary capital, along with a trip to his university print shop, to involve the seniors in his modern British novel class in literature's ties to manufacturing and finances. The last two approaches in the section ask students to consider Woolf's novel in history. Karen Levenback shows how *To the Lighthouse* becomes a war novel when students read all of Woolf's work from the period between the wars, study World War I, and read newspaper accounts and sources detailing the noncombatant reaction to it. In this historical context, many students discover that Woolf's stylistic changes (from the novel's first to its third part) parallel historical changes (from a prewar to a postwar sensibility). In a course on literature written by women, Bonnie Braendlin uses the history of the *Bildungsroman* and *Künstlerroman* genres and the difference between male and female versions to examine how the gender-inflected ideologies embodied in social discourse about life choices are both perpetuated and challenged by literature. Reading *To the Lighthouse* in this context, her students can locate the options Woolf allows Lily, the female artist, within a particular historical moment and a particular social discourse.

The volume ends with "Intertextual Approaches," essays that focus on the ways texts inform each other. As Woolf says, "To continue reading without the book before you, to hold one shadow-shape against another, to have read widely enough and with enough understanding to make such comparisons alive and illuminating—that is difficult" ("How Should One" 267–68). In her modern novel class, for example, Susan Currier uses her students' initial preference for Stephen Dedalus over Lily Briscoe to introduce Carol Gilligan's theories about possible differences in male and female artistic development. Those theories validate both artists' development so that students at least question their desire to rank one over the other. Annette Oxindine's students, comparing *To the Lighthouse* with *Their Eyes Were Watching God* in their class on gender and modernism, never fail to point out important distinctions in the power dynamics displayed in the two worlds. But using Bonnie Kime Scott's "tangled mesh of modernists" as a model (*Gender* 10), they draw many interesting lines of their own between Lily and Janie. In the process, Woolf and Hurston can be seen joining forces across ethnicity and nationality to question standard definitions of modernism. Finally, Vara Neverow has students in both a sophomore women's literature class and a graduate and upper-level undergraduate feminist literary theory class read Adrienne Rich's essay on compulsory heterosexuality with *To the Lighthouse*. As Rich confronts their ideas about homosexuality and Woolf challenges their notions about novels, most students cannot help joining the conversation going on between the two texts. The resulting discussions and papers, as Neverow demonstrates, are powerful.

Although we have tried to sequence and group our contributors' essays in a logical way, we suspect most users of this volume will not read it straight through but will skip around in it to find the approaches most useful or most interesting to them. For example, instructors wanting genre approaches will find them in Paul and Braendlin, and those wanting a focus on female modernism will find it in Currier and Oxindine. The approaches described by Laurence, Folsom, and Oxindine are useful for multicultural classrooms; McNaron and Neverow use lesbian perspectives; and Caughie, McVicker, and Braendlin all confront ideology. Barrett, Pinkerton, Cobb, and Pratt focus closely on language. Experiential strategies can be found in Pratt and Bishop, with some of Pratt's strategies possible even in large classes, and Braendlin and Hussey both suggest possible connections to popular culture. DeSalvo, Pratt, Davis, and Neverow suggest possible paper topics, and Hussey, Levenback, Pratt, DeSalvo, and Bazin all pair Woolf's novel with other of her primary works. Fruitful discussions occur across the essays, too, such as when Folsom says that Woolf mutes her anger in *To the Lighthouse* and Yunis argues that anger is the novel's subject or when DeSalvo, Caughie, McVicker, and Laurence disagree about how Woolf portrays and uses Mrs. McNab. Readers, of course, will discover reverberations, arguments, and conversations of their own.

Readers looking for cutting-edge criticism or radical pedagogies will not find them here. What they will find instead are instruction and approaches that aim to help undergraduates new to Woolf's novel become the readers Woolf ultimately wants: open, curious, sensitive, active. Given Woolf's attitude about teaching English literature in the university—"But why teach English? As you say, all one can do is to herd books into groups, and then these submissive young, who are far too frightened and callow to have a bone in their backs, swallow it down; and tie it up; and thus we get English literature into ABC; one, two, three; and lose all sense of what its [sic] about. [. . . N]obody reads with open eyes" (*Letters* 5: 450)—if we teachers of *To the Lighthouse* can occasionally help students become readers who read "with open eyes" *within* the academy, that's revolution enough.

NOTE

[1]The edition of *To the Lighthouse* cited in this volume is the 1989 Harvest–Harcourt paperback edition (from the first American edition), with a foreword by Eudora Welty.

How Should One Read
To the Lighthouse?

Teaching *To the Lighthouse* as a Traditional Novel

Janis M. Paul

I have taught *To the Lighthouse* in introductory literature and survey courses, usually to nonmajors or beginning English majors. In general, they know little about novel form, Virginia Woolf, or the cultural and personal history that infuses this work. Given the novel's technical experimentation, which can daunt even experienced readers, *To the Lighthouse* may seem an odd choice for such students. But examining this novel not only teaches students about *To the Lighthouse* and Virginia Woolf, it also offers a historical and biographical context to enrich their understanding of form and genre in all novels. *To the Lighthouse* more than justifies the efforts inexperienced students must make to understand it.

Neophyte readers face two related difficulties when approaching *To the Lighthouse*. First, they need simply to understand what happens in the story: the amorphous structure and wandering prose often make it difficult to determine what is occurring and whose mind they are exploring. Second, students need to understand why these difficult experimental elements exist: to appreciate the scope of Woolf's literary accomplishment, they need to apprehend the historical contribution *To the Lighthouse* makes to the novel as a genre.

The first encounter can be frustrating; to unsophisticated readers, *To the Lighthouse* seems profoundly different from other novels. Therefore, I warn students that what they are about to read will be difficult, and then I ask them to jot down a few sentences of reaction after they have read the first ten sections or so. As we discuss their reactions in class, I inevitably encounter a barrage of criticism and frustration: "Nothing happens." "There's no plot." "No one really talks to anyone else." "I can't tell what anybody looks like." Indeed, most students conclude that *To the Lighthouse* doesn't read like a "real" novel at all.

I assure them that their reactions are appropriate, given certain assumptions about novel form. Then I suggest we explore those assumptions. Perhaps *To the Lighthouse* is, in fact, a "real" novel, a traditional novel, in many ways like those they have read before? When students discover *To the Lighthouse's* strong connections to the novel tradition, they can more clearly understand how and why it also rebels against tradition and forges a new novel form.

To encourage students to examine their assumptions, I ask them what a "real" novel is. Most have read a few conventionally crafted novels, if not Austen or Dickens, then John Grisham or Stephen King. (Or they have seen movies made from these novels.) As we discuss characteristics of the novels they know, we arrive at a definition, agreeing that a novel imitates life by presenting a world—a physical and social milieu where particular people work out significant events: in short, a novel has setting, characters, plot, and theme. (The class discusses all four elements, but I limit my discussion here to setting and character.)

After defining these characteristics, I ask students to find them in *To the Lighthouse*. Most students are pleased to realize that, despite the misty indefiniteness of the novel's language, tone, and form, they can identify many traditional elements of setting, character, plot, and theme familiar to them from other novels. Once they recognize these traditional characteristics, they can see more clearly how Woolf also experiments with them to transform the traditional novel.

Reminding students how much they already know about novels encourages them to understand, rather than fear, the complexities of this one. Furthermore, by moving from the familiar to the unfamiliar, students recapitulate Woolf's literary accomplishment, for she, too, moved from the familiar to the unfamiliar in her fictional experiments. She wanted to transcend the limitations of the past that had defined the novel since its inception: the proscription that novels must concern themselves with the material details of life in society ("Modern Fiction" 104). Woolf's experiments with fiction embody the spirit of rebellion and transformation that defines the preeminent literature and art of the modernist movement, exemplifying her own statement that "in or about December, 1910, human character changed" ("Mr. Bennett" 320).

As these references to modernism suggest, Woolf's experimental novel exists in, and contributes to, a pivotal moment in literary history, and at this point, I place Woolf in a cultural context. For inexperienced students, brief lectures on history and biography provide background. First, I ask them what they think of when they hear the words *Victorian* and *modern*, and a lively free association usually ensues. From there, beginning with Woolf's statement that in 1910 "human character changed," I describe the evolution from the Victorian to the modernist sensibility. In the second half of the nineteenth century, new scientific developments, most notably those of Darwin and Freud, brought with them far-reaching philosophical changes. Darwin's theory of evolution undermined universally held beliefs in God, and Freud's exploration of the unconscious called into question the concept of external reality and the value of human social structures. These and other philosophical changes found artistic expression in the work of Woolf and her contemporaries, who turned their visions away from the chronicling of everyday life in the external social world and instead focused on internal, private reality. Such exploration necessarily engendered rebellion against traditional artistic forms, and *To the Lighthouse* is an enduring example of the formal and thematic experimentation of the early modernist novel.

Such historical background helps students appreciate Woolf's experimentation; similarly, a few biographical points about Woolf help students identify her novel's traditional elements. Woolf had been raised a child of Victorian society: educated at home by her father, the earnest and influential editor Leslie Stephen, and bred into a traditional feminine role by her mother, the noted Victorian beauty Julia Stephen, Woolf never lost her strong connections to the values and traditions of her past, even though she also rebelled against them. The traditional elements of *To the Lighthouse*, then, are the values of Woolf's Victorian past transformed into the material of fiction (Paul).

Conventionally, novels recapitulate the manners and morals that formulate human social life; characters move in society, acting and reacting with other characters in observable events, set against a physical background. In her novels, Woolf questions the manners and morals of traditional society, and so of necessity she also questions the form that contains them. Thus *To the Lighthouse* strikes a delicate balance between tradition and experimentation, between the external world of society and the internal world of consciousness, in essence, between Victorianism and modernism. Once I help students identify this tension between two worlds, many find it possible—indeed rewarding—to tease out the elements of tradition and rebellion in the novel.

We begin with setting. Woolf's settings are often metaphorical, and I explain that many literary critics point to the seascape setting of *To the Lighthouse* as symbolic rather than physical, the sea itself objectifying the modernist expansion of individual consciousness that occurs in the novel. Furthermore, the sea's significance expands to the entire island setting, which affirms freedom from tradition and social restriction: the house with its open doors and windows, the garden, and the gapped hedge leading to a view of the sea symbolize the inner world where the mind roams free, where individual consciousness, emotion, and sensibility are supreme values. The very walls of the house, impregnated with salt and sea, seem anxious to shed their physical being and fade into the mist of consciousness. Even the descriptions of material objects emphasize the world's ephemeral character: "crazy ghosts of chairs and tables whose London life of service was done—they did well enough here [. . .]. The mat was fading, the wall-paper was flapping. You couldn't tell any more that those were roses on it" (26–27; see also 129, 137–41).

Such an amorphous setting and its symbolic implications can present difficulties for inexperienced readers. But when I ask students to extract the physical elements of setting in sections 3–5 of part 1 and then describe where the story occurs, several always bring forth a wealth of physical detail. In so doing, they demonstrate that this setting, like any novel's setting, is simply a place. Whatever its symbolic import, it is also a physical location—an island in the Hebrides, a house, and a garden where activity occurs. Moreover, this particular setting—natural, isolated, away from the quotidian affairs of London life and society—not only symbolizes freedom of consciousness but also generates such freedom. The seascape world eases social restrictions, promoting the freedom of mind that occurs there (19–20). Thus, as in any traditional novel, the setting of *To the Lighthouse* provides the appropriate physical backdrop for the events.

Even more important, this seascape constitutes a shifting, ambivalent setting. Thematically, in Woolf's novels, individual consciousness is always countered by the attraction of society; in essence, the modernist freedom of the individual is countered by the Victorian attachment to external social conventions. *To the Lighthouse* emphasizes that thematic opposition in its setting. I ask students to contrast the daytime setting with the nighttime setting in section 17: the island world alters sharply and significantly between day and night, reflecting the two sides of Woolf's concern. The limitless, open seascape is the daytime setting, where individual consciousness takes precedence. During the day, the Ramsays and their guests walk in the garden, essentially alone with their thoughts; they stop to look through the gap in the hedge at the freedom and openness of the sea. But at night, the sea's limitlessness inspires not freedom from social restrictions but fear of death and oblivion; at night, the characters gather inside the hedge and inside the house, doors and windows closed, candles lit. Their moment of fulfillment comes not from escape into their own inner lives but from the traditional social unity of Mrs. Ramsay's dinner party, symbolized by—and once again physically fostered by—the enclosure of dry land, home, society, and tradition (96–97).

By this point in our examination, students can analyze the elements of *To the Lighthouse's* setting much as they have done with more traditional novels. As they explore the physical characteristics of the daytime and nighttime settings, many perceive a familiar element, the sense of place; when I ask them to consider the implications of place as metaphor, most make the connection to Woolf's thematic ambivalence between modernist rebellion and Victorian tradition. The exploration of consciousness, with its accompanying social freedom, is the hallmark of Woolf's modernist vision. The return to community, with the comfort of its fixed social traditions, demonstrates her attachment to her Victorian roots.

Even students unaccustomed to literary analysis are open to discussions about human nature, and they can usually apply the themes of tradition and rebellion to the characters as well. Critics often interpret Mrs. Ramsay, the fictional representation of Julia Stephen, as the polar opposite of Mr. Ramsay's (or Leslie Stephen's) Victorian factualism; she seems to represent the modern preoccupation with the inner world of the self, of intuition and consciousness, that the novel explores. Her first name unknown, absorbed in the daily rounds of doing for others, she embodies Woolf's indistinct memories of her mother as a "general presence" (*Moments* 83). Indeed, Mrs. Ramsay perceives herself as "a wedge-shaped core of darkness" (62), and Lily Briscoe paints her as a shadow and laments that she can never truly know Mrs. Ramsay (51).

But as always in Woolf's vision, there are two sides to Mrs. Ramsay. I ask students to read closely the two references to the "wedge-shaped core" in Mrs. Ramsay's musings. First she thinks, "All the being and the doing, expansive, glittering, vocal, evaporated; and one shrunk, with a sense of solemnity, *to being oneself, a wedge-shaped core of darkness*, something invisible to others" (62; my emphasis). Here, the image of a core of darkness represents Mrs. Ramsay's sense of her true identity—internal, invisible, and essentially detached from the activity of the external world. But a moment later, she thinks, "*Not as oneself* did one find rest ever, [. . .] but as a wedge of darkness" (63; my emphasis). At this moment, she perceives her essential being as enmeshed in the active day-to-day life of other people and things rather than detached from life; the wedge-shaped core represents not her true self but an escape from that self. Thus, like all aspects of this novel, Mrs. Ramsay vacillates between two worlds—the internal, amorphous and private world of modernist consciousness and the external world of traditional social relations (see 62–71).

Moreover, Mrs. Ramsay depends on the structures of tradition and society to give her life substance and purpose. To illustrate, I read aloud Woolf's description of "The Angel in the House," the paragon of Victorian virtue she criticizes in her essay "Professions for Women" (285). Then we examine the first section of the novel, noting Mrs. Ramsay's angelic and conventional qualities. Like the Angel, Mrs. Ramsay exercises enormous charm and energy in weaving the fabric of social relations, and she exhausts herself attending to the needs of others. And while she sometimes yearns for escape from the ceaseless activity of her daily life, she often desires even more society and structure than already surround her, requiring of herself and of others an excess of community and conventionality. She asks "too many people to stay" (6), and she pressures all of them, especially her children, into conventional social roles: Prue must marry and James shall be "all red and ermine on the Bench" (4). Like her counterpart Julia Stephen, who signed Mrs. Humphry Ward's petition against women's suffrage, Mrs. Ramsay admires men most for their membership in the English patriarchy, and she demands "the subjection of all wives [. . .] to their husband's labours" (11; see also 6-11).

Clearly, Mrs. Ramsay embodies tradition as much as she does rebellion. Exploring her traditional characteristics, many students discover that she is like characters they have encountered in other novels: not an amorphous shadow but a complex, flawed, and human creation, defined as much by her relations in the physical and social world as by her thoughts of immersion in the sea beyond the hedge.

Characteristically, then, Mrs. Ramsay's culminating moment is her dinner party, a transforming moment of social community (see 82–111). No different from a novel by Austen or Dickens, *To the Lighthouse* uses a moment of social interaction to reveal meaning. Like all the structures of tradition in this novel, the dinner party arouses the ambivalence of its guests; they resent the infringement on their private thoughts, and they regret their inability to merge with the others in a moment of social community. Lily, the artist, voices the ambivalence they all feel: she resents the pressure of her feminine social role in conversation with Charles Tansley, but Mrs. Ramsay's overpowering desire for social unity forces Lily to "be nice" (90–92).

Lily questions the value of social tradition because she resents the loss of individuality and honesty that social roles demand. But at the same time, her renunciation helps create Mrs. Ramsay's transcendent "moment" around the dinner table, a "moment" that partakes "of eternity" (105). Furthermore, Lily recapitulates her vacillation between two worlds in her art; she cannot paint "the shapes etherealised"; she must paint the tension between two kinds of reality—"the colour burning on a framework of steel" (48; see also 18-19). Not only Mrs. Ramsay, then, embodies some elements of tradition. Indeed, tradition provides the framework for every aspect of Woolf's novel.

Yet each major element of *To the Lighthouse*—setting, character, plot, and theme—also questions the restrictions of the traditional social world and of the traditional novel that artistically re-creates that world. Virginia Woolf asked such questions because for her the elements of tradition were so patently and powerfully present. In *To the Lighthouse*, she declared that she had laid to rest the ghosts of her childhood, and in so doing she elucidated the strengths as well as the weaknesses of the traditions in her past.

To the Lighthouse offers a surprisingly fruitful experience for readers learning about literary forms. By looking at this experimental work through the novel tradition they know, students come to appreciate the difficulty of Woolf's task as an early modernist writer, and they often see how she projected that difficulty into her form. Just as important, I ask them to consider Woolf's novel from the perspective of genre and formulate for themselves a sophisticated conception of the novel and its elements. Finally, they examine the movement from the Victorian to the modernist sensibility and its personal and cultural effect on Woolf's fiction.

The more students can appreciate about the presence of tradition—historical, biographical, and literary—in *To the Lighthouse*, the more they can value Virginia Woolf's remarkable contribution to the development of the novel and the enduring place of *To the Lighthouse* in literature.

"For Nothing Is Simply One Thing": Knowing the World in *To the Lighthouse*

Mark Hussey

One challenge of teaching *To the Lighthouse* in a large urban university to commuting students who will likely seek jobs in the financial sector is that the students' view of novels is precisely that of the Edwardian novelists Woolf criticized in her 1919 essay "Modern Fiction." Most of my students are "materialists," in Woolf's term (105), looking for plot and action and a neat resolution of conflict at the end. I have taught *To the Lighthouse* in a variety of contexts—sophomore survey, Women in Literature, Twentieth-Century Novel, Virginia Woolf seminar—and always ask students to read "Modern Fiction" before we begin to discuss the novel so that they know Woolf has deliberate reasons for writing as she does.

Students reading *To the Lighthouse* with little or no experience of modernist texts are particularly unsettled by the way nothing seems to "happen." Even English majors struggle with Woolf's narrative technique. Many students get lost in long sentences that expand even further with parentheses and other interruptions. Reading "Modern Fiction" focuses them on the modernist effort to represent in prose what Woolf calls "the flickerings of that innermost flame which flashes its message through the brain" (107).

I tell the class to read the entire novel without worrying about what they do not understand and to finish their first reading of it by the end of the first week of discussion. In the first class I give a minilecture on the cultural context of Woolf's fiction. Referring to "Modern Fiction" and its publication date, I ask what was going on in 1919. Recently, I learned that in 1919 the Chicago White Sox fixed the World Series! Also in 1919, I point out, a solar eclipse confirmed Einstein's relativity theory, making headlines all over the world. Without my explaining the theory, we can usually agree that Einstein revolutionized our understanding of time and space. How might this pertain to Virginia Woolf? Well, in "Modern Fiction" she focuses on how we experience reality and how reality might be represented in fiction, and in *To the Lighthouse* she concerns herself with time and memory.

We discuss our everyday experiencing of experience, what Freud called in 1901 "the psychopathology of everyday life." We all daydream and realize that time seems to go at different speeds: the examples of a forty-minute lecture that seems to last hours or a week's vacation gone in a flash readily bring home the principle. Could Woolf be trying, in her difficult sentences, to represent ordinary human thought? We discuss association, the way the past can suddenly break into consciousness (as it does for Lily Briscoe; see, e.g., 159–61), and our ability to think of several things at once. Possibly, I suggest, some in the room may be listening to what I am saying and simultaneously thinking of something else! Student familiarity with the techniques of cinema (e.g., flash-back, voice-over, or jump cuts) can be a reassuring link to the experience of reading modernist fictions.

When I ask what was going on in 1919, I know that a few students will bring up the First World War, which had just ended. I talk briefly about the war's shattering of Victorian modes and manners and ask whether the book seems to have anything to do with war. If the question does not elicit comment on the three-part structure of the novel, this issue can always be returned to later. Someone may mention modern painting—Cézanne, Matisse, Picasso—and may even explain impressionism and postimpressionism. Thus, we begin to establish that in *To the Lighthouse* Woolf tries to realize a particular "vision" (a word she often uses in her essays to denote the conception that an artist tries to give shape to, whatever the medium) and that this vision was influenced by and contributed to the sweeping changes we call the modernist movement (see the books by Kern and by Chipp for more background material).

Returning to students' discomfort at the novel's apparent lack of action, I suggest we need first to understand how Woolf structures the book and why. On the back cover, the publisher has written: "The subject of this brilliant novel is the daily life of an English family in the Hebrides." Is this so? Quite often students tell me that the book is not about anything. "Nothing happens," they say. A glance at the first two or three pages, where all sorts of things "happen," quickly puts this judgment in question, however. It is even helpful to get students to simply list what is happening: Mrs. Ramsay speaks to James, evoking certain emotions; he is cutting out pictures; his mother fantasizes about his future; his father speaks, evoking other emotions; his mother knits; and so on. These happenings, however, are not the conventional action of a novel, and at first the parts do not seem to relate.

In her notes Woolf sketched the novel as "[t]wo blocks joined by a corridor," drawing the shape (*Holograph Draft*, app. A 48). I propose that we study the first block, "The Window," focusing on Mrs. Ramsay, then the second, "The Lighthouse," focusing on Lily Briscoe, and finally the corridor that connects them, "Time Passes," looking closely at certain passages to see how they relate to one another. This reordering emphasizes that reading in the classroom is different from casual reading. It also reinforces the nonlinearity that is thematic in my introduction to this novel. Again, it can be helpful to make an analogy with the process of assembling a film, where shots taken out of sequence are later assembled to create a sense of continuity. Writers, I point out, generally do not begin at the beginning and write straight through to the end.

In response to the confusion the novel has evoked in students unfamiliar with modernist texts, I offer a hypothesis: *To the Lighthouse* contains within itself a guide to reading it (see Hussey, *Singing* xii, 72–81). A narrowly directed reading of the two "blocks" makes clear why the novel is structured as it is and what its philosophical—or, more significantly, its epistemological—implications are (see *Singing*, ch. 7, for a discussion of the "corridor").

Often, we begin by looking at page 37, the last line of the first paragraph:

"There he stood, demanding sympathy." Then, turning to page 123, we read
Mr. Ramsay: "Will you not tell me just for once that you love me?" (123–24).
Mr. Ramsay's demand for sympathy is met, it seems, when his wife recognizes
that "she had triumphed again" (124). Thus, the line on page 37 begins the arc
of a circle not completed until the very end of part 1. Although the chronological distance between these two points is short, that circle contains a rich and
complex amount of memory that far exceeds what can be measured by the
clock. Referring to students' own daydreaming, I suggest that *To the Lighthouse* represents how rich in thought and feeling a very brief measure of time
can be. Consideration of the word *moment*, so important to this novel, usually
leads to the idea that a moment measures emotionally experienced time as well
as chronological time. As several students bring to the discussion examples of
how different emotional states, often triggered by a specific event, can color an
entire day, many grasp what Woolf continually attempts in her prose: to represent this coloring.

When Lily asks Andrew about his father's work, she is told it concerns
"[s]ubject and object and the nature of reality" (23). Going to section 6 (30–
36), we discuss the implications of the various images used to describe Mr.
Ramsay's thought: an alphabet, a heroic quest, a piano's keyboard. His linear,
positivist thinking contrasts with his wife's more sensuous, intuitive way of
being in the world. Subject and object are quite discrete in Mr. Ramsay's philosophy; for Mrs. Ramsay, they can merge. Some students may have read
Descartes and have an idea of what constitutes the "logos" of Western epistemology. (If not, I sketch the outlines of Cartesian thought with reference to a
general history of philosophy, such as Copleston, or to works on Descartes,
such as those by Caton or Keeling.) Woolf undermines this Cartesian dualism
in her novel by involving readers in an experience that demands they put
together "echoes and fragments" to arrive at truth.

The phrase is from "Impassioned Prose," an essay that Woolf wrote in 1926
while at work on *To the Lighthouse*. In it, she describes how Thomas De
Quincey captured in his writing "states of mind in which, often, time is miraculously prolonged and space miraculously expanded" (171). At the conclusion
of "Impassioned Prose," she writes that "it is not the actual sight or sound itself
that matters, but the reverberations that it makes as it travels through our
minds. These are often to be found far away, strangely transformed; but it is
only by gathering up and putting together these echoes and fragments that we
arrive at the true nature of our experience" (172).

In *To the Lighthouse*, images of James cutting up and arranging pictures in
a catalog and, later, Mrs. Ramsay picking up these pieces and putting them
together demonstrate what the reader must do: select and gather the echoes
and fragments (the novel contains many such metaphors of itself). Images of
fragments coalescing into momentary wholes and then breaking apart once
more, like waves on a beach, appear throughout the novel. For example, Woolf
uses exactly the same terms to describe Mrs. Ramsay in her reverie and Lily

Briscoe when she paints. Each of them has an affinity with the natural world (but Mrs. Ramsay cannot get her husband to notice the flowers in the garden), and each experiences moments in which personality dissolves, along with the boundaries of a stable "ego," of a sense of self. In "The Narrow Bridge of Art," an essay published the same year as *To the Lighthouse*, Woolf wrote, "Every moment is the centre and meeting-place of an extraordinary number of perceptions which have not yet been expressed. Life is always and inevitably much richer than we who try to express it" (229). *To the Lighthouse* expresses this excessive richness of ordinary experience.

At the dinner party (section 17), Mrs. Ramsay acts as an artist of the social. At the start, "Nothing seemed to have merged. They all sat separate" (83). Manners, gender roles, and social conventions are described (90–91). Eventually, the "moment" begins: a sense of unity develops among the guests and family in contrast to the dark chaos outside; they are "composed, as they had not been in the twilight" (97). By talking about the common patterns of their own successful social gatherings—initial awkwardness eventually resolving into a kind of harmony—many students again see this novel as not so far removed from their own lives as they had first thought.

As Mrs. Ramsay looks at what she has brought together, we focus on why Woolf's sentences are so frequently expanded by interruptions: "Just now (but this cannot last, she thought, dissociating herself from the moment [. . .]) just now she had reached security" (104). At this point, we discuss how Woolf wants to represent the simultaneity of various thoughts and their interruptions through the multiple parentheses.

The paragraph ends, "Of such moments, she thought, the thing is made that endures" (105). The language is necessarily vague, for what Woolf tries to represent is an experience rather than an object. In her talk entitled "How Should One Read a Book?" (also written during the composition of *To the Lighthouse*), she describes how the book "as a whole is different from the book received currently in separate phrases" (267). Reading is necessarily linear; we move along each line, word by word. But as we do, we build up an impression of the whole work that can be recalled when we have finished the book. Talking about *To the Lighthouse* in these terms may help students with the difficulty of reading a book whose action is not linear. Woolf places great demands on the reader's memory; like Lily, like Mrs. Ramsay, readers must become artists, gathering up fragments to create momentary wholes. Woolf's essays make clear to most students, though, that these narrative strategies are a deliberate working out of her aesthetic philosophy.

To help readers become artists, Woolf often uses what I have termed "descriptive homologies" (Hussey, *Singing* xix) to draw together fragments of her fiction in the reader's mind, creating juxtapositions in memory that transgress the linear sequence of sentences. For example, Mrs. Ramsay thinks at her dinner party, "Of such moments [. . .] the thing is made that endures" (105). Ten years after that dinner, in part 3, Lily tries to make "of the moment something permanent" (161). Most of us are familiar with the difficulty of moving from conception to realization; most of us, like Lily, have stared at blank space, be it a canvas, page, or computer screen: "She could see it all so clearly, so commandingly, when she looked: it was when she took her brush in hand that the whole thing changed" (19). In the first part of the book, Lily's problem is defined as that of filling space. She wants to paint "colour burning on a framework of steel; the light of a butterfly's wing lying upon the arches of a cathedral" (48). When Lily returns to her painting (with a fresh canvas) ten years later, she thinks it must be beautiful and bright, "one colour melting into another like the colours on a butterfly's wing; but beneath the fabric must be clamped together with bolts of iron" (171), another metaphor for the book itself.

We can easily read Lily's painting as an analogue to the novel. Early on, Lily understands that her problem has to do mainly with relation: "if there, in that corner, it was bright, here, in this, she felt the need of darkness" (52). The great difficulty lies in bringing a personal conception into the world in such a way that others can share it. Their struggles as writers give many students immediate insight into what Lily is experiencing. In her diary in 1926 Woolf described the "greatest book in the world" as that which would be made

> entirely solely & with integrity of one's thoughts. Suppose one could catch them before they became "works of art."? [sic] Catch them hot & sudden as they rise in the mind [. . .]. Of course one cannot; for the process of language is slow & deluding. One must stop to find a word; then, there is the form of the sentence, soliciting one to fill it.
>
> (*Diary* 3: 102)

The "form of the sentence" and the "blank space" of Lily's canvas are analogous, and Lily's wish for her painting to be simultaneously fluid and solid aptly describes the form of *To the Lighthouse*. What seems at first evanescent, wandering, impressionistic, and vague becomes, on closer inspection, a rigorously structured and carefully composed narrative.

Section 3 of "The Lighthouse" (156–62) focuses on Lily's painting. I point out in it several descriptive homologies between Lily's state of mind when painting and Mrs. Ramsay's in her reverie. In Lily's realization that the "great revelation perhaps never did come" occurs yet another self-reflexive image of the book: "Instead there were little daily miracles, illuminations, matches struck unexpectedly in the dark" (161). The criticism that "nothing happens" may now be revised to "nothing conventionally heroic or climactic happens." Both Lily and Mrs. Ramsay attempt to "[make] of the moment something permanent" (161), knowing that doing so is impossible, for time passes, a fact confirmed in the novel's final phrase, "I have had my vision." Lily's present perfect tense shows that the vision cannot be prolonged. A momentary achievement, experienced as she makes the final brush stroke, the line "there, in the centre" (209), completes our reading, finishes the painting, and marks the conclusion of the journey to the lighthouse.

In "The Lighthouse," Mr. Ramsay's belated journey with Cam and James is interwoven with Lily's painting in the garden. Her brush strokes and the strokes of the waves against the boat combine rhythmically. Sections in "The Lighthouse" repeat on a larger scale what happens throughout the book at the sentence level: characters' thoughts are interrupted and expanded by memories and questions. Lily finally reveals the ecstasy of the ordinary: "One wanted, she thought, dipping her brush deliberately, to be on a level with ordinary experience, to feel simply that's a chair, that's a table, and yet at the same time, It's a miracle, it's an ecstasy" (202). In "Modern Fiction" Woolf asks novelists to "[e]xamine for a moment an ordinary mind on an ordinary day" and "record the atoms as they fall upon the mind in the order in which they fall, [. . .] however disconnected and incoherent in appearance" (106–07). In *To the Lighthouse* she does just that, gently but persuasively detaching us from certainty about the answers to those grand questions posed in "Time Passes" and repeated rather banally in Lily's "What is the meaning of life?" (161).

If we focus on moments that describe consciousness, the artist's state of mind as she or he creates, or the way perceptions construct reality, *To the Lighthouse* may lose some of its mystery for student readers unfamiliar with modernist texts. For Mr. Ramsay, knowledge is the straightforward black and white of the keyboard or what Woolf elsewhere termed the strict "railway line of [the] sentence" (*Letters* 3: 135). On the voyage out to the lighthouse, though, James Ramsay perceives a different metaphor for knowledge (and reveals another metaphor for the book itself):

> The Lighthouse was then a silvery, misty-looking tower with a yellow eye, that opened suddenly, and softly in the evening. Now—
> James looked at the Lighthouse. He could see the white-washed rocks; the tower, stark and straight; he could see that it was barred with black and white; he could see windows in it; he could even see washing spread on the rocks to dry. So that was the Lighthouse, was it?
> No, the other was also the Lighthouse. For nothing was simply one thing. The other Lighthouse was true too.   (186)

To the Lighthouse, I believe, undermines the binary logic of our dominant, positivist epistemology and works against the linearity and conclusiveness instilled in the majority of students from an early age by the discipline-bound, content-based education they receive. When they understand that nothing is simply one thing, they share in James's revelation and Lily's creativity and understand that this novel is "about" how we know the world.

Returning to the Lighthouse:
A Postmodern Approach

Pamela L. Caughie

Since the late 1970s, critics have been rereading modernist writers from the perspective of postmodern literature and literary theory, elucidating how modernists anticipated, even inaugurated, postmodernism while challenging received definitions of modernism that have shaped the canon of twentieth-century British literature. While such revisionary readings have become common in critical practice, however, their implications have had little effect on pedagogical practice. This essay considers what a postmodern approach to teaching a classic modernist text like Woolf's might entail—how and why postmodernism challenges our tasks as teachers, changing the questions we ask and the goals we hope to achieve in teaching *To the Lighthouse*.

My title signals my first difficulty in teaching *To the Lighthouse* from a postmodern perspective. How do I convey to students the experience of *returning* to a novel that many are reading for the first time? How do I teach them what postmodernism means when they come to my classes in twentieth-century literature with little or no understanding of what modernism was?

I could begin by defining these terms, treating modernism and postmodernism as distinct literary periods and distinguishing between the different formal features, aesthetic interests, and cultural crises characterizing each. (See the essays by Paul, Hussey, and Yunis in this volume for definitions of modernism. See Waugh, *Metafiction* 21–28; Hutcheon, *Politics* 1–29; and McHale 1–11 for definitions of postmodernism.) At the risk of oversimplifying, I could say that modernist fiction makes us self-conscious about the narrative perspective and the form of the work, while postmodernist fiction makes us self-conscious about conventions of representation, the very production of the work. If modernist writing seeks to give us multiple perspectives on reality— "One wanted fifty pairs of eyes to see with" (198)—postmodern fiction presents reality as itself the product of representation. Postmodern novels emphasize writing rather than consciousness, narrative plotting rather than time, intrusive narrators rather than the dissipation of narrative authority. Where the strategies of modernist fiction can be discussed in relation to Einstein's theory of relativity, Freud's discovery of the unconscious, or Bergson's concept of subjective time, the discontinuity, indeterminacy, and parody of postmodern fiction can be discussed in connection with quantum theory, Derrida's deconstruction of binary oppositions, Lacan's decentered subject, and Lyotard's repudiation of metanarratives—theories that undermine the notion of stable, predictable systems and that seek out the instabilities of any discourse (Gaggi 49–51, 157–87; Marshall 6, 81–119; Lyotard 27–41, 55–57).

Such definitions would encourage students to look for modernist or postmodernist elements in Woolf's novel. For example, Lily Briscoe's discussion of her painting with William Bankes neatly encapsulates a modernist-formalist aesthetics (52–53), while the novel's self-reflexivity (the way it turns in on itself, making the creation of an artwork part of its subject) or the indeterminacy of Lily's final brush stroke (Is it a horizontal line connecting the right and left sides of the painting? Is it a vertical line dividing the canvas?) could illustrate a postmodern aesthetic. Similarly, one might contrast Augustus Carmichael's modernist understanding of art, validating the artist's activity in terms of the thing that endures—"nothing stays; all changes; but not words, not paint"—with Lily's more postmodern understanding, emphasizing the creative process itself, valuing the artwork as disposable—"it would be rolled up and flung under a sofa" (179). Or one might compare passages that typify a modernist sensibility—such as where Mrs. Ramsay, alone and "[l]osing personality" (63), becomes "a wedge-shaped core of darkness" (62)—with lines that represent a postmodernist understanding of the mediated nature of subjectivity. For example, the line "We are in the hands of the Lord" (63) reveals even one's innermost desires as the effect of cultural conditioning (Minow-Pinkney, "Reading" 241).

If the approach I have sketched out above seems legitimate as a way to teach *To the Lighthouse* from a postmodern perspective, if most students would feel comfortable with an approach that encourages them to identify the novel's postmodern themes and features, it is precisely because that approach is so familiar, relying as it does on a pedagogy more characteristic of a modernist reading practice than a postmodernist one. Drawing distinctions between two things, isolating and identifying the common features of each, treating the text as representative of a certain kind of aesthetics, reading the novel as a reflection of its author's consciousness or its historical moment—these seemingly common pedagogical tasks correspond to a modernist-formalist practice. Postmodernism, however, questions the assumptions on which such a pedagogy rests: for example, that the novel is an autonomous entity existing prior to and apart from the act of reading; that all texts grouped under a common term share certain features; that these features are properties of the texts themselves; and that the appropriate pedagogical tasks are to describe a work as a coherent whole, to interpret its meanings, and to define its form.

Thus, my dilemma: my students need and expect definitions of modernism and postmodernism, yet the postmodern theory underlying my pedagogy challenges the very act of definition (Caughie, *Postmodernism* 16–19; Marshall 3–4). Defining concepts, delineating literary periods, and classifying texts—familiar pedagogical tasks—have been challenged by postmodernism, which questions the boundaries endemic to any definition by asking how and why certain boundaries have been drawn and whose interests those boundaries serve. Postmodernism makes us acutely aware of our own implication in the discourses and histories we attempt to explain. "There is no 'outside' from which to 'objectively' name the present," or the past (Marshall 3).

So how do I get students to approach the novel from a postmodern perspective when their literary training, like ours, has largely been based on modernist assumptions? How do I keep a postmodern approach from becoming an exercise in mining the novel for postmodern features? What precisely does a pedagogy based on postmodern assumptions attempt to teach?

By way of answering these questions, let me return to the problem of returning to a novel being read for the first time. That dilemma, which gave rise to the need for definitions, is in fact a false one. For literary history is made, not recorded. "Returning to the lighthouse" does not mean recovering "that which was already there" (Foucault 78), for what was "there" (in this case, Woolf's novel) is always only the effect of a certain kind of narrative, told from a particular point of view for a particular purpose. What we single out as "features" of a literary period or style are not properties of the texts themselves but the values created by our approach to literature.

The false start of this essay, then, where I begin with a problem that turns out to be illusory, is analogous to the false start I take in my classes on Woolf, where I perform the difference a postmodern reading makes. I introduce *To the Lighthouse* by providing an overview of Woolf's life and writing. Then I stop abruptly in the middle of my remarks and read a passage from Catherine Belsey's *Critical Practice*: "Books [and seminars] about authors often begin with a brief biography discussing the influence of the family, the environment or the society." Belsey names the ideology behind such an approach "expressive realism," where "to understand the text is to explain it in terms of the author's ideas, psychological state, or social background" (13). Along with a formalist reading practice, which locates meaning in the words on the page, expressive realism, which locates meaning in "something anterior" to the text (13), has been the reigning paradigm in literary pedagogy since modernist literature entered the canon. Those critical practices shore up the belief that there *is* some*thing* called modernism. My performative opening seeks to jolt students out of their complacency, to make them aware of the noninnocent nature of reading and thus self-conscious about the assumptions, questions, and values that inform readings of *To the Lighthouse*.

To illustrate this point, I compare reading practices. As an example of the making of modernism, I assign Erich Auerbach's now classic essay on *To the Lighthouse*, "The Brown Stocking," after our reading of part 1. Auerbach establishes Woolf's novel as a modernist classic not only by including it in his monumental history of Western realism, *Mimesis*, but also by describing its narrative method in terms of a modernist-formalist aesthetics: the use of multiple and shifting perspectives, the subjective rendering of time, and the tracing of the mind's inner processes. Modernism's seeming hostility to historical reality, evident in the way Woolf's novel neglects the "great changes [and] exterior turning points" of history, such as World War I (546), and in its critique of mimetic representation ("the picture was not of them, [Lily] said" [52]), provides an antidote, Auerbach says, to increasing diversity and the collapse of old value systems between the wars.

Auerbach's essay lets me explain not only what modernism was but, more

important, how it has been made. For Auerbach's reading method is an analogue of the very modernism he defines, and it responds to the same historical
forces. As he admits, he could never have written anything so ambitious as a
history of Western representation unless he (like Woolf) had eschewed large
historical explanation, focusing instead on a close reading of certain motifs in a
few randomly selected texts representing the whole of Western realism (548),
as Woolf (in Auerbach's reading) exploits the "minor, unimpressive, random
events" (546) of everyday life to achieve a new kind of cultural and aesthetic
harmony. Auerbach's narrative of Western realism relies on a modern
(Hegelian) concept of history as a progression of events toward some telos and
on a dialectical approach that resolves contradictions on a deeper or higher
level, revealing the commonalities in what appear to be conflicting positions.
Although Auerbach assumes his is an objective, disinterested description of
Woolf's novel, his method inadvertently undermines this assumption because
it depends on and perpetuates the very values he has located in this work—
unity, coherence, and synthesis.

To help students consider the implications of Auerbach's reading, I then
assign Barbara Johnson's reading of his essay in *A World of Difference* (164–
66). Johnson points out that "what Auerbach calls 'minor, unimpressive, random events'—measuring a stocking, conversing with the maid, answering the
phone—can all be identified as conventional *women's* activities" (165). Thus
when Auerbach says that Woolf's focus on the minor and trivial events of daily
life signifies an "approaching unification and simplification" (553), his seemingly neutral values of unity and simplicity reveal, Johnson argues, "an urge to
resubsume female difference under the category of the universal, which has
always been unavowedly male" (165–66). Not only does Auerbach neglect to
consider gender differences, but his reading functions structurally to negate
female difference by, on the one hand, presenting difference as a loss of commonality and, on the other hand, appropriating activities historically associated
with women's roles to index the "elementary things which *men* in general have
in common" (Auerbach 552; my emphasis).

This exercise does not aim to dismiss Auerbach as sexist; he did include a
woman in the canon of great Western writers. Nor does it aim to compare two
interpretations of the novel, for Johnson does not provide a reading of *To the
Lighthouse*. Rather, it aims to change the assumptions many students bring to
this novel and the questions they ask of it. Johnson's approach is postmodern
in that it seeks out what is excluded by Auerbach's, with its emphasis on unity,
harmony, and synthesis. Johnson's essay makes us aware of the politics of interpretation, the motivated and therefore noninnocent nature of reading. Johnson's reassessment of Auerbach lets me turn students' attention from what
Auerbach says about the novel to what his essay does, from its content to its
function, from the formal achievements of the novel to the structural exclusions produced by any reading that emphasizes continuity in history and values
commonality in human experience. A postmodern pedagogy, then, seeks to

make students aware of how any discourse produces its own nonknowledge and of what results from such ignorance.

"What structural exclusions does Woolf's novel produce?" I ask students as we begin our reading of "Time Passes." This section is difficult for many students, who keep asking Lily's question, "What can it all mean?" (145). I encourage them to focus instead on how this part functions in the overall narrative. Part 2 has long been read as marking a transition between the Victorian past (pt. 1) and the modernist present (pt. 3) of the novel. From a postmodern perspective, however, "Time Passes" functions less as a transition from a pre- to postwar order than as a problematizing disruption in the narratives constructed in parts 1 and 3: a family romance narrative modeled on Freud's oedipal theory of infantile development (most clearly evident in pt. 1, sec. 7) and a modernist narrative of the artist's achievement of transcendent vision (dramatized in Lily's closing words). Part 2, I suggest, reveals what these modern narratives cannot account for.

"Time Passes" narrates the gaps between the acts of history, not just in presenting the minute particulars of the passage of time over major historical events (Auerbach's emphasis) but also in testifying to what has not been narrated in history or in fiction—specifically, the memories and interior monologues of Mrs. McNab, the woman who tends the Ramsays' summer home. *To the Lighthouse*, like much postmodern fiction, presents the stories of those marginalized by history (the mother, the woman artist, the housekeeper). But how, I ask students, is Mrs. McNab included in the narrative? We read section 5.

> As she lurched (for she rolled like a ship at sea) and leered (for her eyes fell on nothing directly, [. . .] she was witless, she knew it), as she clutched the banisters and hauled herself upstairs and rolled from room to room, she sang [. . .] something that had been gay twenty years before on the stage perhaps, [. . .] but now, coming from the toothless, bonneted, caretaking woman, was robbed of meaning, was like the voice of witlessness, humour, persistency itself [. . .].   (130)

"What does it mean to be 'robbed of meaning'?" I ask, drawing on Mary Lou Emery's reading of part 2. Students often comment on Mrs. McNab's simplicity and the natural imagery used to describe her. As a working-class woman, Mrs. McNab is presented as part of time's natural cycle, one of the natural forces, like the little airs that work on the empty house, one who, like Faulkner's Dilsey, endures. Unlike the organic spirit of Mrs. McNab, the Ramsays succumb to time and the forces of history, and Lily Briscoe changes, as a woman and an artist, over ten years. Thus, the narrative perspective in part 2 is far from impersonal. Indeed, Woolf's narrative admits its own difficulties in imagining the inner life of a lower-class woman who is outside history:

> Visions of joy there *must have been* at the wash-tub, say with her children [. . .], at the public-house, drinking; turning over scraps in her drawers.

> Some cleavage of the dark there *must have been* [. . .]. The mystic, the visionary, walking the beach on a fine night, stirring a puddle, looking at a stone, asking themselves "What am I," "What is this?" had suddenly an answer vouchsafed them [. . .]. But Mrs. McNab continued to drink and gossip as before.   (131; my emphasis)

Auerbach first pointed out such narrative uncertainty as characteristic of the novel as a whole. However, the objective of Auerbach's modernist practice is to describe and classify the narrative techniques; the objective of our postmodernist practice is to interrogate their function. The narrative uncertainty does not produce the same effect throughout. The speculations offered about Mrs. Ramsay in part 1 endow her with an aura of secrecy and a depth of meaning ("Was it wisdom? Was it knowledge?" [50]), while those offered about Mrs. McNab confine her to representing the lower classes and their supposed simplicity: "But Mrs. McNab continued to drink and gossip as before."

Vision, so important for the artist, is denied Mrs. McNab. When Mrs. McNab remembers Mrs. Ramsay, she envisions concrete things: "boots and shoes," "a brush and comb," "her grey cloak," "a plate of milk soup" (136). In contrast, when Lily remembers Mrs. Ramsay, she tries to imagine "her thoughts, her imaginations, her desires. What did the hedge mean to her, what did the garden mean to her, what did it mean to her when a wave broke?" (198). The concrete "crumpled glove in the corner of a sofa" stirs Lily's imaginative pursuit of "the essential thing," the spirit of Mrs. Ramsay (49). Mrs. McNab's memories consist of isolated things; Lily puts things together, "write[s] them out in some sentence" (147), a process that in this novel defines vision, the ability to forge relationships out of disparate experiences, "to feel simply that's a chair, that's a table, and yet at the same time, It's a miracle, it's an ecstasy" (202). Although Lily's closing words, "it was finished," first used in reference to Mrs. McNab's cleaning (141), connect the artist's work with the cleaning woman's, only Lily is allowed vision (209). To be "robbed of meaning" is to be denied vision, the power to imaginatively reconstruct the past and thus fulfill some present desire, as Lily does in part 3. Given a voice in this novel, Mrs. McNab is still denied narrative agency, the ability to select and order events into a meaningful sequence, as Lily does in one medium and Woolf in another.

Far from recuperating Mrs. McNab's story, Woolf's narrative seems to acknowledge the limits of its vision. *To the Lighthouse* may tell a different story, eliding historical events and focusing instead on women's daily existence and everyday family life, but as long as the writer desires to bring all into harmony with a dominant theme (see Woolf, *Diary* 3: 102), the narrative will necessarily produce its own exclusions even as it attempts to narrate what has been excluded. Harmony, unity, vision—the values created by a distinctively modernist narrative—elide the crisis in modern culture that "Time Passes" represents: the tension produced by the historical need to acknowledge diversity in the general public and the equally compelling psychological need to seek unity in a common culture. "Time Passes" marks the eruption of that tension into this modernist narrative. Mrs. McNab's daily life intrudes on the story of the Ramsays, calling attention to what cannot be brought into harmony with its vision. Like the report in brackets (sec. 6) that intrudes on Lily's vision of Mrs. Ramsay in part 3 (180) and resists the narrative's tendency to sentimentality, "Time Passes" marks the narrative's self-resistance, its structural awareness of its own exclusions.

A postmodern reading seeks to sensitize students to the tensions in any discourse and to the structural exclusions produced by efforts to resolve them. It reveals the question "What does it mean?" to be, as Lily recognizes, "a catchword [. . .], caught up from some book" (145), a loaded question, not an innocent one. Returning to *To the Lighthouse* from a postmodern vantage point can result in a simple reversal of values, where difference, indeterminacy, and discontinuity become the valued features of a new mode of writing. But such an approach subsumes postmodernism to the contours of a modernist paradigm. Difference, discontinuity, and indeterminacy are not the ends of a postmodern practice; rather, they are the effects produced by a different kind of inquiry. A postmodern reading is less concerned with defining a modernist classic like *To the Lighthouse* than with interrogating how and why it has been defined as it has; less concerned with tracing the evolution of modernism than with tracing the conflicts and motives behind its emergence as a literary concept and as a course topic; less concerned with interpreting the novel than with scrutinizing what is at stake in any interpretation (Marshall 9–12). Any pedagogy seeking to make students self-conscious about how they read cannot simply reproduce the same reading again and again; instead, it must provide a way to displace the authority of its own position and to reveal its own forms of ignorance. Toward this end, teaching *To the Lighthouse* is valuable less for what it tells students about Woolf or modernism than for how the novel's very structure produces a rupture in the narrative consciousness, thereby displacing the authority of its own narrative dynamics.

A postmodern pedagogy takes risks. If you perform the difference postmodernism makes, you risk that your students won't get it; if, instead, you make that difference explicit, reducing postmodernism to a set of themes or positions, then *you* don't get it. For a fundamental insight of postmodernism is that no one can be a postmodernist since any position is necessarily constituted by what it must displace in order to take hold (Butler, "Foundations" 8). What are the lessons returning to *To the Lighthouse* can teach? That "nothing is simply one thing" (186) and that one can never simply return.

The Language of Fabric in *To the Lighthouse*

Eileen Barrett

> Or do I fabricate with words, loving them as I do?
> —Virginia Woolf, *The Diary of Virginia Woolf*

In *A Room of One's Own* Woolf declares, "It would be a thousand pities if women wrote like men" (88). In my modern British fiction course, we discuss Woolf's statement, asking how women's writing might differ from men's. The predominantly lower-middle-class students in the course reflect the multicultural population of California State University, Hayward, a campus serving the San Francisco Bay area. Many (primarily women) are returning to school after years of working, raising a family, or both; most work twenty to forty hours a week. These students talk fluently about plot and character, sharing their diverse experiences to create lively class discussions that frequently bring out their feminism. They are less proficient, however, in discussing how writers use language and imagery to convey meaning.

I have two goals in teaching the following directed sequence of classes on *To the Lighthouse*, then: to continue the analysis of gender and language central to our readings of James Joyce, D. H. Lawrence, and Katherine Mansfield but, more important, to focus on Woolf's language of fabric as a way to model the skill of close reading. Students practice that skill on their own during the remainder of the course.

Before we begin the novel, we read Elaine Showalter's "Piecing and Writing" or Elaine Hedges's "The Needle or the Pen: The Literary Rediscovery of Women's Textile Work." Not only do these essays demonstrate how gender might influence writing, they also create a critical context for our analysis of Woolf's textile imagery. Additionally, I assign Alice Walker's "In Search of Our

Mothers' Gardens" or Jane Marcus's "Invisible Mending." These autobiographical essays provide contemporary models of the woman-identified relationship Woolf portrays between Lily and Mrs. Ramsay. They also generate discussion of the roles that gender, class, and ethnicity play in creating arbitrary distinctions between art and craft.

Woven throughout the novel, Woolf's language of fabric invites close reading. We focus on this language in passages from three major scenes: Mrs. Ramsay at the drawing room window (38), Mrs. Ramsay at the dinner party (106), and Lily at her canvas (171). At the same time, we trace references to fabric throughout the novel, enabling us to connect "Time Passes" to the other two parts. Once discovered, the language of fabric helps students appreciate the integrity of Woolf's novel and unravel complex feminist themes.

I first ask students to notice how *To the Lighthouse* opens: Mrs. Ramsay sits behind the drawing room window knitting a stocking while Lily Briscoe stands outside on the lawn painting Mrs. Ramsay (3–30). This connection between Mrs. Ramsay's knitting and Lily's painting serves as Woolf's narrative warp. Each woman works with a fabric, Mrs. Ramsay with her stocking and Lily with her canvas, and Woolf weaves these fabrics together to create her text. Further, Woolf uses materials like Mrs. Ramsay's shawl as symbolic devices to enhance her own narrative fabrication.

At this stage, I ask students to supply meanings for *fabricate* and emphasize the importance of their definitions by writing them on the board. Someone invariably notes that it means to work with fabric or other materials to produce something; another student volunteers that it means to make up, create, or invent; and yet another remarks that it can mean to lie or to deceive.

No one knew better than Woolf did, I then explain, about the connections between writing and working with fabric. As an amateur bookbinder and cofounder of the Hogarth Press, she was keenly aware of the material quality of the *text*—a word that, she was certain to know, derives from the Latin for "fabric." I read aloud Woolf's description of her daily activities to illustrate the point: "when nothing is written one may safely suppose that I have been stitching books" (*Diary* 2: 141). Using Diane Gillespie's *The Sisters' Arts*, a text central to my informal lectures, I elaborate on Woolf's interests in painting, writing, and working with fabric and describe her relationship with her sister, the painter Vanessa Bell. Perhaps Woolf's collaborations with Bell reminded her of the text's textuality, the connections among writing, painting, and working with fabric.

Like other women of her class and time, Woolf learned to sew, knit, and embroider during her youth. In later years, she claimed that knitting was "the saving of life" (*Letters* 1: 491) and that embroidery was a soothing diversion (*Letters* 3: 202). Vanessa Bell, along with other artists, elevated similar crafts to art. During the second decade of the century, Bell not only painted but also created designs for clothing, rugs, and screens, decorated plates, and worked cross-stitch cushions for the Omega Workshop. To enhance students' understanding of the sisters' artistic relationship, I show them slides from *Bloomsbury*, Gillian

Naylor's beautiful collection of Omega artwork, including Bell's portrait of her sister knitting; I also show them photographs of Woolf dressed in clothes that Bell designed (Morrell) and reproductions of Bell's woodcuts embroidering the margins of Woolf's "Kew Gardens" (Gillespie, *Sisters' Arts*).

I return to Lily and Mrs. Ramsay's artistic relationship by calling attention to Vanessa Bell as a model for Lily Briscoe. Not surprisingly, Bell admired Lily, commenting in a letter to Woolf, "Surely Lily Briscoe must have been rather a good painter—before her time perhaps, but with great gifts really?" (*Letters* 3: 573). Bell also mentions that Woolf modeled Mrs. Ramsay after their mother, Julia Stephen: "you have given a portrait of mother which is more like her to me than anything I could ever have conceived of as possible" (*Letters* 3: 572). In my classes, however, I want to emphasize the artistic relationship between Lily and Mrs. Ramsay, so I note that Woolf also used her artistic sister as a model for Mrs. Ramsay. In fact, responding to Bell's letter, Woolf writes, "Probably there is a great deal of you in Mrs. Ramsay" (*Letters* 3: 383).

As many students soon realize, Mrs. Ramsay is complex. Embodying the contradictions and duplicities marriage required of Victorian women, including its willed passivity and feigned weakness, Mrs. Ramsay patterns her choices after the options set forth in Sarah Stickney Ellis's nineteenth-century writings for married women. After warning her audience that some men "are not, strictly speaking, noble, nor highly enlightened, nor altogether good," Ellis insists that a true wife should "exhibit by the most delicate, but most profound respect, how highly she is capable of valuing her husband [. . .]. Not [. . .] merely to comfort him by her endearments, but actually to raise him in his own esteem [. . .]" (125–26). I use this passage to show students that Mrs. Ramsay sustains her marriage by artfully lying or fabricating.

With this picture of Mrs. Ramsay established, we do a close reading of our first passage, where Mrs. Ramsay reflects on her life and marriage as acts of fabrication:

> Immediately, Mrs. Ramsay seemed to fold herself together, one petal closed in another, and the whole fabric fell in exhaustion upon itself, so that she had only strength enough to move her finger, in exquisite abandonment to exhaustion, across the page of Grimm's fairy story, while there throbbed through her, like the pulse in a spring which has expanded to its full width and now gently ceases to beat, the rapture of successful creation. (38)

While Mrs. Ramsay's act climaxes with "exquisite abandonment" representing the "rapture of successful creation," a few students quickly notice her perilous position. As a part of the marriage as well as its creative knitter, she is the fabric folding in exhaustion, the pulse ceasing to beat; both images prefigure her death. Still, her marriage is her art. She embroiders it, insisting that Lily must marry (49), yet knowing she insists because she needs to legitimate her own choices: "she was driven on, too quickly she knew, almost as if it were an escape for her too, to say that people must marry; people must have children" (60).

Woolf deepens Mrs. Ramsay's ambivalence by repeatedly associating her with images of twisted fabric. I ask students to search "The Window" for such images, and they find several examples. Lily knows Mrs. Ramsay by her crumpled glove with its twisted finger (49), a synecdoche that captures the "faint touch of irony that made Mrs. Ramsay slip through one's fingers" (175). Indeed, Mrs. Ramsay's art depends on artifice—"she would adroitly shape; even maliciously twist" (49). For instance, she protects James from the disappointment of a canceled trip to the lighthouse with false assurances about the weather, while making "some little twist of the reddish-brown stocking she was knitting, impatiently" (4).

Similarly, she protects her husband. Although Mr. Ramsay envisions himself on a chivalric expedition (36), a few students notice that this knight protects his wife only because she allows it: "For he wished, she knew, to protect her" (65). Thus when Mrs. Ramsay listens to the men talk, envisioning a "masculine intelligence" beyond her ken, I direct students to the way Woolf has Mrs. Ramsay unconsciously qualify her admiration in our second passage:

> [S]he let it uphold and sustain her, this admirable fabric of the masculine intelligence, which ran up and down, crossed this way and that, like iron girders spanning the swaying fabric, upholding the world, so that she could trust herself to it utterly, even shut her eyes, or flicker them for a moment, as a child staring up from its pillow winks at the myriad layers of the leaves of a tree. Then she woke up. It was still being fabricated.
>
> (106)

Nearly all my students pause when the narrator describes the "fabric of the masculine intelligence," knowing that Mrs. Ramsay's hands hold the knitting needles. When the narrator compares that intelligence to "iron girders," we assume that Mrs. Ramsay believes it upholds the world. But these girders span "the swaying fabric," reducing masculine intelligence to a design within a more complex pattern. Childlike, Mrs. Ramsay trusts this "masculine intelligence," some of my students point out, but by shifting to the figurative meaning of *fabricate*, the narrator also suggests that on some level, Mrs. Ramsay realizes that the patriarchy invents it: "It was still being fabricated."

Mrs. Ramsay's green cashmere shawl also plays an important part in Woolf's narrative fabric. Students eagerly peruse the text for shawl images. Lily sees Mrs. Ramsay knitting her stocking through the window, framed in part by the green shawl (30). Protected by the shawl, Mrs. Ramsay willingly goes to Mr. Ramsay (65). At dinner, she pulls it around her as if to hide her temporary absence of feeling (94). Like the glove, the shawl functions as a synecdoche for Mrs. Ramsay: through its unfolding, time passes and major events are conveyed; its presence in the house reminds us that even after her death, Mrs. Ramsay's essence remains.

By now, accustomed to Woolf's play on the language of fabric, a few students suggest other metaphoric fabrications, such as the way Mrs. Ramsay knits people's fates through her marriage plotting. Reminding them of the artistic unity Woolf suggests between Mrs. Ramsay and Lily in the opening scene (3–30), I ask if Mrs. Ramsay and Lily shape reality in similar ways, and we analyze Woolf's textile images to find out. When we discuss the dinner party, for example, students practiced in tracing the language of fabric notice that Lily fixes her gaze on some needlework (85). The floral design embroidered in the tablecloth helps Lily solve an aesthetic problem in her painting (84–85, 102). Meanwhile, Mrs. Ramsay looks at the fruit bowl and juxtaposes colors and shadows; arranges curved, ridged, and round shapes; and becomes upset when someone spoils the aesthetic pattern (108–09).

Moreover, just as Lily must shed "her impressions as a woman" (53) to paint, Mrs. Ramsay discards images of herself as wife and mother, losing "the fret, the hurry, the stir" (63). Furthermore, Woolf suggests that Mrs. Ramsay achieves her epiphany through her skillful fabrication; the narrator interrupts Mrs. Ramsay's acute awareness of herself as "a wedge-shaped core of darkness" (62) to tell us that she "accomplished here something dexterous with her needles" (63). Lily then captures and paints this wedge image on her canvas (52).

Woolf also suggests the artistic connection between Lily and Mrs. Ramsay in a scene with the shawl as a central image. Bidding her youngest children good night, Mrs. Ramsay finds her daughter Cam frightened by the boar's skull that James insists remain hanging on the nursery wall. Mrs. Ramsay wraps her shawl around the skull, thereby transforming this emblem of death into a fairy garden for Cam. Meanwhile, she assures James that "the skull was still there under the shawl" (115), thus finding a "razor edge of balance between two opposite forces" similar to what Lily seeks in her painting (193). Discussion of this scene also prepares students for Woolf's use of Mrs. Ramsay's shawl in "Time Passes."

Some students point out that Mrs. Ramsay's shawl unravels three times in "Time Passes," exposing the frailty of life's fabric while seamlessly unifying the narrative. To signal Mrs. Ramsay's death, the narrator notes that "one fold of the shawl loosened and swung to and fro" (130). Prue's death in childbirth unwinds another fold of the shawl, which "hung, and swayed" (133), while the war and Andrew's death further loosen the shawl (133). Finally, when Mrs. McNab leaves the house to decay, "the swaying shawl swung to and fro" (137). Why, then, I ask, does this section end with Lily? Usually students grasp that whereas Mrs. Ramsay was only half awake to life's fabrications (106), Lily is ready to see through their complex patterns: "Here she was again, she thought, sitting bolt upright in bed. Awake" (143).

In "The Lighthouse" we continue to trace the language of fabric. As Lily reflects on the Ramsay marriage, for example, the narrator assures us, "She was not inventing; she was only trying to smooth out something she had been given years ago folded up; something she had seen" (199). Some students remember that Mrs. Ramsay sees in Lily a "thread" of "something of her own" that she likes "very much" (104). Rather than leave a crumpled glove to Lily, Mrs. Ramsay recognizes their common artistic thread and bequeaths an image of her marriage as folded fabric.

Lily achieves creative unity when her final brush stroke brings her a moment of ecstasy, exhaustion, and vision. But before she can paint her canvas, Lily must also smooth out Mr. Ramsay's "heavy draperies of grief" (152). Resisting his demands for sympathy, she praises his boots (153). Some astute student usually notices that Lily's compliment inspires Mr. Ramsay's eloquence about another fabrication; celebrating the craft of making boots, Mr. Ramsay can shed his grief. Thus relieved, he proceeds to the boat that carries him, by means of another kind of canvas, to the lighthouse. A few of my students delight in pointing out that now the sea and sky form for Lily "all one fabric," the air becoming "a fine gauze which held things and kept them softly in its mesh" (182). Suddenly, Mrs. Ramsay appears to Lily, "flick[ing] her needles to and fro, knit[ting] her reddish-brown stocking" (202).

By remembering Mrs. Ramsay's creative rather than maternal and wifely aspects, Lily answers her personal and aesthetic questions. Although she imagines Augustus Carmichael as a male artist telling her that everything in life vanishes "but not words, not paint," she as a female artist fears that her painting will "be rolled up and flung under a sofa" (179). But by unfolding and unraveling Mrs. Ramsay's fabric and acknowledging her as an artist, Lily completes her painting. Drawing the line in the middle of her canvas, Lily achieves her razor edge of balance.

Many of my students find Lily's vision at the end of *To the Lighthouse* satisfying. But to complete our discussion of Woolf's language of fabric, we turn to one more passage for close reading:

> Beautiful and bright it should be on the surface, feathery and evanescent, one colour melting into another like the colours on a butterfly's wing; but beneath the fabric must be clamped together with bolts of iron. It was to be a thing you could ruffle with your breath; and a thing you could not dislodge with a team of horses.　　　　　　　　　　　　　　(171)

I want students to see that, like the fairy garden Mrs. Ramsay created for Cam with her shawl, Lily's painting is "feathery and evanescent." Similarly, like the skull that Mrs. Ramsay reassured James was there, horses cannot dislodge Lily's painting. Whereas the iron girders of masculine intelligence merely spanned the swaying fabric (106), Lily's bolts of iron clamp and secure her canvas. We need not fear for her painting; it will not be forgotten.

Many students appreciate the way Woolf's novel weaves female experience with a language of fabric, and their close readings inform our later discussions of gender differences in writing. And when a student proudly wears her handknit sweater to the last day of class, I know that Woolf's validation of often forgotten or trivialized women's arts has affected more than classroom discussions.

Reading Provisionally:
Narrative Theory and *To the Lighthouse*

Mary Pinkerton

Years ago, when I read *To the Lighthouse* for the first time as a college student, I was puzzled and bewildered. So that now, when I teach it, I try to remember that response, to put myself in my students' place, incorporating their responses to the novel into class discussion. I have discovered that narrative theory gives students ways to approach this complex modern novel: tools for provisional reading and interpretation.

By using narrative theory, along with the assumptions of reader-response criticism and the work on cognitive development done by William Perry, in *Forms of Intellectual and Ethical Development in the College Years: A Scheme*, and by Mary Field Belenky, Blythe McVicker Clinchy, Nancy Rule Goldberger, and Jill Mattuck Tarule, in *Women's Ways of Knowing: The Development of Self, Voice, and Mind*, I hope to encourage students to develop cognitively toward what Perry calls "committed relativism" (136–37) and Belenky et al. call "constructed knowledge" (134). Put simply, narrative theory helps students begin to see that multiple interpretations are possible but that some are more explanatory than others. My approach is eclectic, bringing in historical and biographical context, feminist theory, intertextual references, and a variety of other critical approaches. In emphasizing narrative theory, however, I have found that many students begin to move away from asking questions that implicitly seek straightforward answers from an authority figure (such as "What does the lighthouse symbolize?") to generating their own reading strategies and interpretations.

I have taught *To the Lighthouse* in a twentieth-century women writers course and also in a course on the modern British novel. Both are upper-division courses taken by English majors with an emphasis in literature, writing, or education to fulfill a distribution requirement. The women writers course also attracts women's studies majors and a handful of students taking it as a humanities elective. Between twenty-five and thirty-five students (including three or four returning students) generally enroll in these classes, allowing me to use a combination of small discussion groups, class discussion, and lecture. In the modern British novel course, we usually begin with a novel that demonstrates features of conventional realistic fiction (Hardy or early Forster), and then we move to impressionism (*The Good Soldier*, perhaps) and a novel with a single character filter (*A Portrait of the Artist as a Young Man*, for instance). In the twentieth-century women writers course, I might begin with Wharton (more conventional and realistic) and then move to Mansfield, assigning a story with a single character filter. In both classes, such a progression helps prepare students for Woolf's complexity.

I encourage students to read actively, raising questions and responding honestly to the works we're studying, and that desire for active student involvement has uncovered some of the difficulties they face in reading Woolf. In either reading journals or short (two- to three-hundred-word) responses, many students reveal their frustrations with *To the Lighthouse.* They have trouble keeping the characters straight, complain about seeing no plot development, and are baffled by what they call a confusing point of view. One student, for example, wrote, "Would so much be lost by telling the reader who is thinking? During the dinner party the reader is left hanging at several points, forced to 'backpedal' several paragraphs in a sometimes feeble attempt to understand whose thoughts are being exposed." A couple of students in the women writers class reflect many of their classmates' views when they lament that they read *A Room of One's Own* and thought Woolf was a feminist but find Mrs. Ramsay so conventional. In my classes, I attempt to take these first problems and reactions as a starting point, to work with them.

Students' initial frustration involves the lack of a story about external events: "I don't know what's happening." "How can Lily be painting on the lawn one moment and throwing herself on Mrs. Ramsay's knee the next?" It may be a critical commonplace that Woolf downplays external events (E. Auerbach 546), but many students are not used to exploring subjective responses to situations triggered by random external events. What helps? Because I remember my relief when a professor outlined "events" in *Mrs. Dalloway,* we first summarize external events in *To the Lighthouse*—Mrs. Ramsay knitting the stocking, visiting the village with Charles Tansley, getting dressed for dinner, and so on. With this framework on the board, students can see that external events do exist but that they are only a small part of the story. Perhaps, I suggest, Woolf downplays external events for a reason, complicating the relation between external and internal.

Here, narrative theory enters our discussion. Because narrative theory differentiates between story elements (character, setting, events) and discourse (how the story gets narrated), it helps students account for some of their difficulties in reading an author who downplays story. But since the students are a mixed group and these courses are not focused on theory, I must be careful to discuss narrative strategy with basic terms, ones understandable to a beginner. Seymour Chatman's work (*Story and Discourse: Narrative Structure in Fiction and Film, Coming to Terms: The Rhetoric of Narrative in Fiction and Film,* and "Narratological Empowerment") provides instructors with an introduction to narrative theory and its potential for classroom use, but his approach is also accessible to undergraduates, clearly written and free from highly technical jargon. His textbook, *Reading Narrative Fiction,* shows how narrative theory can be used even at the freshman level. Instructors interested in pursuing additional theoretical contributions and detailed readings will also want to read the work of Gérard Genette, Shlomith Rimmon-Kenan, Mieke Bal, and Dorrit Cohn (*Transparent Minds*). Though narrative theory examines many textual features to analyze discourse, I focus my discussion with students on the role of narrative voice and the use of perspective (focalization or character filter, in Chatman's terminology). As a result, many begin to understand their own frustrations and to recognize the complexity of Woolf's techniques and her emphasis on subjective response to experience.

Thus, in my classroom, we concern ourselves not only with what happens but also with how we learn what happens. I begin by defining the key terms from narrative theory that will frame our problems and analysis: narrative voice and character filter. Narrative theory distinguishes between the narrator (the one who speaks) and the character filter (the one who sees or perceives). In *To the Lighthouse*, for example, the narrator is largely faceless and covert, and the character filter keeps shifting. J. Hillis Miller has recognized the difficulty of following such a voice: "Exactly who, or what, is the narrator of *To the Lighthouse*? Where is she, he, or it located? What powers does the narrator have?" This narrator, he adds, is "nowhere and everywhere, located at no identifiable time" and "has none of the characteristics of a person except voice and tone" (172–73). It should not be surprising, then, that many students feel thwarted by a narrator who neither guides the reader into certain perceptions about individual characters nor generalizes about human behavior as a nineteenth-century narrator might. We need to reexamine our expectations as readers to accommodate this narrative voice.

Problems with voice and with story are inextricably intertwined. Woolf represents the multiplicity of subjective response while downplaying both the external event's importance and the narrator's authority. However, by looking at this narrator's limitations and by distinguishing between narrator's slant (who speaks?) and character filter (who sees?), students can unlock some narrative complexities and begin to evaluate subjective responses between and among characters instead of relying exclusively on the narrator.

The students' initiation into these difficulties begins on the first page of "The Window," where they face questions, uncertainty, and deferred information. Readers must be alert. "'Yes, of course, if it's fine tomorrow,' said Mrs. Ramsay. 'But you'll have to be up with the lark,' she added" (3). Dialogue is initiated without preparation and is accompanied by minimal narration. We are given only simple tags: "said Mrs. Ramsay"; "she added." Whom does Mrs. Ramsay address? What has preceded her affirmative but hypothetical response? What are the circumstances? One question resolves itself in the following sentences: she is speaking to her son, whose name appears much later, embedded within a sentence of an astonishing one hundred words. The complexity of this particular sentence plunges the reader immediately into some of the novel's crucial problems. Who speaks here? Presumably a narrator. But do these perceptions belong exclusively to the narrator, or do they include the perceptions of the character filter, James, whose emotional response is carefully recounted? What is the relationship between the narrator and the character filter? And what is the relationship between James and Mrs. Ramsay?

These problems are exacerbated on the very next page, where the reader assumes that James's perceptions are being recounted: "The wheelbarrow, the lawnmower, the sound of poplar trees, leaves whitening before rain, rooks cawing, brooms knocking, dresses rustling [. . .]." Before the sentence ends, however, this catalog of perceptions breaks off, and the narrator generalizes: "all these were so coloured and distinguished in his mind that he had already his private code, his secret language" (3–4). And by the close of the sentence, perceptions are filtered through Mrs. Ramsay, a shift that students may not recognize at first: "so that his mother, watching him guide his scissors neatly round the refrigerator, imagined him all red and ermine on the Bench or directing a stern and momentous enterprise in some crisis of public affairs" (4). The shift from James as filter character to the distanced perspective of the narrator and then to Mrs. Ramsay as filter creates uncertainty. Readers can't rely on the narrator, they wonder about the source of their information, and they realize they must pay attention to how information is conveyed. I work through these initial pages carefully in the first class, sentence by sentence, to show students how Woolf differentiates between the narrator and the character filter.

Some students soon realize that relying on the narrator's authority and looking for a causal chain of plot events are simply not enough. They must learn to identify the character filter, follow the shifts between narrator and character filter, and be aware of the subtlety of such shifts. In other words, they must develop strategies for provisional reading. They must formulate tentative interpretations, realizing that those interpretations will almost certainly need to be adjusted or reopened to include new information. One student, describing her reading experience, noted that she paid special attention to pronouns and proper names in an effort to sort out the perceptions of various character filters. Because the character filter may shift from one paragraph to the next with little or no warning, she learned to pick up the shift from male to female pronouns (or vice versa) and then wait to see the pronoun confirmed with a proper name. The reader must also learn very quickly to pay attention to tags: "said his father," "(James thought)," "said Mrs. Ramsay," "she would ask" (4–5). I point out another fairly consistent pattern: one character observes another, and then the observed person becomes the filter. Students who learn to differentiate between narrator's voice and character filter not only understand their earlier bewilderment but also begin to admire the complexity of Woolf's technique.

Sometimes, however, students must struggle to distinguish between narrator and character filter. For example, the narrator may adopt a character's vocabulary and angle so that the voice becomes ambiguous and attribution a problem. These cases of double-voiced discourse have implications for interpretation, complicating even further the relationship between narrator and character filter. In "The Window," for example, a series of questions follows the narrator's identification of Mr. Ramsay as a character filter: "Mr. Ramsay squared his shoulders and stood very upright by the urn" (36). The leitmotif in the sequence that follows is blame, public opinion, and the possibility of heroism: "Who shall blame him, if, so standing for a moment, he dwells upon fame, upon search parties, upon cairns raised by grateful followers over his bones? Finally, who shall blame the leader of the doomed expedition [. . .]?" (36). Are these questions the narrator's observations and speculations? or Mr. Ramsay's narrated monologue? It is difficult, if not impossible, to decide. The passage seems mediated by the narrator, yet the self-justification (or even self-pity) and romantic overstatement belong to Mr. Ramsay. The narrator thus raises questions rather than comments, guides, or judges as a more conventional nineteenth-century narrator might, and students need to develop provisional reading strategies to deal with this narrator as well as with the characters. They must piece together Mr. Ramsay's views of himself (his progress from Q to R [33–35]); his thoughts about others, particularly Mrs. Ramsay (31); other people's thoughts about him, particularly those of Mrs. Ramsay, Charles Tansley, and William Bankes; Tennysonian allusions; and Victorian gender issues to arrive at statements such as "Mr. Ramsay has romantic delusions" or "Mr. Ramsay overvalues facts," because the narrator never says such a thing.

This process of reading provisionally, of working from an analysis of recorded thoughts to an understanding of character and that character's place within a net of intersubjective responses, applies not only to Mr. Ramsay but to most of the other characters as well. Early in the novel, for example, Mrs. Ramsay notices Lily painting on the lawn. Woolf frames Lily's internal experience between two acts: considering her painting and replacing her paint brushes in the box to join Bankes on a walk (18–19). Within this frame, Lily's fears, the difficulty and courage required to move from artistic conception to execution, her love for Mrs. Ramsay and Mrs. Ramsay's way of life, as well as her intense ambivalence about the older woman, come to us in undigested fragments, with little or no mediation from the narrator. Presented without comment, Lily's confusion and ambivalence puzzle many students. Again, I encourage them to recognize how Woolf uses external markers to place Lily, and I ask them to consider the discrepancies between the way Lily sees herself and the way other characters, particularly Tansley and Mrs. Ramsay, view her. Through Lily's thoughts, Woolf offers resistance and an alternative to conventional gender roles, but her alternative involves contradiction and struggle.

By the time students reach "Time Passes," most have learned to follow the shifts from one character filter to another and to recognize double-voiced discourse in which the narrator adopts the vocabulary and mental angle of the character filter. While the narrator continues to be covert in this part, Woolf also deprives us of a character filter. Who perceives the changes wrought by the passage of time? Who tells us information? The narrator even calls our attention to the difficulty of locating the source of our perceptions when she says, "Listening (had there been any one to listen) [. . .]" (134). The "certain airs, detached from the body of the wind" or the "sliding lights" (126) provide something of a filter through which the house is described, but because this filter is nonhuman, many students distrust the voice. Further, the tentative tone and proliferation of questions used by the narrator in much of this part contrast with the certainty used in reporting the embedded parenthetical events. As we learn how inadequate the facts of Mrs. Ramsay's death, Prue's marriage and subsequent death in childbirth, and Andrew's death are, as we rely on Mrs. McNab for the limited subjective responses in the section, we feel the loss of that fully articulated and interwoven set of subjective responses we have come to expect. As one student wrote,

> In the first part of the story, we have gotten to know Mrs. Ramsay, Prue, and Andrew. When their deaths are barely mentioned in part two, it is hard for readers because we wonder how these deaths came about and how they affected everyone else. It is almost more sad for the reader because of it.

In the third part, "The Lighthouse," Woolf returns to the narrative strategy of "The Window." In my experience, most students have become comfortable with Woolf's technique by this point, alert to shifting character filters and multiple subjectivity. As a result, they understand and appreciate the passage where Lily admires Mr. Ramsay's boots and the sections that interweave the thoughts of James and Cam in the boat.

Because it emphasizes reading as a provisional process, this approach to reading *To the Lighthouse* calls attention to the destabilized authority of the narrator, stresses the mediation of the character filters, and does not result in oversimplified or univocal interpretation. Once I point out exactly how Woolf downplays external events and substitutes a wealth of subjective responses, many say they understand the points she makes in "Modern Fiction" and "Mr. Bennett and Mrs. Brown." To arrive at meaning for the novel, most students learn that they must use the thoughts and impressions of a range of characters as those characters think about themselves and others. The relation between external "reality" and subjective response is problematic, but using the tools of narrative theory helps students understand the aesthetic of modernism, the subtlety of Woolf's feminism, and the importance of the reader's response within a modern text. Most important, they gain tools that help them generate a range of interpretations, all based on careful reading and analysis. For example, students in my classes have used this approach to explore variant reactions to Mr. Ramsay, the evolving relationship between Mrs. Ramsay and Lily, James and his relationship to his father, and the way in which the theme of loss is handled. One writing-emphasis major even went on to use some of these techniques in a creative writing class in a short story he wrote about his relationship with his mother.

So in my experience, some basic concepts from narrative theory help students develop a provisional reading strategy, generate readings, and become aware of fictional technique. Most rewarding, this reading strategy helps students experience the richness and depth of *To the Lighthouse*. No longer frustrated, many now even acknowledge the novel's readability!

"Some Rope to Throw to the Reader": Teaching the Diverse Rhythms of *To the Lighthouse*

Patricia Laurence

Teaching Virginia Woolf isn't easy these days, perched as she is—a white, upper-middle-class British literary lady, with a whiff of experimentalism, feminism, lesbianism, and colonialism about her—on a shelf with other, mostly male, writers in the modernist canon. In teaching *To the Lighthouse* to English majors at a large, public, urban university, I have observed that student resistance to it stems not only from the frustrations of reading an experimental novel but also from stereotypes growing out of different cultural and economic backgrounds.

Part of the mission of New York's City College since its founding in the middle of the nineteenth century has been to give the talented poor (we have a minority population of 77% and an international population of 9%) an opportunity to enter the middle class through education and careers. The students who make it in the college undergo rapid and difficult psychological and cultural change compressed into one generation. The force of this change produces an unusual kind of educational atmosphere in which students have a heightened sensitivity to questions about money, careers, lifestyles, class, education, and the reality of characters they read about. My urban students, most of whom Woolf would call "outsiders," are preoccupied with identity. African American, Hispanic, Asian, Haitian, they read Woolf's novel in terms of their ethnic, class, and gender identity, observing out loud how their lives differ from the lives described in the text: "Mrs. Ramsay has servants. Why do you say she is overworked and tired?" "How does Lily earn money so that she has all that time to paint?" "Did she sell that painting at the end of the novel after she spent all that time on it?" "Do the Ramsays have two homes? They must be rich."

Yes, observe this British society's privilege and differences, I say, but notice also how this family becomes part of a narrative experiment that projects many kinds of difference. Because I know that many of my students are sensitive to fairness and justice in our society, I also urge them to observe other kinds of difference inscribed in the characters. Although they are in the same community and class and seem to share the same experiences, the men, women, children, bachelors, housekeeper, students, artist, father, and mother in this novel each see daily events differently.

How, I say, does Woolf's presentation of these characters from the inside reveal to us the difference between how they feel and think and then how they act on the outside? How does Lily feel remembering Charles Tansley's sneer, "Women can't paint, women can't write" (48), for example, when she is struggling to finish her picture? Or what is the emptiness that Lily feels when she silently cries out, "Oh, Mrs. Ramsay!" after she realizes that Mrs. Ramsay will never come back (178–80)? Doesn't Woolf show us that a flat description of someone's social and economic category differs from a novelist's narration or from what characters think and feel? How are thoughts and feelings both bound by gender, class, or ethnicity and unbound by Woolf's narration? I grasp for ways of broadening students' sense of difference among people and of life beyond social categories.

Often, Woolf provides some answers. In her *Diary*, she notes "by way of advising other Virginias with other books that this is the way of the thing: up down, up down—& Lord knows the truth" (4: 262). Intended for novice writers, this advice also applies to student readers because up-and-down rhythms pervade *To the Lighthouse*. Using Mikhail Bakhtin's theory of the novel's "multi-voicedness," I invite my students to move into the rising and falling patterns of mind, image, voice, and action of Lily, Mrs. Ramsay, Mr. Ramsay, and Mrs. McNab, to experience what Bakhtin calls the "unity of the polyphonic novel" ("Polyphonic Novel" 43).

Students, however, unused to reading according to a rhythm instead of a plot, can drown, and their comments in class reflect their anxiety. One student says, "Sometimes I stop and ask myself what is happening. I never know." Another says, "Often when I hear the thoughts of a certain character, I lose a sense of where I am and what the novel's time and setting are." Experiencing Woolf's rhythms of consciousness, this student fears she will not surface into what she calls the real landscape of the outer world. Naturally, past reading experiences shape expectations, and students trained to read for "realism" and "plot" in many high schools feel uneasy without unity of plot and logic in character. These students rightly sense Woolf's reluctance to shift back to a real scene, forcing them to question how they read and, indeed, what is real. The novel invites this split in reading consciousness, and, in fact, students' comments reveal their sensitivity to the two levels (or kinds of being) required by a sensitive reader of Woolf. The reader must learn the rhythm of movement in Woolf (and in many modernist writers) from a surface event in life to an inner reflection or associative thought or feeling about that event. Yet like many beginning readers of modern or postmodern texts, students fear letting go and taking pleasure in the up and down of consciousness: they do not want to lose their loyalty to social class or to a plot that anchors their reading experience and "always gives you," as one student commented in class, "something to say."

While writing *To the Lighthouse*, Woolf wrote to Vita Sackville-West that rhythm is essential: "Style is a very simple matter; it is all rhythm" (*Letters* 3: 247). As a teacher, then, I help my students break out of the easy certainties of reading according to ethnic, social, or economic categories and become more comfortable participating in the pleasure and the music of Woolf's style that "goes far deeper than words" (*Letters* 3: 247). An experimental novel, after all, needs an experimental reader. And the teacher needs, as Woolf herself advises, "some rope to throw to the reader" (*Letters* 4: 204). So I ask students to search for rhythmic passages from the novel in which they can follow the movement of character from action to introspection, from a spoken to an inner voice, from an individual or private voice to a social or public one, or from an animate to an inanimate state—and back again.

Then my students who like to read aloud perform these passages that show the movement or rhythm from outer to inner states or from private to social experience in one of the characters. They capture differences between and among the characters' voices, minds, rhythms. Unwittingly, they perform Bakhtin's theory of polyphony taken from his essay "Dostoevsky's Polyphonic Novel and Its Treatment in Critical Literature." In this essay, Bakhtin speaks of the "multi-voicedness" of the world as we experience it and its extension into the novel. As Rosa, a student from the Dominican Republic, reads in her lilting Hispanic accent Mrs. Ramsay's reflections after her children have gone to bed, I hear a "multi-voicedness" in the novel that I haven't heard before—or, I am convinced, that Bakhtin didn't imagine as part of his theory. Bakhtin urges us toward a closer inspection of any novel, because within it, the author has consciously or unconsciously inscribed voices representing different social classes, genders, professions, states of mind, and languages of society's strata ("Discourse" 289). When my Haitian student reads the opening sentence of the novel in rapid French rhythms—"'Yes, of course, if it's fine tomorrow,' said Mrs. Ramsay. 'But you'll have to be up with the lark,' she added" (3)—Woolf's language takes on the flavor of the reader's language. Accents familiarize Woolf's language for my students, a fourth of whom speak English as a second language, and then Woolf's novel pulses not only with the multi-voicedness she embodies in her characters but also with the sociology of consciousness and the accents of my students.

In performing these and other passages that I suggest, many students begin to appreciate Woolf's representation of and sympathy for people with varying casts of mind and position, even within the same class or gender. They see her sympathy, for example, for women like Lily, the new woman, who chooses not to marry and struggles against society's prejudices toward women who want to become artists. They recognize her pity, at times, for Mr. Ramsay, who feels that he is a failure in life because he has not come up with a grand philosophical theory or published enough papers as a professor. Or they understand the hatred of the boy, James, who resents his father's cold responses and treatment of his mother. The reading of these passages restrains the facile assumption—"Woolf is an elitist"—that students sometimes voice.

As they read aloud, many students experience the novel's up-and-down rhythms of consciousness, the songs and countersongs of the characters' consciousness, a new music for them. After reading her chosen passage, for example, one student said she heard the waves in it, something Woolf surely intended. Reading also helps them begin to hear in new ways the concord and discord between Mr. and Mrs. Ramsay as husband and wife or the rhythms of Lily's mind and paintbrush. While listening to Mr. Banks speak of Mr. Ramsay, the narrator notes:

> Suddenly, as if the movement of his hand had released it, the load of her accumulated impressions of him tilted up, and down poured in a ponderous avalanche all she felt about him. That was one sensation. Then up

rose in a fume the essence of his being. That was another. [. . .] All of this danced up and down, like a company of gnats, each separate, but all marvellously controlled in an invisible elastic net—danced up and down in Lily's mind [. . .].   (23–25)

Lily captures these movements of hand, eye, and mind in rhythmic strokes of her paintbrush, which pauses and flickers, moves up and down, and "attain[s] a dancing rhythmical movement" (158). Even the space Lily encloses on her canvas becomes musical as, "lightly and swiftly pausing, striking, she score[s] her canvas" (158). When Lily first faces her canvas, it floats "up" and places itself "white and uncompromising directly before her," a surreal landscape. But as she stares at it, she recaptures life's pulse in her relations with Mrs. Ramsay, the "relations of those lines cutting across, slicing down" (156–57). At novel's end, she takes "up" her brush to finish her picture, has her vision, and lays it "down" (208–09).

Rhythm influences Lily's paintbrush, just as it does Woolf's writing and Mrs. Ramsay's mind as she reads poetry. Knitting, reading at random, Mrs. Ramsay feels she is "climbing backwards, upwards, shoving her way up under petals that curved over her, so that she only knew this is white, or this is red. She did not know at first what the words meant at all" (119). Her mind goes "up and down, up and down with the poetry" (122) or with the knitting or with the long slow strokes of the lighthouse: "When life sank down for a moment, the range of experience seemed limitless. [. . .] Beneath it is all dark, it is all spreading, it is unfathomably deep; but now and again we rise to the surface and that is what you see us by" (62). Her thoughts, usually interrupted (88), seem somehow motionless, suspended, unlike Mr. Ramsay's methodical train of thought. Her mind's rhythms, ebbing in the slowly spreading depths of consciousness, also contrast with Lily's dancing rhythms of thought, eye, and hand. Yet human relations uphold Mrs. Ramsay (106) just as the "relations of those lines cutting across, slicing down" (157) sustain Lily's artistic vision.

Mrs. Ramsay's movements of mind also adjust to Mr. Ramsay's walks "up and down, up and down the terrace" (5) where, without the interruption of children or the preparation of dinner, he waxes on matters philosophical with Charles Tansley: "Every throb of this pulse seemed, as he walked away, to enclose her and her husband, and to give to each that solace which two different notes, one high, one low, struck together, seem to give each other as they combine" (38–39). Mr. Ramsay's peripatetic walks are metaphors for his "splendid mind" (33), that mind like a keyboard or the alphabet. Embodied in his methodical tread, a sound that paces Mrs. Ramsay's and even Lily's heart and mind, his masculinity echoes the sound of male footsteps across the centuries. After Lily praises his boots, he wheels about, leading the way to the boat "with his firm military tread" (154). These rhythmic marchings of boots and mind capture the tyranny of Mr. Ramsay's demands, affecting the minds, art, and peace of the women around him.

In "Time Passes," Mrs. McNab, the housekeeper, also moves in an up-and-down motion while housecleaning. Lurching and leering, cleaning the summerhouse to prepare for the Ramsays' arrival, she is bowed down by class and work. Her voice is

> like the voice of witlessness, humour, persistency itself, trodden *down* but springing *up* again, so that as she lurched, dusting, wiping, she seemed to say how it was one long sorrow and trouble, how it was getting *up* and going to bed again, and bringing things out and putting them away again. [. . .] Bowed *down* she was with weariness. How long, she asked, creaking and groaning on her knees under the bed, dusting the boards, how long shall it endure? but hobbled to her feet again, pulled herself *up* [. . .].   (130–31; my emphasis)

Here, Woolf presents the semiotics of bodily and class pain: the difficulty of getting up every morning and then going down on one's knees to clean each day. Noting these class differences, some students can yet see how Mrs. McNab's movements and reflections compare with Mrs. Ramsay's meditations at the dinner table:

> But what have I done with my life? [. . .] and so, giving herself the little shake that one gives a watch that has stopped, the old familiar pulse began beating, as the watch begins ticking—one, two, three, one, two, three. And so on and so on, she repeated, listening to it, sheltering and fostering the still feeble pulse as one might guard a weak flame with a newspaper.   (82–83)

Both women dread life and guard a certain rhythm, retreating to the safety of "all the being and the doing" (62). Comparing their up-down rhythms reveals class differences but gender similarities, especially when we consider Mr. Ramsay's habit of spending hours thinking about Shakespeare, the existence of a slave class, and life: "thinking up and down and in and out of the old familiar lanes and commons" (43). Born of training in university "commons," his mental and physical marching clearly differs from Mrs. McNab's stooping in other people's parlors and Mrs. Ramsay's meditating to the pulse of the lighthouse.

If students can hear Woolf's songs and countersongs of characters' bodies and minds, they can become in *accord* with those characters, with all the connotations of that word: *cor, cordis* ("heart," "heart to heart," "heartstrings," "nerves"); *chorda* ("the strings of a musical instrument" and "three or more simultaneous notes"); and *cord* ("to bind together with a string"). Experiencing the novel's polyphony unconsciously, many students feel in accord with Woolf's patterning of the novel: a rhythm "behind the cotton wool" of experience (Woolf, *Moments* 73) that allows voices, states, and sensations of mind and body to participate in a metadialogue about life. These students experience the polyphony of Lily's dancing creativity, Mrs. Ramsay's meditative sinking, Mr.

Ramsay's intellectual marching, and Mrs. McNab's domestic struggling. Using Bakhtin as a rope to help themselves ride the waves of *To the Lighthouse*, students learn to go up and down, up and down, moving with mind and pulse in accord with the mental, bodily, and social rhythms of the characters.

Reading *To the Lighthouse* through Bakhtin's theory of the multi-voicedness of the novel and hearing the "multi-voicedness" of my students reading Woolf led to the democratization of Woolf for me. Strange though it may seem, I, an American student, had constructed a British cocoon bound by theory during my years of doctoral study, and in my consciousness I separated my teaching of composition and introductory literature courses from my intense and wide-ranging study of the theory and history of the British novel. When I finally had the opportunity to teach Woolf to the students described here, they brought my teaching and scholarly selves into a healthier relation. The sociology of consciousness in Woolf filtered through the rhythm of my students' voices has made my experience as a teacher, a reader, and a scholar much richer.

Twenty Years to the Lighthouse:
A Teaching Voyage

Annis Pratt

During my twenty years at the University of Wisconsin, Madison, I always eagerly anticipated teaching Virginia Woolf. My enjoyment did not come from feeling I'd mastered her opus or, as the years went on, from the comfort of having taught the course so many times before; instead, I looked forward to the zany surprises that would occur if I coaxed a new group of students to read her for themselves.

I remember one morning, for example, when I heard strange incantations coming from my classroom. Peering around the door, I discovered three students perched on the big wooden desk; two others, crouched on the floor below, were chanting phrases representing the contents of Cam's and James's streams of consciousness. These voices were counterpointed by two on the desktop, who were speaking what Cam and James actually say. Mr. Ramsay, in the bow of the desk, was bent over a book of poetry, muttering to himself, while the students on the floor writhed in their choreographic rendition of waves.

Two things about this scene reassured me that my teaching method was working. First, I wasn't in the room yet. That crucial move from professor-centered teaching (focused on what was inside *my* head) to student-centered ownership of the text was taking place without me, amid peals of laughter that told me my students were bridging the considerable gulf between twenty-year-old midwesterners and a difficult British modernist text. Second, as students argued about how to act out the scene, their right as well as their left brains were in cognitive play.

How did my students, who often found themselves unable to use *I* in their first papers, learn to trust their own instincts about *To the Lighthouse* so thoroughly? It was not ever so. In my early years of teaching Virginia Woolf, I, like many college teachers who had no pedagogical training whatever and who had not thought very much about the relation between authority and the acquisition of knowledge, assumed that the most useful knowledge about Woolf's works resided in critics' writings. Thus, when I was given an all-Woolf honors course to teach in 1972, I assigned oral reports on the criticism. If you think about what was available then (before Quentin Bell's biography came out and before any second-wave feminist had noticed Woolf) and if you have ever heard students report on secondary material they cannot identify with, you will appreciate why, in their evaluations, they begged me to abandon reports they characterized as "droning and boring." They wanted more discussion of the books: to hear more of each other's opinions, to develop their own questions, and to be allowed to finish their sentences! These comments inspired my life-long attempt (never entirely successful) to restrain my New York verbosity and to put my pedagogy where my mouth was.

Let me explain how I abandoned professor-centered teaching and developed a student-centered method that brought students' understanding of Woolf out of their own heads. First, I recalled my dissertation director's approach to *To the Lighthouse*. William York Tindall, an iconoclast in the profession who advised us against attending MLA conventions lest the originality of our ideas be compromised by other people's theories, insisted on close readings of texts and respect for individual responses: "What the reader gets from a symbol depends not only upon what the author has put into it, but upon the reader's sensitivity and his consequent apprehension of what is there" (17). Tindall's attitude matched Woolf's respect for the common reader, whom Woolf defined as "guided by an instinct to create for himself, out of whatever odds or ends he can come by, some kind of whole" of his or her own (*Common Reader* 1).

My teaching method was grounded in this personalized relationship between a student reader and the text and a respect for the student's thinking processes and the life experience those processes grow out of. This approach is hardly a new idea in the United States, having been outlined in 1916 when John Dewey published *Democracy and Education*. More recently, such teaching has been related to critical thinking and paying attention to the phases of student cognitive development described in pedagogical studies like that of William G. Perry, Jr. ("Different Worlds") and adapted for African Americans by W. E. Cross and for women by Nancy Downing and Kristin Roush. My own version of pedagogical empowerment requires four teaching techniques: relating the verbal to the visual, sequencing the syllabus, enhancing discussion, and focusing on images. By explaining how I used these strategies to change my teaching of *To the Lighthouse*, I hope to demonstrate how students can learn to trust their own ability to develop close readings of the novel.

Visual Language: Lily Briscoe and Modern Art

Early in my Course for Majors, I handed out a list of left-mode and right-mode ways of knowing to my thirty-five students: verbal versus nonverbal, symbolic versus concrete, abstract versus anagogic. One reason Woolf is "hard" for many students is that she cannot be read with mere logic: students need to experience her texts intuitively, concretely, and visually. During the years I taught Woolf, I discovered not only that viewing art contemporary with her fiction helped the students grasp her prose but also that encouraging them to sketch and chart her fictional structures for themselves led them to the heart of her texts. Such visual activities can range from the simple (underlining all kinesthetic images in green and all light images in yellow) to the more complex (rendering the structure of "Time Passes" in many colors) to the even more sophisticated (writing term papers on the cubist elements of Lily's painting or on the montage and images in motion in "The Window").

I also encouraged such visual and verbal connections by having a slide show about Virginia Woolf and modern art early in the course and by accompanying the show's images with readings from Woolf, Roger Fry, Clive Bell, Desmond MacCarthy, and other commentators on the art scene in England from 1910 to 1920 (see Rosenbaum's *A Bloomsbury Group Reader* for a good selection). For example, I read Woolf's famous passage on examining an ordinary mind on an ordinary day ("Modern Fiction") as I showed slides of Seurat and Monet; Roger Fry on Cézanne with Cézanne (*Vision* 256–65); Sergei Eisenstein's concepts of images in motion and montage with Picasso (45–63, 72–83); and Woolf on how all novels begin with the expression of character ("Mr. Bennett") with Edvard Munch, who used color and shape to render emotion. In addition, I accompanied slides of Matisse, Chagall, and Gris with readings from Woolf's diaries and letters of 1918 and 1919 that reveal how modern art suggested new methods to her for composing her fiction.

Syllabus Sequencing

How could I get college undergraduates to trust their own ideas enough to abandon their subjugation to authority, the norm in most of their other classes? I arranged my syllabus so that by the time they read *To the Lighthouse*, they had completed a sequence of assignments designed to help them feel competent as critical readers of Woolf. I am convinced that teachers should never introduce Woolf with a full-length novel (especially in introductory literature courses) but with short stories such as "The Haunted House," "Kew Gardens," and "An Unwritten Novel." Before class discussion of these stories, I handed out definitions of descriptive images, similes, and metaphors, along with Tindall's definition of the modern symbol as grounded in concrete sensation. Then I asked for lists of these figures from each story, such as "the bitterness of her tone was like lemon on cold steel" and "as though the skin on her back were as a plucked fowl's in a poulterer's shop-window" ("Unwriten Novel" 113).

During these short story assignments, we continued to look at the relation between Woolf's fictional techniques and methods of impressionism, post-impressionism, expressionism, and cubism, particularly as they influenced the decorative style of the Omega Workshops in which Woolf's sister, Vanessa Bell, and their friends participated. I assigned two discussions of "Kew Gardens," one before and one after the slide show on Woolf and modern art outlined earlier, and we paid special attention to Vanessa Bell's cover designs and illustrations for the Hogarth Press edition of the story.

After class discussion of "An Unwritten Novel," I gave out the first writing assignment, an ungraded exercise in which students observed a real person and then wrote a character sketch using the same techniques Woolf used to portray Minnie: descriptive images used as objective correlatives to suggest the character's state of mind. Consistently, if I assigned the ungraded Woolf imitation first, at least sixty percent of the students received A's on the next paper, a critical analysis of imagery in a short story; students were to choose a Woolf story we had not analyzed in class and discuss one image (e.g., color, light, a flower, fire, water, sewing, waves, bells, clothing, the motion of circling or stroking, rising or falling) to demonstrate how Woolf weaves it into a text's structure as a thematic image. Why did they do so well on this paper? Having to imitate Woolf had detoxified them from their panic that Woolf was ultrasophisticated and difficult; developing objective correlatives for their own character descriptions helped them grasp the centrality of sense imagery in Woolf's texts; and participating in the sorts of discussions described below enhanced their confidence in their own ideas.

Since I handed out grades as well as comments on this second paper, I should include here a comment on grading for empowerment. The shock of getting a bad grade after only one attempt is a kind of intellectual guillotine, fostering discouragement. As a result, in addition to the grammatical corrections I always insisted on, any paper with less than an A– could be rewritten over and over until the next-to-last week of classes. I made this permission to rewrite less onerous for me by insisting that individual sentences be corrected right on the paper, paragraphs on a facing page, and longer revisions on new pages attached to the original copy. I refused to accept clean rewrites. That way, I was not burdened with piles of new papers to grade from scratch but could skim the revised versions with my suggestions on the originals in front of me.

As for outside readings, I developed (and continually updated) a large collection of primary and secondary materials on the reserve room shelves, urging students to keep up with Woolf's letters and diaries but only assigning criticism for the term paper. Any critical articles I might bring to their attention were hypotheses—leads they might use in interpreting Woolf for themselves. Although the term paper required reading a critical chapter or essay on one novel, I insisted that they focus on their reading of it: I used a grading system that reinforced this requirement, awarding A's for success in coming up with their own ideas and giving lower grades for summarizing plot or parroting critical authorities, including me.

Discussion Enhancement

Much influenced by Virginia Woolf's scorn for the "vain and vicious system" of lecturing about English literature (*Three Guineas* 37, 155–56n30), I lectured for only ten minutes a session, except for the day after a paper was due, when I introduced a new unit. Instead, I used an active learning method suggested by Martin Bickman. With this method, I spent a lot of time preparing sheets of questions or tasks for my students to use with their reading assignments and then in their discussions: "Find every use of motion in section 7 of part 1," for example, "and figure out how these kinesthetic images relate to the characters and interactions of James, Mr. Ramsay, and Mrs. Ramsay." On the first day of class, I divided my thirty to forty students into permanent groups of ten, who then moved their chairs together during every session to tackle the particular question or task assigned to them. After ten to twenty minutes of discussion, members from each group told the class about its discoveries and conclusions, along with any additional issues that had come up as they talked. I quickly learned that group members police each other, as in "George! This is the fourth time you haven't done the reading and we've had to use up time telling you about it!" and "You always report back, Barbara—let some of the rest of us have a turn!" This group discussion method is not limited to smaller classes, by the way; Bickman describes leading small-group discussions in classes of a hundred students.

We plunged into *To the Lighthouse* section by section, using questions handed out ahead of time, often on specific images. A day's discussion might have groups working on various aspects of section 17, for example: listing the progression of moods Mrs. Ramsay goes through during the dinner, outlining the dinner's structure in terms of descriptive images and submerged archetypal motifs, assessing Lily's state of mind at the table according to the images of motion associated with her stream of consciousness, and so on. As the groups reported, the class analyzed that section, with me tying things together, mediating disagreements, and outlining our conclusions on the board. During my ten-minute "lecture" that began the next session, I reminded students where we had got the session before and then set the sequence in motion again: small groups discussing preassigned questions, groups reporting back, class discussing the groups' findings, tying everything together.

Image Focus

After that disastrous first Woolf course, I had decided that the only way to teach *To the Lighthouse* was to read it with the students, choosing for each class session short passages to analyze. I remembered Tindall telling us that if we started with a single descriptive image, observed the way Woolf first worked it into metaphor and then into concrete modern symbol, and kept track of how she wove these into larger archetypal patterns, we would discover the key to the novel's structure. So we started with passages from sections 1–11 in "The Window," searching for concrete sensations of color, motion, heat and cold, shape, and so on. If we took the time to focus carefully on those passages in class, sentence by sentence and image by image, students learned to use this close reading skill throughout the rest of the novel.

In fact, most students emerged from this focus on imagery remarkably at home with the abstract "Time Passes." After I introduced some of Woolf's statements about how it fits into the novel's structure (*Diary* 3: 36, 75–76, 106–07; *Holograph Draft,* app. A 48) and students found the images of light or of mirrors or of rising and falling, I sent them off to design charts showing how the middle part of the novel proceeds "from what through what to what" (a formula Tindall had adapted from Kenneth Burke). Did things go in a straight line? Could a plot or narrative sequence be sketched on paper? Students, having drawn their charts and outlines of structural interpretations on the board for class discussion, often realized that the pattern characterizing "The Window"—plunging down into the unconscious and then back up into the everyday world—also undergirds "Time Passes."

When they turned to "The Lighthouse," they could see how Woolf reiterates the thematic images of "The Window" and how the whole novel mirrors its middle section, with its motion down into death or dissolution and then up into life or restructuring. Here I brought my feminist archetypal work to their attention, suggesting that the resurrection of the house parallels the rebirth of Mrs. Ramsay in Lily's mind, an archetypal pattern deeply grounded in the Eleusinian mysteries that Jung characterized as an empowering mother-daughter and daughter-mother quest (see Jung; Jung and Kerenyi; J. Harrison; Bolen; C. Downing; Pratt, *Patterns*). Knowing that my book carried authority, however, I kept myself open to alternative hypotheses.

For example, some students were more interested in the images of woman-woman relationships and where to locate Lily and Mrs. Ramsay on a lesbian continuum. And despite the centrality of the Lily–Mrs. Ramsay relationship in "The Lighthouse," many students (like those writhing around, on, and under the desk on that memorable day!) preferred to focus on images of Cam and James and Mr. Ramsay sailing to the lighthouse, perhaps because, in age, they were much closer to that adolescent-father conflict than they are to the relationship between Lily, an adult woman, and the older and now dead mother figure she had once revered.

A student-centered pedagogy thus takes into account the relation between students' developmental stage and the material. It allows students to explore their own reactions to what they read, encourages them to undertake such explorations by using all their senses and both sides of their brains, and builds their competence (and confidence) by providing a sequence of skills and assignments. As Woolf herself suggests, the pedagogy modeled on the lecturer-divine standing on a raised platform and funneling knowledge from the book to students, all of whom are threatened with academic damnation if they don't catch every word, no longer seems either appropriate or effective. Why create classrooms in which instructors practice "the arts of dominating other people" (*Three Guineas* 34)? Why not create classrooms full of open-minded, confident, even laughing common readers reading *To the Lighthouse* for themselves?

After I retired, I heard from the student who had played Cam in the classroom skit. In the class, she had gone on to paint Lily Briscoe's painting for herself and then turn it in as an accompaniment to a brilliant term paper on the last section of *To the Lighthouse*. As we recalled her project, she mentioned that she hadn't had such fun since kindergarten, a sentiment that made me glad that, all those years ago, I had renounced lecturing and begun my quest for a student-centered pedagogy fostering multiple facets of cognition.

Reading and Writing: Helping Students Discover Meaning in *To the Lighthouse*

Laura Davis

Located in the economically rusty Steel Belt, the East Liverpool campus of Kent State University is populated by first-generation college students, typically enrolled full time to qualify for financial aid and majoring primarily in two-year technical programs. These students, with twins and a newborn at home or a full-time job at the local Giant Eagle, usually see studying literature as time-consuming, peripheral, and frustrating. These are not future English majors, nor have they had much exposure to literature. First-year students may ingenuously comment that they have never before read a "book." They lack confidence as readers and writers and are unpracticed in the skills that allow one to successfully approach a work of literature, particularly a complex, novel-length work. Yet as sophomores, they may be reading *To the Lighthouse* for a course that will fulfill a liberal education requirement. They react to Virginia Woolf's novel with dismay. A student who complained about Hemingway cries, "Give me back *The Sun Also Rises!*" Another asks, "What is this '*Some one had blundered*' stuff and why is the phrase printed differently in the text?" Yet another wants to know, "Why are the sentences so long?" ("Wait until Faulkner," I tease.) "How can we possibly read the novel twice when it takes so long to read it once?" "I can't believe we have to write on this novel," they lament. They'll read the novel—reluctantly—wanting to be told what it means or even just what the action is. On the first point, I resist. I'll comment on mysteries of plot, but the meaning of the novel they must discover for themselves.

Such students can make meaning out of *To the Lighthouse* when taught a practical technique—selective indexing. Indexing works because it enables students to break a complex and unwieldy job into steps familiar to them from the writing process: prereading (like prewriting), quick reacting through brainstorming, making associations through clustering or grouping, finding a focus, and rereading. After reading with a focus and taking selective notes, many students can more successfully choose a topic and thesis for a critical essay on the novel and support their views with relevant information that they have already gathered from the text. While indexing, many students discover meaning by making connections within the text and thus with the text. One reader, for example, told the class that she found herself repeatedly abandoning her vacuum cleaner to record her visions of the novel's structure and that she wrote at her dining room table with the sound of a grandfather clock breaking into her consciousness, ticking "time passes, time passes." This student, like others who approached the novel through indexing, was able to discover what held the most meaning for her in *To the Lighthouse*.

In the semester course in which students read *To the Lighthouse*, Major

Modern British and American Writers, we spend a week and a half on each of several other novels and three weeks on *To the Lighthouse*. In addition to reading *To the Lighthouse* for class discussion, students also index the novel to prepare for writing a critical paper. For class discussion, we approach *To the Lighthouse* as we do each work, by focusing on central concerns shared by modern works. We also spend part of each class during the first week on *To the Lighthouse* discussing how to selectively index. Students prepare for indexing by prereading at least a quarter of *To the Lighthouse* as a prelude to discussing the novel's key elements. The first of several in-class brainstorming sessions during that first week (the next step in the indexing process) encourages students to voice (or vent) their reactions to the novel—to note what most strikes them or to identify what makes *To the Lighthouse* difficult to read.

In a second brainstorming session after further discussion of the novel, students list elements of *To the Lighthouse* that have caught their attention. Some lists may be dominated by the concrete and observable—rocks, colors, fish, water, boots, the connection between Mrs. Ramsay and the lighthouse, and the significance of the Ramsays' being called "Mr." and "Mrs." Other lists may emphasize the abstract and interpretive: "son hates his father," "mother seems gentle but stern," "compassionate interaction," and "Mrs. R. constantly trying to please." Still others may focus on the novel's technical aspects: "the speaker changes," "not a lot of action," "very detailed about feelings—not about physical/material things," "unclear, long sentences." After students and I brainstorm some more on our own, we share what we have found in class, brainstorm further, and talk about broad terms for labeling elements in the novel. We then combine students' lists of elements in *To the Lighthouse* to form a master list, with items arranged in groups, as in this sampling: images and objects (from sharp instruments to Mrs. Ramsay's shawl); characters (including relationships between pairs of characters and positive and negative qualities of a character); themes, issues, and ideas in the novel (isolation, jealousy, conflict, admiration, changing emotions, time, the past, memory, and ritual); and technical features (narrative structure, point of view, and setting). If students don't suggest certain significant thematic or stylistic elements, especially ones that would serve particularly well as paper topics, I add them to the list during our discussion.

At the end of the first week on *To the Lighthouse* (or earlier, if possible), each student selects ten items to index from the class-compiled master list. Some students will have finished a first reading of the novel; others will be about halfway through. Everybody is asked to begin over again at this point, to reread the novel slowly and thoughtfully, tracing the appearance of the elements each has chosen and keeping notes on index cards. Students indicate the title of the novel in the upper left-hand corner of the card and write the element being traced and a number for the card in the upper right-hand corner. Numbers of pages from which notes are taken run down the left-hand side of the card, with the note written to the right, as in this student sample:

6   Mrs. R. "had the whole of the other sex under her protection" [Why?!] & all
            women should feel that way.
10–11   Mrs. Ramsay insinuated to Mr. Tansley about men being so smart & women
            subjected to them. [She thought opposite.]
24   [Everyone felt bad for W. Bankes because he had no wife & children.]
41–42   Mrs. R. feels snubbed by Mr. Carmichael; she suspects "this desire of hers to
            give, to help, was vanity."
47–48   Lily looks at Mr. Bankes looking at Mrs. R. [Love of men for women].
49   Mrs. R. said no matter what, "an unmarried woman has missed the best of
            life."

Indexing allows students to read for meaning, focusing their attention on
selected items. As they index, they are compiling potentially usable notes for
their papers on *To the Lighthouse*. I recommend that students bracket their
own remarks so that they can later distinguish between text and interpretation.
The brackets around the note for page 24 show, too, that the student has pre-
read the novel; not until page 84 does the text mention Mrs. Ramsay's pitying
William Bankes for not having a wife and children. The reader has concluded
that "everyone" feels sorry for Mr. Bankes. On subsequent index cards for
"Men vs. Women," page numbers out of sequence show that this writer worked
recursively, circling back through the text to pick up additional notes on this
topic. This student writer also filled in what may appear to be gaps in the "Men
vs. Women" index notes by tracing related elements, as in the notes on "Changing feelings between Mr. & Mrs. R":

31   "the folly of women's minds enraged him."
32   Mrs. R. thought that to tell James what Mr. R. thought to be the truth with-
            out considering his feelings was awful . . . Then he said he'd ask Coastguard.
            "There was nobody whom she reverenced as she reverenced him."
33   The sight of his son & wife "fortified him and satisfied him."
37–38!!!   She protects & renews him.

Other elements this writer traces, such as "Marriage" and "Mrs. Ramsay's
thoughts on life," also relate to "Men vs. Women" and "Changing feelings."
The writer has thus developed a good base for her essay, and the exclamation
points highlight an item that will probably appear in it.
    Students compile their indexes over a two-week period. During the third
week, as we are finishing our discussion of *To the Lighthouse*, students generate
topics and possible thesis statements for their six-page essays. Because a short
critical analysis usually focuses on one aspect of a novel, students must move
from their list of elements to a focused paper topic to a thesis. Helping them
through this process, I point out even the self-evident, first recommending that

they sit quietly and think about what they might say about the novel. Then I suggest that they reread all of their index notes. Rereading the notes helps students connect ideas that may lead to a thesis. At this point, students again brainstorm, phrasing potential thesis statements and identifying related points. Here they begin to realize that their index notes will provide the evidence needed for a supporting discussion. I assure them, however, that they should not try to use everything in any given index in their papers. Like all writers, they must choose details and let go of others to achieve a unified piece of writing; they must continue to be selective.

Selectively indexing demystifies reading and writing about *To the Lighthouse*. It makes explicit what good readers and writers do implicitly—cataloging, grouping, keeping a running tab and commentary going in one's head, and focusing on those elements that seem most interesting or significant. Many students are relieved to find out that they will not have to master every element in the novel while indexing, and they often get excited about individual elements that they trace. Some feel distracted by taking notes while reading, but others find that doing so sharpens their eye for detail. They also discover that indexing helps them keep track of ideas that surface over and over. Once they have gone through this process, most students agree that prereading as much of the novel as possible first and indexing it during a second reading ultimately save time by helping them locate supporting details during the writing phase. Time isn't wasted, as one student put it in class, "scrounging around in the novel." Indexing gives students control and works better than other techniques they have tried; it allows them to see connections and prevents the horror of facing 135 pages with undifferentiated yellow highlights.

Indexing *To the Lighthouse* as a part of the reading process certainly helps many students become better writers about the novel and also provides opportunities for reviewing concepts related to writing. As we compile the list of elements, for example, I help students distinguish between "details" and "elements" in *To the Lighthouse*. That Mr. Ramsay says "Damn you" to Mrs. Ramsay (32) is a detail that can be recorded on a card labeled for any of these elements: "the relationship between Mr. and Mrs. Ramsay" or "conflict" or "the need to assert." Moving back and forth between the particular and the general, as well as sorting out facts from commentary on those facts, gives students valuable practice for writing. Indexing done during reading prepares for and makes easier our later discussions about amply developing and supporting the main idea of a paragraph. While explaining the indexing process, I also review the differences among direct quoting, paraphrasing, and summarizing. As we talk about restricting or broadening a topic, some students say that they are going to have to go back through *To the Lighthouse* to trace another relevant element. But earlier practice in classifying and sorting the text's information makes such backtracking much less painful and time-consuming. Once they have completed their indexes, students may also share notes for a particular item in the text, and we then talk about the way to acknowledge the help that classmates or I provide.

Indexing aids students in at least one other significant way: to write a critical essay about *To the Lighthouse*, students must find a focused topic and then discuss its meaning within the whole text. Indexing helps them avoid what novice writers often submit to: the "tyranny of the text."[1] They have been told the warning sign—drafting an analysis with the book open, turning the pages one by one. Looking at details already sorted on cards that can themselves be shuffled helps students discover their own order, one that best suits their views of the novel. They have an opportunity to share those views during an in-class revising and peer-editing session after we have completed *To the Lighthouse*. I meet individually with students, too, to discuss drafts of their essays, which are due about a week after we finish the novel.

Indexing works for many students and for me as well. I began indexing when I got bogged down in preparing *The Red and the Black* for a great books course. Grouping and tracing a focused list of elements in that novel gave me a workable method for leading class discussions. I continue to index most novels I prepare to teach, including *To the Lighthouse*. I can lead a discussion on Mrs. Ramsay's relationship with her daughters, for example, or on the images of hands, modeling what students do as they compile their indexes and what they will do to compose their essays. I also use indexing to illustrate modernism in *To the Lighthouse*, most notably to locate the effects of the war and what students find aptly expressed in *The Norton Anthology of English Literature* as the "weakening of traditional stabilities" (Abrams 1683). Finally, we look for common elements in all of the novels we read for the course, making connections and working from both the top down and the bottom up as we define modernism.

In fact, using indexing to help students see connections both within *To the Lighthouse* and among modern works has overcome my resistance to teaching the novel. Until I approached *To the Lighthouse* with indexing, I was wary both of sharing this novel with a less than enthusiastic audience and of imposing my views on student readers. With indexing, students can relate to the text and make connections, if not to works outside the course, at least to works inside the course and to life. They discover and can articulate their own points of view on the novel. One reader, struck from the beginning by the relationship between Mr. Ramsay and James, saw the Freudian conflict between the two but gave a more contemporary reading of Mr. Ramsay as abusive. A young woman successfully resisted (still difficult for me) the seductiveness of Mrs. Ramsay and wished that her mother and sisters could see their own passivity in Mrs. Ramsay. Instead, as this student sat revising at the kitchen table, her mother read over her shoulder and harrumphed, "Nobody's like that." The daughter concluded her essay: "*To the Lighthouse* demonstrates that through total devotion and subservience to men, women give up themselves, the essential part of adequacy, fulfillment, and happiness. Woolf's comment on the subservient woman could be summed up as, Lily was happy; Mrs. Ramsay was dead."

These readings of Mr. and Mrs. Ramsay show me that I have found a practical way to step to the side so that students can discover meaning in *To the*

Lighthouse for themselves. Through selective indexing, inexperienced readers and writers have responded to the text in deeply felt ways, and my learning what the hedge, the garden, and a wave breaking on the shore mean to them has added to my reading of *To the Lighthouse*.

NOTE

[1]"Tyranny of the text" is a turn upon W. W. Greg's phrase "tyranny of the copy-text." Greg's advice to textual editors to maintain "liberty" when choosing among variant readings for an edition of a literary work may be adapted into advice to student writers to control the selection of information from a novel that they will use for evidence in a critical essay (22, 26).

Look Again: Reading *To the Lighthouse* from an Aesthetic of Likeness

Toni A. H. McNaron

Teaching Virginia Woolf from a lesbian-feminist perspective means more than pointing out possible lesbian characters in her novels or affirming her liaisons with other lesbians. On a theoretical level, it involves accenting an aesthetic founded on likeness rather than on opposition. As a lesbian-feminist, I choose to affirm images, relationships, and situations in which such likeness or mirroring is present. By likeness I do not mean sameness, since I agree with the current critical emphases on the dangers of essentialism and the power of diversity in art and life. I mean that seeing someone like me representationally (another woman) in the bathroom glass, across a table, or in bed produces a response very different from that of seeing someone representationally unlike me (a man) in the same locations. Because heterosexist values and assumptions drive our culture, we learn that like pairs are far less interesting, erotic, or exciting than opposite pairs. Since Woolf actively cut against cultural assumptions and preferred spending time with other women, I believe my lesbian-feminist affirmation of likeness (despite its paradoxical difference from other critical stances) has genuine value.

When the students in an undergraduate seminar entitled Virginia Woolf's Major Novels first encountered *To the Lighthouse*, they found what they had been trained to see. Eighteen motivated, bright juniors and seniors, predominantly English or women's studies majors, made up the class. All of them—even the two or three lesbians—entered the course reading from unexamined positions, including the pervasive heterosexist one: that is, the profound and fundamental acceptance of heterosexuality to the exclusion of any other approach to human intimacy. Concomitant with this position is the belief that difference is more exciting and powerful than complementarity.

Given this entrenched conditioning, these students at first saw Mrs. Ramsay and Lily Briscoe as polar opposites. Their early written reactions to the novel defined Mrs. Ramsay as mother and matchmaker. Those who did not find her a romantic figure of nurturance and protection (the more feminist members of the class) judged her a shallow figure of domestic fiction. Lily, however, they saw as an ungiving young woman in danger of becoming a spinster, that worst of all female roles. A few students agreed with Lily's assessment in her self-doubting moments, that the result of her efforts to paint would be rolled up and stored in someone's attic. At the end of our first session, many students concluded that the two characters were diametrically opposed.

My task as a teacher, then, was to shift student perception from an ingrained affirmation of difference toward a reading both more faithful to the text and consistent with lesbian-feminist literary theory. A lesbian-feminist perspective expands and challenges the more accepted heterosexual feminist ethic (with its emphasis on female friendship) by finding erotic and sexual excitement within same-sex interactions. Such a lens is important in a Virginia Woolf course because Woolf was both deeply woman-identified, proclaiming in a letter to Ethel Smyth, "Women alone stir my imagination" (*Letters* 4: 203), and ambivalent about the women she called "Sapphists." To gain understanding of her fiction, students separated from Woolf by time, culture, and attitudes toward language need to expand their frameworks for recognizing intimacy and connection.

Effecting a paradigmatic shift in reader attention from a heterosexist to a more sexually and erotically inclusive position demands a classroom climate within which such a new look becomes possible. From the start, I stressed how important it would be for students to voice their opinions, even if they clashed with mine. Use of weekly small groups from which I was absent allowed the class to bond quickly. To contextualize Woolf's fiction, I set up research teams that prepared reports on her family background and her relationship with her mother, her sister, Vita Sackville-West, and Ethel Smyth. The reports were excellent, relying on biographical and critical sources such as Louise DeSalvo and Roger Poole.

Before reading *To the Lighthouse*, students had studied *Night and Day* and *Orlando*. In those earlier discussions, I pointed to the often charged atmosphere between female characters. At the end of our work on *Night and Day*, I asked students to name a moment that would linger in their minds. The majority listed a scene in which Mary Datchett rests at Katharine Hilbery's feet, fingering the hem of her dress as the two women sit quietly, not needing words to communicate their deepest feelings (278). I knew then that my approach was making sense to the class.

To begin *To the Lighthouse*, we had the open-ended discussion mentioned earlier because I wanted to hear how they interpreted the novel. Near the end of class, I announced that a lesbian-feminist reading of likeness might yield a fresh interpretation of Mrs. Ramsay and Lily Briscoe's relationship. Shocked, some students showed me passages in which Woolf articulates categorical differences between them. As we continued talking, however, they realized that it was usually Mrs. Ramsay who spoke of those differences. I suggested that we might focus on Lily and the narrative voice instead.

Believing that I had elicited honest responses on the first day and that I could now shift our thinking, I lectured at the second class meeting. I noted the hegemonic dictum that judges maturity in relationships by whether or not a protagonist succeeds at heterosexual marriage and family life. For many female characters, adjusting to this belief entails a shrinkage of creative potential and/or intellectual development. I canvassed the students for canonical novels in which this shrinkage is a prerequisite to the denouement: *Portrait of a Lady*, *The Great Gatsby*, *The Bostonians*, *Pride and Prejudice*, *Middlemarch*. They followed this sobering exercise by listing fiction in which the female character resists such shrinkage but winds up mad or dead for her troubles: "The Yellow Wallpaper," *The Awakening*, *Madame Bovary*, *Clarissa*, *Wuthering Heights*.

Once students recognized this covert cultural demand, most seemed more open to new theoretical information. Beginning with Freud's classic argument that an appreciation of likeness is a sign of immaturity and narcissism ("On Narcissism"), I outlined an alternative, a way to think about likeness that would allow for serious consideration of relations between members of the same sex—our mirror images.

The class had read *A Room of One's Own* just before *To the Lighthouse*, so I reminded them that in 1929 Woolf had posited a historical function of women as mirrors in which men could find themselves reflected at twice their actual size (35). As someone who minored in mathematics, I understand only two paths to this fantasy: either a woman must dwarf herself by half so that the viewer may maintain an illusion of greatness without having to do anything or she must inflate her responses to whatever her needy looker does so that usual acts seem grand. In both instances, the work done by the image-making woman involves her in a lie so close to the bone that she runs the risk of destroying whatever separate self she might have. Several students easily provided personal examples of their being expected to fulfill this function.

I ended my lecture by reading the passage in *A Room of One's Own* where Woolf muses about how radical it would be if novelists were to write about Chloe's liking Olivia (82–85). She proposes a shift from gender difference to gender likeness as a governing narrative and aesthetic principle. Her excitement about scenes in which Chloe watches Olivia stack bottles in their shared lab or in which two women speak directly to one another without the usual male-centered filter indicates that she felt the charge present in relations based on likeness; Woolf wanted literature to work against our cultural belief that only "opposites attract." I recalled our discussion about *Night and Day* and the erotic energy between Katharine and Mary, who, on the narrative surface, were falling in and out of love with the same young man.

Having established room for an alternative possibility in approaching the relationship between Mrs. Ramsay and Lily, I turned to the novel. Early in *To the Lighthouse*, Mrs. Ramsay herself speaks about difference: "Strife, divisions, difference of opinion, prejudices twisted into the very fibre of being, oh, that they should begin so early [. . .]. It seemed to her such nonsense—inventing differences, when people, heaven knows, were different enough without that" (8). Yet she also periodically underlines the gulf between Lily and herself because she has known the pleasures of marriage and motherhood while Lily remains alone and unattached. She muses that Lily may not appeal to most potential male partners: "There was in Lily a thread of something; a flare of something; something of her own which Mrs. Ramsay liked very much indeed, but no man would, she feared" (104). I asked students to hear in the phrase "something of her own" Woolf's deep commitment to women's needing private space. Lily's retention of something inviolable and completely intimate about herself for herself attracts Mrs. Ramsay, undercutting the official energy directed at marrying Lily off to someone like the older William Bankes. Mrs. Ramsay herself desires such a core self, complicating romanticized readings of her as a natural caretaker who finds self-fulfillment in service to others.

Wanting to provide some cues to look for when foregrounding likeness, I asked students to study scenes in which two (or more) women were pictured alone, since such scenes often function as dramatic asides, revealing an insider's view; to notice where such scenes were and what they expected to happen in such sites; and to pay attention to linguistic echoes from one character to another. We then looked at one such scene, Lily and Mrs. Ramsay alone in Lily's bedroom.

> Arriving late at night, with a light tap on one's bedroom door, wrapped in an old fur coat [. . .], [Mrs. Ramsay] would enact again whatever it might be [. . .]. All this she would adroitly shape; even maliciously twist; and, moving over to the window, in pretence that she must go, [. . .] half turn back, more intimately, but still always laughing, insist that [Lily] must, Minta must, they all must marry, since [. . .] there could be no disputing this: an unmarried woman [. . .], an unmarried woman has missed the best of life.
> (49)

Some students commented that Mrs. Ramsay's distinctions reflect cultural messages, so I showed them how, as Lily attempts to answer this pressure, her words are few and halting: "oh, but, Lily would say, there was her father; her home; even, had she dared to say it, her painting. But all this seemed so little, so virginal, against the other" (50). Together we agreed that if the syntax is taken literally, Lily cannot name her best defense against Mrs. Ramsay's pity, her art. She can only think it, having internalized what her surroundings have told her. But Woolf does not leave the two women in such an imbalanced and contrasting place. Instead, she suspends the scene, allowing readers to watch as the women stay together even after the frontal attack on Lily's isolation from the human family: "Yet, as the night wore on, [. . .] gathering a desperate courage she would urge her own exemption from the universal law; plead for it; she liked to be alone; she liked to be herself; she was not made for that [. . .]" (50).

Through careful analysis of this scene, we discussed how Woolf complicates the case for difference by extending the contact between the two women and by maintaining intimacy between them despite internal or verbal arguments. Finally, she gives Lily the last laugh: "Then, she remembered, she had laid her head on Mrs. Ramsay's lap and laughed and laughed and laughed, laughed almost hysterically at the thought of Mrs. Ramsay presiding with immutable calm over destinies which she completely failed to understand" (50). Our discussion focused on several salient points: Lily is intimately affectionate with Mrs. Ramsay, who has abandoned her impulse to exit in a righteous huff; Lily laughs just as Mrs. Ramsay did earlier when trying to show Lily the error of her solitary ways, a linguistic act that draws the two disparate characters together; and Lily can see both sides, making her psychologically convincing and on a level with her mentor.

Having felt the rewards of reading for likeness in this scene, students eagerly sought other exemplary scenes. Many came to the next class awed by Woolf's having Mrs. Ramsay define her essence in terms corresponding to Lily's remarks on her painting. I delighted in their discovery (not telling them that many critics have remarked on the similarity between Mrs. Ramsay's "wedge-shaped core of darkness" [62] and Lily's "triangular purple shape" [52]) because it marked a watershed in my attempts to open their vision to a lesbian-feminist aesthetic broader than content or characterization. They were coming to understand how Woolf subtly asserts a fundamental connection between Mrs. Ramsay and Lily Briscoe, despite all surface differences. Excited about being guided toward this understanding, most students appreciated participating in a rigorous deconstruction of the novel despite their initial unexamined heterosexist assumptions. Those who resisted did so from uneasiness, making me suspect that my theoretical framework had dislodged their usual way of reading.

To conclude our exploration of how an aesthetic of likeness might influence a reader of *To the Lighthouse*, we discussed Lily's final execution of her painting, interrupted by a world war, several family crises, and the death of her idol. Late in the novel, Lily muses about Mrs. Ramsay's power of bringing together disparate pieces of life:

> But what a power was in the human soul! she thought. That woman sitting there writing under the rock resolved everything into simplicity; [. . .] brought together this and that and then this, and so made out of that miserable silliness and spite [. . .] something [. . .] which survived, after all these years complete, [. . .] and there it stayed in the mind affecting one almost like a work of art. (160)

Underscoring the assertion of artistry, Lily recalls how Mrs. Ramsay adroitly brought unlike persons and moods into a single frozen frame: "Mrs. Ramsay saying, 'Life stand still here'; Mrs. Ramsay making of the moment something permanent (as in another sphere Lily herself tried to make of the moment something permanent)—this was of the nature of a revelation. In the midst of chaos there was shape" (161).

Meeting in small groups to discuss this passage, students praised Woolf's skill at collapsing perceived differences between Lily and her adopted muse and mother. They argued that "bringing together" is precisely what Lily tries to do as a painter. Several students who had earlier resisted my reading now pointed out that by saying Mrs. Ramsay made something, Woolf valorized a character thoroughly caught up in domestic webs. To support their work, I told them that in Woolf's journals, she often referred to her aesthetic process as a "making up" from disparate sensual elements (see, e.g., *Diary* 3: 282, 4: 143, 5: 291).

By using the same linguistic formulations for Mrs. Ramsay's domestic and Lily's aesthetic labor, Woolf affirmed what late-twentieth-century writers like Alice Walker theorize ("Search"). Domestic labor has within it the same impulses and discipline as more formally defined art forms: a garden or quilt or beautifully planned home reflects an artist working in the medium available or allowed to her. So a giver of elaborate dinner parties can be depicted as an artist as surely as can a woman at an easel with brushes and paints.

By examining such linguistic echoes, my students could see how Woolf refused the very differences she articulated. By so doing, she asks readers to shift their evaluation, bringing likeness from background to foreground. Woolf's call for an aesthetic re-formation implicitly protests unexamined critical norms. It also puts her into the postmodern posture of critiquing her own characters: her superficial portrayal of Mrs. Ramsay conforms to cultural expectations of the perfect wife and mother, while that of Lily Briscoe works to support similarly stereotypical images of the unmarried woman; her subtler representations of these two figures, however, work against the stereotypes while revealing their ultimate likeness to one another.

My lesbian-feminist orientation encouraged me to lead students into new territory, to shift their critical position toward *To the Lighthouse*. Using the aids I supplied, most of them saw just how often the text affirms complementarity and the power of likeness rather than reinscribing a narrowly heterosexist aesthetic. My students went away from the novel less sure of its final significance and more open to the precise language of the text. For the most part, they seemed hungry for such ambiguities, even if occasionally uneasy about giving up their comfortable lenses. They came to see that accenting likeness rather than difference can enrich an already challenging text.

What Teaching *To the Lighthouse* Taught Me about Reading Virginia Woolf

Louise DeSalvo

"How can a one-armed man hang a circus poster?"

The question came from a student in the back of the room in a course called The Novels of Virginia Woolf that I teach at New York City's Hunter College. I was talking about the temporal structure of *To the Lighthouse* and Mrs. Ramsay's trip with Charles Tansley into town to visit the poor. On their way, Mrs. Ramsay sees a one-armed man "pasting a bill. The vast flapping sheet flattened itself out, and each shove of the brush revealed fresh legs, hoops, horses, glistening reds and blues, beautifully smooth, until half the wall was covered with the advertisement of a circus" (11). Mrs. Ramsay observes that it is "terribly dangerous work for a one-armed man, [. . .]—his left arm had been cut off in a reaping machine two years ago" (11), but she quickly buries her pity in a plan to attend the circus.

"What?" Fixed on Woolf's brilliant structure, I hadn't paid any attention to the content of Mrs. Ramsay's observation.

"What Woolf says the one-armed man is doing is impossible. Think about it. Try to make the picture," she said, just as I did whenever we confronted a difficult Woolfian passage.

I tried to make the picture and saw instantly what my student meant: a one-armed man not being able to hang a circus poster; every time he tried, it fell onto his head.

Most students agreed that the one-armed man would have struggled to do his job; not one believed the poster would have been "beautifully smooth." My questioning student believed that because Woolf cared more about the circus poster than about the one-armed man, she had erred in using the phrase "beautifully smooth." Although they agreed that Woolf expressed concern for the working class by including working-class characters in the novel, many believed she didn't comprehend the difficulties of working-class lives. Unable to fully escape her upper-middle-class bias, they said, she could describe the working class only from the outside.

All term, we tested this hypothesis against the evidence of the novels, diaries, and manuscripts. Using this same hypothesis, Kathleen Dobie, another of my students, systematically studied *Jacob's Room*; she has published her findings in a model essay, "This Is the Room That Class Built: The Structures of Sex and Class in *Jacob's Room*."

Until that discussion, I hadn't explored class in Woolf's works, although ironically, I had been hired in part because I, like Charles Tansley and my Hunter students, had been raised in a working-class family. Although tuition at Hunter is low compared with that at other colleges, it is still hard to afford for much of the student population; a majority of students receive some form of need-based aid. Many are single parents, many are self-supporting, and most work, some at two jobs, while attending college, even those with full-time course loads. Hunter is racially and ethnically diverse; many students come from the latest wave of New York City immigrants. They range in age from the late teens to over eighty (the average age is twenty-five), and several are activists: members of Act-Up, leaders of student protest movements, labor organizers, members of programs helping prostitutes. Before my teaching focus changed as a result of my students' prodding, I was interested in the Ramsays, not in Charles Tansley, and certainly not in Marie, the maid who cannot get back to Switzerland to see her dying father. After the circus poster discussion, however, I realized that what you focus on when you teach a literary work should depend on whom you teach.

When you look, you discover a *To the Lighthouse* filled with class issues and working-class characters. Indeed, working-class characters or issues occupy a significant amount of fictive space: Mrs. Ramsay takes credit for the *boeuf en daube*, which has taken Mildred, the cook, three days to prepare (100–01); Mrs. Ramsay claims it is her grandmother's recipe, though it is probably her grandmother's *cook's* recipe (100); Mrs. Ramsay interacts with her servants infrequently, often sending orders through Cam (grown women are ordered around by a child) (54); Mrs. Ramsay ducks responsibility and blames a servant for not taking down the skull in the nursery (114); Mr. Ramsay believes a slave class is necessary for the greater good of humankind (the upper class) (43); the image of a queen washing a beggar's foot suggests a reign preoccupied with gestures rather than with authentic care for the poor (7); Mr. Ramsay would disinherit his daughter if she married Charles Tansley (66); Charles Tansley reflects the complexities of a self-made man (12); Mrs. Ramsay doesn't want to hear too much about his suffering (12); the fisherman Macalister praises James for his good sailing before his father does (204); Macalister's son must fish while the Ramsays go to the lighthouse (163, 169, 180) because it is a desperate time for the fishermen, many of whom have emigrated; Mrs. Ramsay uses scratchy, cheap wool for the stocking (30); she sends to the lighthouse whatever she finds littering the room, rather than carefully chosen gifts (5); and Mrs. McNab and Mrs. Bast work to save the house ("Time Passes").

The following sketch of how a discussion focusing on class might proceed combines my experiences from many of the classes I have taught. I use a close reading method, paying attention to the words on the page, supplemented with research I or my students undertake in Woolf's diaries and manuscripts. Here, I refer to Mr. Ramsay, James, and Cam in the sailboat with Macalister and his boy on their way to the lighthouse, section 4 of "The Lighthouse," a scene that illuminates Woolf's treatment of class in the novel.

Mr. Ramsay asks Macalister "some question about the great storm at Christmas" (164). Macalister responds that the storm was terrible, that "ten ships had been driven into the bay for shelter," and that, finally, "they had launched the lifeboat, and they had got her out past the point" (164).

"What does Macalister's story depict?" I ask. A few students respond that

Macalister tells a story of great courage and genuine heroism, indicating the dangerous work fishermen perform daily.

"Is Woolf sympathetic to the dangers of fishermen's lives?" I ask. "Yes," most students respond. "Is Mr. Ramsay?" Here, they disagree: some argue that he is genuinely engaged; others are not so sure.

I ask why Mr. Ramsay "relished" the idea of "fishermen striving there" (164). Some students immediately answer that Mr. Ramsay ignores the tragedy of Macalister's story: the fishermen are in danger of drowning; many of them *do* drown. "Striving" is inappropriate; it denies and misrepresents what's happening.

"Does Mr. Ramsay acknowledge Macalister's heroism?" I ask. Most agree that Mr. Ramsay simply doesn't hear Macalister's description of the perils of a fisherman's life. Most important, he does not acknowledge Macalister's heroism; he elides it. Some students suggest that he might feel competitive, others that Macalister's heroism reinforces Mr. Ramsay's sense of inadequacy. Mr. Ramsay observes that he "liked that men should labour and sweat on the windy beach at night; pitting muscle and brain against the waves and wind; he liked men to work like that, and women to keep house, and sit beside sleeping children indoors, while men were drowned, out there in a storm" (164). "Does this passage show empathy?" I ask. Quite obviously not. But why not?

Using Macalister's story to support his belief in separate spheres for men and women is strange. "Can he really be so callous about fishermen drowning? What does that say about him?" I ask. Although Mr. Ramsay thinks a slave class is necessary, this passage indicates a more chilling attitude: a working-class life has no value. "What does Mr. Ramsay never express?" I ask. He never expresses empathy for the men who died.

"Are there any analogues in the novel?" I ask. Yes, in the story of Steenie's drowning that Mr. Ramsay reads in Sir Walter Scott. Macalister's story remains a story to Mr. Ramsay: he does not conceptualize the fishermen as people, as real. He also thinks of dying as heroic, which isn't Macalister's message at all. Macalister describes the reality of hardship, risk, loss, and death, the inverse of heroism. But Mr. Ramsay co-opts Macalister's experience; he acts as if he were "a peasant himself" (164). He looks "proudly" at the spot where Macalister points, where a ship has gone down, where men have died.

"Who is Mr. Ramsay proud of? Of Macalister?" I ask. "No," the students reply. Mr. Ramsay slips into Macalister's story, becoming a hero to his daughter Cam, who desperately idealizes him. She believes that "had he been there he would have launched the lifeboat, he would have reached the wreck [. . .]. He was so brave" (164–65).

"Is her perception accurate?" Of course not. Mr. Ramsay could not possibly have launched a lifeboat; he can't even sail to the lighthouse by himself. Macalister, the hero who did launch the lifeboat, is unacknowledged by these privileged characters, who don't believe that common folk can be heroes. Yet even Macalister does not consider his act heroic. So when Mr. Ramsay intones, "We perished, [. . .] each alone" (165), he slips into Macalister's role and subsequently ignores him. He appropriates Macalister's story, incorporating it into his own delusory sense of himself as the leader of a failed expedition.

Such discussion sparks interest in what Woolf recorded about class in her diaries while writing *To the Lighthouse*, so I encourage students to read them to prepare for further discussion. Woolf's diaries and manuscripts show that by the time she recorded her detailed plan for the novel, she placed class at her design's center: she planned to write the "Episode of taking Tansley to call on the poor. How they see [Mrs. Ramsay]. The great cleavages in to which the human race is split, through the Ramsays not liking Mr. Tansley. [. . .] How much more important divisions between people are than between countries. The source of all evil" (*Holograph Draft*, app. A, 48–49). So Woolf intended the novel to be about not only the Ramsays as portraits of the Stephens, St. Ives, and childhood but also Britain's class division as the source of all evil (thus anticipating her class critique in *Three Guineas*); she intended to use the Ramsays and their class prejudice toward Charles Tansley as demonstration.

In July 1925, when she hoped to begin writing her novel, Woolf was also gathering material for "Lives of the Obscure"; she wanted to tell the "whole history of England in one obscure life after another" (*Diary* 3: 37). *To the Lighthouse* displays this concern: Charles Tansley, Lily Briscoe, the servant Marie, the cook Mildred, the gardener, Mrs. McNab, Mrs. Bast, Macalister and his boy, the lighthouse keeper and his son—Woolf weaves all these obscure lives into the novel's fabric, illuminating the substantial but unacknowledged contribution each has made to English history.

Paradoxically, however, throughout her work on the novel, her diary entries show that Woolf could not fully acknowledge the contribution her own servants made to her well-being. She was in the "throes of the usual servant crisis" (*Diary* 3: 41; see also *Diary* 3: 359, 367 of the index for other pertinent entries). Though in "Time Passes" she penned one of the most eloquent descriptions of a charwoman's work ever written, Woolf herself hardly acted as a beneficent employer: she manifested the very behavior she criticized.

Woolf saw the "servant question" as an unfortunate carryover from her parents' age (Zwerdling 87–119). Yet she expected the women in her employ, Lottie Hope and Nelly Boxall, to do her bidding unquestioningly, to not complain, and to be grateful for whatever they got. This attitude, despite her leftist politics, echoed that of her mother, Julia Stephen (J. Marcus, *Woolf and the Languages* 97). Julia Stephen had written an article on the "servant question" (248–52); in it she insisted, as Alex Zwerdling summarizes, that "there was nothing degrading in domestic service, that the mistress was responsible for the welfare of her servants, and that she must therefore keep a constant watch over them" (Zwerdling 98).

Complicating the class issue still further, the general strike proclaimed by the Trades Union Congress in support of striking miners (*Diary* 3: 77n1) affected Woolf's composing of "Time Passes." The strike made it impossible to lead a normal life—Leonard Woolf said that it disrupted life in London more than World War I had (*Diary* 3: 80)—and Woolf changed "Time Passes" dramatically as a result.

Woolf first conceptualized "Time Passes" on 18 April 1926, just before the strike began on 2 May 1926. She described finishing it, "sketchily I admit" on 25 May 1926 (*Diary* 3: 88), which means that she drafted "Time Passes" throughout the strike. Before the strike, she planned to delineate only "an empty house, no people's characters, the passage of time, all eyeless & featureless with nothing to cling to" (*Diary* 3: 76). No mention of Mrs. McNab or Mrs. Bast.

But the strike demonstrated unequivocally to London's middle and upper classes exactly how much society depended on the work of laborers. Concurrent with planning and writing "Time Passes," Woolf kept a diary about the strike's effects: "nobody is building," "everyone is bicycling," "at 11 the light was turned off," she wrote on 5 May 1926 (*Diary* 3: 77). Virginia and Leonard Woolf also quarreled about it. Although she doesn't specify the exact nature of their quarrel, she wrote that she disliked the "tub-thumper" in Leonard and that he disliked the "irrational" Christian in her. Leonard vowed that if the state won and smashed the trade union movement, he would "devote his life to labour" (*Diary* 3: 80–81). Presumably, then, they quarreled about how much the labor cause should be supported and about Leonard's pessimism and Virginia's optimism that discourse and negotiation could solve the current confrontation. After they resolved their differences, Leonard and Virginia petitioned the government to reenter negotiations with the strikers (*Diary* 3: 81n11). In this regard, Woolf's activist socialist politics and her writing were congruent.

In addition, she shifted her focus in "Time Passes" after the strike—from "no people's characters" to an implicitly political description of the "gradual dissolution of everything," "Hopeless gulfs of misery. Cruelty. The War. Change. Oblivion. Human vitality. Old woman Cleaning up" (*Holograph Draft*, app. B, 51). After the strike, seeing how seriously altered her life was without the services of the working class, she wrote the portrait of Mrs. McNab, the "principle of life, & its power to persist; & its courage, & its assiduity, & its determination, denied one entrance, to seek another" (*Holograph Draft* 211). Though romanticized, Woolf's paean nonetheless values servants' work. My most radical students, however, dislike the implicit message in Mrs. McNab's portrait—the upper-class belief that you can always hire a poor woman to clean up your mess, to set to rights what you've let go to ruin.

Although Woolf penned the portraits of Mrs. Bast and Mrs. McNab to reflect her activist understanding of the strike, she did not change her attitude toward her own servants. On the contrary, she reports repeated fights, showdowns, leave-takings, and compromises. On 31 May 1929, she was "shocked" to discover that both she and Nelly Boxall wanted the Labour Party to win the general election that had just taken place: "why? partly that I don't want to be ruled by Nelly. I think to be ruled by Nelly & Lottie would be a disaster" (*Diary* 3: 230). Supporting Labour seemed a good idea in theory, but in practice, having the working class actually running a government was too much.

When she heard that Labour had, in fact, taken a majority, she wrote in resignation, "So we shall be ruled by labour" (*Diary* 3: 230).

Asking students to compare Woolf's attitudes about class in her fiction and in her life provoked much controversy. Some students believed that writers' lives are irrelevant, that only the work counts. Others believed that writers who evidence classist, racist, anti-Semitic, or homophobic attitudes in private will necessarily, even if unconsciously, reveal those attitudes in their work. We discussed how paradoxical writers' behavior can be and how difficult it is to translate political ideals into daily behavior. Students also debated whether one ought to read works by writers with despicable personal ideologies; whether a "bad" person can write a "good" book; whether literature, with its capacity to uplift, also has the capacity to harm; whether reading racist, classist, anti-Semitic, or homophobic works harms readers; and whether teachers have a moral obligation to inform students of writers' political beliefs and actions.

Inspired to draw parallels between Woolf's time and our own, many of my students became much more interested in her work because they were discussing issues that affected them. Teaching Hunter students helped me see Woolf's complex, contradictory, often reprehensible attitudes to the working class in her work and life. Had I not been privileged to teach working-class students who read Woolf in the context of their experience, I might have continued to overlook the working-class strands of meaning in Woolf's work, or I would have romanticized her interest in the working class and her depiction of working-class characters in her novels. I might have continued to read Virginia Woolf with the blinders of class on.

Reading *To the Lighthouse* as a Critique of the Imperial

Jeanette McVicker

Cultural and literary theory, of which postcolonial theory is a part, has radically altered readers' views about the construction and narration of ethnicity, class, gender, and power relations. With critics as diverse as Jane Marcus, Fredric Jameson, Patrick Brantlinger, Kathy Phillips, Janet Winston, Gayatri Chakravorty Spivak, and Mary Lou Emery recognizing that Woolf's texts reveal important connections between the aesthetic project of modernism and the discourse of imperialism, breaking down students' initial reaction to *To the Lighthouse* as a novel in which "nothing happens" becomes an exciting challenge. Studying *To the Lighthouse* as a critique of the imperial impulse helps students discover how everyday language, common beliefs, and domestic relations are fraught with the same violent impulses that manifest themselves abroad as colonialism, thus increasing their awareness of cultural differences and the struggle of "others" to articulate their own national narratives. As we discuss how Woolf's novel discloses the imperial project as a continuum generated, advanced, and maintained through Western metaphysics, the patriarchal family, academic institutions, and art or culture, and as students begin to understand how an indissoluble relay of sites (a phrase used by my friend William Spanos in conversation) works to construct the myth of the nation (and the British Empire growing out of it), they and their worldviews become dislocated. However, seeing how Woolf contested the authorizing discourses of her culture also encourages them to contribute to the "renegotiation of those times, terms and traditions" (Bhabha 306) pervading their own culture. Thus, their learning ultimately extends far beyond the classroom.

This approach can be used successfully in several classroom situations, from upper-division literature courses to women's and cultural studies courses. While I have taught *To the Lighthouse* in a women's studies and English elective called Major Women Novelists, I most often teach it in a world literature course that serves as both an English core elective and a humanities elective in the college's general education curriculum. Novels and Tales primarily draws sophomores from multiple majors with little exposure to literature beyond high school. My students at Fredonia, a four-year liberal arts college in the state university system, are almost exclusively white, middle-class upstate New Yorkers. They encounter *To the Lighthouse* about midway through the semester on a syllabus that includes Native American creation stories, African American folklore, short stories by nineteenth-century Romanian writers and contemporary Latin American women, and novels by Franz Kafka, Milan Kundera, J. M. Coetzee, Chinua Achebe, and Italo Calvino. Because *To the Lighthouse* is often the only twentieth-century Anglo-American text they read, they believe that it will be somehow familiar. Instead, it baffles them: a few students always remark that they wish they had an interpreter, so unfamiliar is this novel's language to them.

Such a response is fairly typical and derives, I think, from two interrelated factors. Most students are generally unable to ascertain a plot and therefore think that the novel is "about nothing." That view, however, is itself generated from their deep inscription in a culture grounded in values and ideologies that are the legacy of the imperial impulse. By focusing almost immediately on Woolf's novel as a critique of that impulse, I invite students to reconsider her "domestic" narrative while simultaneously "unhoming" their own perceptions of the world and their places within it. While any approach asking students to rethink their values will be met with resistance, this one zeros in on some of the most comfortable (and thus the most unthought about) ideas they have about the world. Yet I'm convinced that it is worthwhile to expose students to texts that compel them to examine their investment in such ideas and ideologies (and to encounter their resistance), as I watch them grapple almost daily with racism, sexism, homophobia, and other social biases. I have learned that ungraded response papers, together with background lectures, focused discussions, and small-group sessions, work best in encouraging students to look at difficult questions. We also sit in a circle all semester, an arrangement that not only helps stimulate conversation but also symbolically demonstrates the process of rethinking traditional authority.

I use the first class session (out of six) to introduce the important concepts we will use as a framework for our discussions of the novel; it is the only session in which I lecture. Because I have already assigned a response paper on "The Window," I know they have begun reading and probably feel frustrated; writing about their reading experience before this session allows them to articulate their frustration, and their reading experience becomes important to subsequent discussions. Because they have now confronted Woolf's "strange" style, I begin with a summary of the traditional aesthetic interpretation of *To the Lighthouse*. Indicating that this approach obscures the social and political ideas in the novel, I move to a general background on modernist literature and art. To place modernism in a historical context, which also provides background for later discussions of Lily's art, I show them slides of famous paintings depicting the shift from realism to impressionism to postimpressionism. I also distribute a handout that includes Woolf's famous statement from "Mr. Bennett and Mrs. Brown" about the modernist rupture: "in or about December, 1910, human character changed" (320). She goes on, "All human relations have shifted—those between masters and servants, husbands and wives, parents and children. And when human relations change, there is at the same time a change in religion, conduct, politics, and literature" (321).

To introduce ideology and hegemony, concepts crucial for students' understanding of how the imperial functions and is maintained through an indissoluble relay of sites, the handout also contains passages from Raymond Williams's classic, *Marxism and Literature*, which is as overtly theoretical as we will get.

Conveying that hegemony is a lived process functioning at the level of everyday experience, Williams (expanding on Antonio Gramsci's work), explains it as

> a saturation of the whole process of living [. . .] to such a depth that the pressures and limits of what can ultimately be seen as a specific economic, political and cultural system seem to most of us the pressures and limits of simple experience and common sense. [. . .] It is a whole body of practices and expectations [. . .], our shaping perceptions of ourselves and our world. It is a lived system of meanings and values [and] thus constitutes [. . .] a sense of absolute [. . .] reality beyond which it is very difficult for most members of the society to move [. . .].   (110)

Our upcoming discussions now have a framework that brings together art and culture, everyday experience, and Woolf's own suggestion that all human relations are relations of power; students have now encountered the idea that power functions as a continuum or field or relay of sites. In the remaining minutes, we look at the novel's first scene together, and I ask students to pay particular attention to the Ramsay family dynamics and to jot down questions with which we will begin the next session.

Students often have questions about Mr. Ramsay, who seems a bit "odd" or "mean," and about the italic passages in the text. We start, then, with a recital of Tennyson's "Charge of the Light Brigade" and an explanation of its origin. Mr. Ramsay functions for most of the novel as the primary agent of the imperial through three ideologically determined (and privileged) roles: empirical philosopher (in the tradition of Locke, Hume, and Berkeley) who sees being— "subject and object and the nature of reality" (23)—from above or beyond it, thus spatializing it and making it graspable; patriarch, dominating his wife and family; and Cambridge professor, training the ranks of civil servants needed for the functioning of the British Empire. In these three roles, Mr. Ramsay generates and maintains the "truth" that informs daily living by embodying imperialism's need for reason, truth, order, stability, and logic. He demands these from himself, his wife, his children, his students—the world. Section 6 of "The Window" demonstrates this demand with great clarity. Mr. Ramsay storms around porch and garden mumbling "*Some one had blundered*" (18), while the topic of going to the lighthouse is discussed inside by Mrs. Ramsay and James. Through the window, that porthole of domesticity, Mr. Ramsay "snapped out irascibly" that there would be no trip. "How did he know? she asked. The wind often changed" (31). He directs his anger not simply at his wife's optimism, which she displays for James's sake, but also at her irrationality in the face of facts ("the barometer falling and the wind due west"), "the folly of women's minds" (32, 31). The imperial poem he recites, which at first appears marginal, is at the core of his being in all its functions: philosopher, husband and father, professor— colonizer. Mr. Ramsay is committed to a logic that privileges reason and order and thus represses any "other" that would disrupt this imperial "truth."

In the same session and continuing into the third, we discuss how Mrs. Ramsay intuits these ideological imperatives embedded in her family's daily lives and senses the outrage and brutality of such demands. Woolf's images reinforce the point: Mrs. Ramsay feels as if she is "dazed and blinded, [. . .] pelt[ed by] jagged hail [and . . .] dirty water" (32). Not only does she feel physically assaulted by her husband's lack of consideration for her feelings (and the feelings of any others who might threaten his authority), but she is also punished because she does not conform, ideologically, to "right reason." Because many students pity Mrs. Ramsay and identify with her at this point, they are surprised by my next question: How does Mrs. Ramsay inscribe the imperial impulse at the site of family? After all, her continual efforts to create domestic peace, play the matchmaker, and soothe her husband's ego are just as necessary to the smooth functioning of imperialism as Mr. Ramsay's demands for reason. This seeming contradiction—how Mrs. Ramsay can be both victim and perpetrator of the imperial truth discourse—provides the crucial moment in students' understanding of imperial ideology and the way it functions. Here, it is helpful to show students Woolf's description of the Victorian "Angel in the House" from her speech to the London National Society for Women's Service in January 1931. In a passage remarkably similar to one in the novel, Woolf makes the imperial continuum clear:

> The Angel in the house was the ideal of womanhood created by the imaginations of men and women at a certain stage [. . .]. They agreed to accept this ideal, because for reasons I cannot now go into—they have to do with the British Empire, our colonies, Queen Victoria, Lord Tennyson, the growth of the middle class and so on [. . .].   (*Pargiters* xxx)

This passage recalls for students how human relations change and how hegemony works: the institutions that make up society—the family, the academy, art and culture, the government—all perpetuate ideology, working together, as a continuum, to promote the "truths" a nation asserts. Mrs. Ramsay intuits this web of ideology in moments of self-reflection, though of course she never names it: "Indeed, she had the whole of the other sex under her protection; *for reasons she could not explain*, for their chivalry and valour, for the fact that they negotiated treaties, ruled India, controlled finance [. . .]" (6; my emphasis). She imagines James "all red and ermine on the Bench" (4), a propagator of empire. Her daughters may mutely question "deference and chivalry," "taking care of some man or other," and "the Bank of England and the Indian Empire," but these are "infidel ideas" (7, 6). So while Mr. Ramsay oppressively demands adherence to facts, reason, and truth from all those who circulate around his center, Mrs. Ramsay constructs a domestic haven and demands that her daughters do the same. Together, they reinforce specific (and ideological) norms of behavior for themselves and others, thus revealing the imperial impulse at work. Woolf's vivid portrayal of this continuum in *To the Lighthouse* asks all of us, teacher and students, to see how ideology pervades our world and how important it is to become aware of its pervasiveness.

In our fourth session on the novel, we first carefully consider the "Q-R" passage, which reveals the metaphysical foundation for the imperial truth discourse. The passage demonstrates Mr. Ramsay's obsession with mastering reality and further illustrates Woolf's critique of the imperial as derived from Enlightenment philosophical thinking. The narrator likens thought to an organized series of letters, that is, the alphabet, and says that Mr. Ramsay's "splendid mind had no sort of difficulty in running over those letters one by one, firmly and accurately, until it had reached, say, the letter Q" (33). Many students have a tough time making sense of this metaphor, and as we talk about the metaphysical tradition, their sense of uneasiness increases. As an empiricist, Mr. Ramsay attempts to master thought in an orderly, correct way: if one can only picture, or spatialize, reality in a chart or graph, then one can somehow master or domesticate it. His professional interests thus ideologically undergird the British Empire. When I compare Mr. Ramsay's philosophy to Mendel's genetic table in biology or Mendeleyev's periodic table of elements in chemistry, some students connect the Enlightenment's efforts to map out nature with Woolf's portrayal of metaphysics as advancing the manipulation of knowledge. Of course, the empire ultimately gains power over all "exotic others" through such knowledge, the "civilizing mission" of colonialism. Mr. Ramsay's philosophy, which he *lives*, thus embodies the repressiveness of the entire academic tradition. This discussion helps students begin to understand why the United States and British educational system generally barred university attendance for the poor, women, and people of color well into the twentieth century, and they are profoundly disturbed by discovering a double meaning for the phrase "knowledge is power." Contemplating how they themselves are implicated in the imperial impulse through the education they are at that very moment gaining, many students embark on their own journey to the lighthouse or toward awareness, the starting point for resistance or counterhegemony.

At this point, I break the class up into several small groups and ask each one to consider how Mr. Ramsay sees his quest for R, his effort to master reality step-by-step, in terms of being an expeditionary hero (34–36) and how Mr. Ramsay and his quest compare and contrast with characters and situations in one of the previous texts we have read. Because we have just discussed the linear metaphor of the alphabet as the spatialization of knowledge, some students discuss the ways the expedition metaphors reinscribe the Enlightenment impulse to chart and domesticate the great natural frontiers, and others note that the same impulse worked to repress Native American traditions and African folkways. After we have come back together as a class and students have shared their various insights about Mr. Ramsay and quest motifs, I ask, "What does Woolf imply by linking the heroic ideal with what is essentially an imperialist mission? For what other reason do nations send brave men out to post the national flag if not to claim the land and its inhabitants for king and

country?" The students who have been most willing to let go of their preconceived notions of power discover Woolf's humor: she undercuts the entire
imperial project by leaving Mr. Ramsay not only stuck at Q but also imagining
himself as the "heroic" leader of doomed expeditions!

Having begun to feel more comfortable with the text and its critique of the
imperial, some students once again express their bafflement when we discuss
"Time Passes" in our fifth session. Here I suggest that Woolf symbolically
stages a dual end of the imperial impulse: the collapse of imperialism proper
in the catastrophe of World War I (sec. 6) and the collapse of civilization itself
in the near destruction of the Ramsay house and family. Despite imperial
efforts to measure time, domesticate nature, dominate the other, and thus master reality itself, time, nature, the colonized, and reality refuse to be controlled.
This central "truth" of the novel, and of human existence, cannot be ascer-
tained and mastered systematically, letter by letter. Situating this cosmic struggle in the center of the book, Woolf asks readers to recognize the limits of
civilization and power while implying that the society we create determines the
context within which we confront those limits. As Gillian Beer suggests, *To the
Lighthouse* is "an elegy for a kind of life no longer to be retrieved—and no
longer wanted back. [. . .] Everything is in flux, land as much as sea, individual
as well as whole culture" (*Woolf* 159). The students who have begun to connect
their experience of reading the novel—moving from dislocation to comfort and
back again—to its content understand the strange parenthetical deaths of Mrs.
Ramsay, Prue, and Andrew and the effect those deaths have. We can then discuss how these experiences of comfort and dislocation may parallel participa-
tion in and resistance to a culture and how difficult and yet how crucial it is to
envision society in new ways.

Lily Briscoe's struggle to finish her painting in "The Lighthouse" further
illustrates the complexity of Woolf's critique. While many students initially perceive Lily as slightly confused (one called her "an airhead") and unsure of herself, I use this perception by suggesting, still in our fifth class, that Lily, too, is
affected by the imperial impulse, particularly by the ideological pressures of
the angel in the house. Some students sympathize with Lily's uneasiness over
her "lack" of traditional feminine virtues as they talk about "acceptable" gender roles in our own society. They also realize that Lily cannot complete her
painting as long as she perceives her lack of conformity to the ideological
model as a failure. Only when she gains confidence in her own model, one that
resists the claims that "women can't paint, women can't write" (48), can Lily
achieve the clarity necessary for her "vision" (209). But before these students
turn Lily into a feminist rebel, I ask them to reconsider the examples of modernist art we began with. Lily's abstract representation of mother and child, of
her emotional relationship to Mrs. Ramsay, seems to achieve the modernist
aim, defined by many critics as an attempt to break with traditional artistic
forms and to express a profound sense of alienation and fragmentation by pro-
jecting a momentary sense of order. It also recalls "Time Passes" and its

attempt to frame the fluid and the chaotic within art. But Lily's achievement—
"With a sudden intensity, as if she saw it clear for a second, she drew a line
there, in the centre. It was done; it was finished" (209)—is ambiguously pre-
figured by Mrs. McNab's retrieving the summerhouse from ruin: "At last, after
days of labour within, of cutting and digging without, [. . .] the front door was
banged; it was finished" (141). It is as though Woolf uses these scenes to suggest that time is a greater power than any human effort—artistic or domestic—
to contain it. Perhaps, I say to my students, Woolf herself, as modernist artist
and daughter of a "real" Victorian angel, is ambivalent about art's ability to
resist the imperial impulse.

If some of my students, especially the women, are slightly annoyed with my
dampening of their enthusiasm for Lily here, that's okay, because it requires
them to move beyond the simplistic either-or interpretation that sees characters as villains or heroes. Then they can see that each of the novel's main characters expresses positive and negative ideological positions, just as we all do,
and they are better prepared to discuss the Ramsays' landing at the lighthouse
in our last session. My focus, then, is on transition and transformation, which
again recalls our earlier discussion of how hegemony works as a lived, everyday process and how change in human relations occurs; therefore, as we reori-
ent our discussion toward James and Cam, my students' optimism usually
returns, if a little muted. Agreeing that Lily is of course changing the model
for what it means to be a woman, departing from the role of Victorian angel
that had helped promote the British national narrative, I also suggest that as
an artist, Lily has a sense of arrival or of aesthetic wholeness that also rein-
scribes, at some level, the same imperial impulse. But what about James and
Cam? Though they have been groomed by their parents and their culture to
continue the imperial tradition, "all human relations have shifted." As Beer
says, "The long backward survey to the politics of Edwardian family life, to
England before the First World War, which began to unravel through the
image of the abandoned house in 'Time Passes' here reaches conclusion: 'It is
finished.' [. . .] Things have come to an end. The period of empire is drawing
to its close. [. . .] The parents' England is gone" (*Woolf* 158). Coming to a silent
understanding of their father after vowing to fight the tyranny he had represented, James and Cam may write, Woolf hints, a different narrative of the
nation—and thus of the future. This session gives the students a wonderful
moment, allowing them to feel that they, too, have reached the lighthouse.
"This is really a hard novel to read," said one student in class, "but it has helped
me think about how different my life and times are from my parents' and why
they still don't understand multiculturalism." It is a moment for the instructor
to savor, too.

When students consider the imperial context of *To the Lighthouse*, they
begin to read the cultural, social, and political narratives that inform the Western tradition and to understand how these narratives require everyone's par-
ticipation through a continuum of everyday situations as well as institutional

pressures. Once students think about power in this way, and not simply as outright suppression by force, many also begin to recognize how we are all inscribed by such pressures; indeed, the "end" of the British Empire as marked by Hong Kong's return to China or the president's call for a national discussion on race no longer seems detached from the small, everyday incidents they observe, participate in, or react to on campus. Woolf resisted, as best she could, the demands of power exerted at various sites in the imperial continuum: in works such as *A Room of One's Own* and *Three Guineas,* in her commitment to pacifist socialism, and more subtly, but finally more fundamentally, in her fiction. As students search, like Cam and James, for a more equitable future, Woolf's model can be liberating. And while this approach can often be frustrating, for students and instructor, student responses over the years—one student told me that all teachers should "shock" their students!—ultimately make it worthwhile.

Autobiographical Approaches

Articulating the Questions, Searching for Answers: How *To the Lighthouse* Can Help

Nancy Topping Bazin

At Old Dominion University, English majors must take one of the following courses—Postcolonial Literature, Literature by Minorities, African-American Literature, or Women Writers. In each course, our majors encounter new materials and perspectives. I teach Virginia Woolf's *To the Lighthouse* in Women Writers, a course in which students expect to explore feminist perspectives. Students range in age from nineteen to sixty, but most are in their twenties or thirties. Frequently the first in their families to attend college, many come from conservative homes where *feminist* is a derogatory word. Therefore I find that the best way into a feminist novel like Virginia Woolf's *To the Lighthouse* is through biography and autobiography, and I point out that Woolf noted the autobiographical nature of this novel in her letters, diaries, and autobiographical fragments. Despite differences in class, national culture, and time period, most students can successfully relate to the concerns about marriage and work expressed by Woolf. Discovering links between and among her life, the novel, and their own lives helps them see, and empathize with, her feminist perspective.

Many students initially dismiss Mrs. Ramsay and the inner conflicts felt by Lily Briscoe as old-fashioned and thus irrelevant. For them, women are now liberated and can easily have a career and a family. Other students, subscribing to the beliefs of the local Christian Coalition, are unsympathetic to Lily Briscoe, who chooses work over family. A more feminist group tends to dehumanize the oppressive husband, Mr. Ramsay, thereby failing to perceive the extent to which Woolf admires his intellectual and emotional courage. Moving students beyond these initial reactions requires accuracy in reading but also occurs most readily when students connect what they read with their own lives. To become intellectually and emotionally involved with this book, students must care about its content. I have learned that I can encourage students to relate to the novel personally without promoting true confessions or group therapy, however; common sense tells me when our discussion should return to the text.

Indeed, many students make some general connections right away, such as when they relate Lily Briscoe's struggle to their own tensions between devotion to family and commitment to work. Through analyzing the text in their journals and in class, others begin to see how Woolf's insights apply to them. For example, several female students desiring to enter professions said they feared that getting married would mean giving up their ambitions and happiness for someone else's, and they could not imagine a time when having a baby would not interfere with their careers. Many male students in the class discovered they experience these work and family tensions, too, but usually not to the same degree that women do. However, both a single father and a man who had chosen to be the primary caretaker for his child argued that the tension is, in fact, role-related rather than gender-related. This point enriched the discussion, for it allowed students not only to recognize the validity of the point but also to see these two men as exceptions to the still strong social rule that the principal caretaker be female.

Many students have told me that they understand *To the Lighthouse* better once they learn more about the situation of women during Mr. and Mrs. Ramsay's lifetimes, so in my class of forty-five students, of which ten are usually graduate students, I ask two of them to report on the women's suffrage movement in Great Britain. I suggest they start with Emmeline Pankhurst's *My Own Story*, Christabel Pankhurst's *Unshackled: The Story of How We Won the Vote*, Ray Strachey's *The Cause*, and Patricia Branca's *Women in Europe since 1750*. Then the whole class reads (and sees the video of) Woolf's long essay *A Room of One's Own*. Discussing this essay prepares students well for reading *To the Lighthouse*.

As indicated in *A Room of One's Own*, Woolf wanted women to commit to their own work. She wanted more women to be able to say, as Lily Briscoe did, "I have had my vision" (209). What Lily had seen was the hidden pattern (*Moments* 72), the essence; she had made contact with "reality" (*Room* 114). To create a masterpiece, artists must see human beings "in relation to reality," for great art must have this metaphysical dimension (*Room* 114). But not until women are freed from gender inequities, not until they have money and rooms of their own, will they gain "the habit of freedom and the courage to write exactly what [they] think," the foundations, in Woolf's view, for perceiving the metaphysical dimension (*Room* 113, 114). Therefore, as an artist, Woolf had urgent philosophical reasons for advocating gender equity.

I give students the following quotations from Carol Christ, Simone de Beauvoir, and Woolf to help them understand why Woolf believes equality is a foundation for philosophical speculation. As Carol Christ points out in *Diving Deep and Surfacing*, when women question their designated roles, they also ask, "Who am I? Why am I here? What is my place in the universe?" (8). To consider such philosophical questions, people must feel confident about their right to do so. In other words, women cannot think creatively while being subjected to Charles Tansleys who remark, "Women can't paint, women can't write" (48). As Simone de Beauvoir argues in *The Second Sex*, "[W]e can count on the fingers of one hand the women who have traversed the given in search of its secret dimension [. . .]. Women do not contest the human situation, because they have hardly begun to assume it" (669). Woolf believed that real creativity and spirituality come from being in touch with what she called reality: "it is a fact, that there is no arm to cling to, but that we go alone and that our relation is to the world of reality and not only to the world of men and women" (*Room* 114). Undergraduate reports on chapters 1, 2, and 8 in Carol Christ's book and chapter 25, "The Independent Woman," in Simone de Beauvoir's enrich this discussion, and a report by a graduate student on Mary Daly's *Beyond God the*

Father: Toward a Philosophy of Women's Liberation demonstrates how a belief in equality radically changed not only aspects of Daly's philosophy but her entire worldview.

A similar transformation occurs in *To the Lighthouse* as Lily Briscoe experiments with various ways of seeing, for instance, the Ramsays, William Bankes, marriage, being single, the lighthouse, and her painting, until she is able to arrive at a new synthesis and sense of wholeness (however precarious) at the end of the novel. I begin Women Writers with *A Room of One's Own* and *To the Lighthouse* because together they present so well traditional roles and their consequences for women, challenges to the beliefs governing these roles and the kinds of changes necessary to dislodge them, and, finally, a vision of future possibilities.

I try not to give formal lectures. Instead, I inject information and relevant outside sources into the discussions in response to student comments or questions—for example, about Woolf's life, Bloomsbury attitudes, or what she might mean by "reality" and how that relates to aesthetics and spirituality. The class and I have an ongoing conversation in which I am, at times, a strong participant. However, I further subvert the students' inclination to depend on the teacher for interpretations by having a different student facilitate the discussion during each three-hour class. I choose as facilitators those who plan to be teachers—one for *A Room of One's Own* and two for the two weeks on *To the Lighthouse*. While other students give reports or do special projects, future teachers lead discussions on every work, long or short, assigned during the semester.

In advance, the student leader prepares questions that we discuss privately once or twice before class. I suggest that they first ask for student responses to the novel and then let general discussion develop as much as possible before they ask more specific questions. They know they have to be flexible, to pose questions out of what their peers have been saying, and to insert their prepared questions only when needed to move the discussion forward. Yet they also have to be ready to redirect the discussion to a neglected topic, particularly when omitting that topic may hinder the interpretative process. We also discuss how questions or answers about the meaning of Lily's painting or the lighthouse should be raised not in the beginning but late in the discussion, after students have analyzed how each character functions in the novel and have figured out the overall structure. Given this level of preparation by the facilitator, I intervene in the discussion only when necessary.

Through these conversations, students gradually seem to realize that Woolf raises fundamental questions about how to live, questions they themselves face: whether and whom to marry, what kind of work to choose, which commitments to make, what philosophy to live by, whether their decisions will encourage or discourage a spiritual life. Not just relevant to the nineteen- to twenty-two-year-olds, these issues also confront adults returning to school; they have begun rethinking their earlier decisions about mates, work, and the philosophy directing their time and energy. As Woolf demonstrates, neither

Mrs. Ramsay nor Lily Briscoe has found a perfect solution to the tension between freedom and responsibility, between self and family. Any solution is a compromise, and each individual must negotiate her or his own way.

Because *To the Lighthouse* is autobiographical, I ask students to outline how they might write their autobiographies. We discuss the ways we create meaning and develop a philosophy of life by selecting details from our lives and recollecting particularly significant (even symbolic) moments. We use Woolf's letters and diaries to enrich these discussions with autobiographical details about the writing of *To the Lighthouse*. Her letter of 15 May 1927 to her older sister, Vanessa, conveys how eagerly Woolf awaited Vanessa's response to her depiction of their father and especially their mother, who had died when Woolf was only thirteen (*Letters* 3: 374–77). When Vanessa answered that "it is an amazing portrait of mother" and that she "found the rising of the dead almost painful" (*Diary* 3: 135; see also *Letters* 3: 572), Woolf replied that she was "in a terrible state of pleasure that you should think Mrs Ramsay so like mother." Woolf also wrote: "I was in such a happy state, no tea kettle, no cat, not all the contented and happy creatures in the whole world, were a match for me" (*Letters* 3: 383). After successfully bringing their parents back to life, she concluded, "I was more like him than her, I think" (*Letters* 3: 374). Her kinship with her father was primarily a philosophical one: Woolf shared his "desire to look unflinchingly at life as it is" (Bazin 14).

Lily Briscoe (Woolf's fictional self) studies the virtues and defects of Mr. and Mrs. Ramsay (representing Woolf's parents) to depict the essence of each on her canvas. She begins, as young adults might, by deciding which aspects of her parents' personalities and behaviors to imitate, which to reject. Although Woolf wrote *To the Lighthouse* in her forties, she was still working out, through Lily, how she felt about each parent. I ask the students to reflect in their journals on which parental virtues and defects have influenced their decisions about how they live and what they believe. Then they outline how they might organize an essay on this topic, an assignment that helps students relate to the novel in various ways. They come from a diversity of family structures and resultant influences, some of which include domineering, military-trained fathers; frustrated, unfulfilled mothers; grieving, depressed, or dysfunctional parents; and parents absent for reasons such as military service, alcoholism, mental illness, infidelity, divorce, or death. The loss Woolf suffered (and that Lily and the Ramsays suffer in the novel) becomes much more real when students with absent parents examine the effect of that absence in this ungraded writing exercise. (Of course, any student who is uncomfortable outlining a personal essay may outline a more formal discussion of the novel.)

Woolf clearly suggests that we must reexamine and reevaluate the past to make choices for the future. As Woolf notes in her diary, she was obsessed with her mother and father "unhealthily; & writing of them [in *To the Lighthouse*] was a necessary act" (3: 208). In writing this novel, she claims to have done for herself "what psycho-analysts do for their patients" (*Moments* 81). Abandoning her adolescent love-hate relationship with her parents, she devises a more just and balanced way of seeing them.

Sometime during our discussion of the novel, I insert Woolf's concept of the "Angel in the House" (*Collected Essays* 2: 285–86) and note that in Queen Victoria's reign, when Woolf's parents grew up, strict gender roles prescribed devotion to family for females and a commitment to work for males. Women were admonished to acknowledge the superiority of their husbands simply because they were men (Lilienfeld, "Where the Spear Plants" 151–54). Middle- and upper-class women who chose to work usually had to abandon the possibility of marriage and children. Further, if a mother died, everyone expected the eldest daughter to remain single and devote herself to the family. After both the mother and older sister had died in Woolf's family, for example, Woolf described Vanessa's new role as "part slave, part angel" (*Moments* 125).

Forced to choose between family and work, women of Mrs. Ramsay's generation (and class) generally chose family, but influenced by the vigor of the women's movement between 1865 and 1919 (Branca 179–85), some English women of Lily Briscoe's generation decided to forgo family to devote themselves to work. Like our students, however, many would rather not have had to choose. Woolf, for example, wanted "everything—love, children, adventure, intimacy, work" (*Letters* 1: 496).

Woolf used the tension between devotion to loved ones and time for oneself as the central theme in four of her first five novels—*The Voyage Out* (1915), *Night and Day* (1919), *Mrs. Dalloway* (1925), and *To the Lighthouse* (1927). Only the trauma of her brother's death diverted Woolf to another topic for her third novel, *Jacob's Room* (1922). Since she did not center her novels after *To the Lighthouse*—*The Waves* (1931), *The Years* (1937), and *Between the Acts* (1941)—on this tension between family and self, Woolf evidently felt satisfied with how she had articulated and tried to settle the key questions about such tension in that novel.

Nearly all of today's students struggle with the same questions that Woolf addressed in *To the Lighthouse*. Although discussions of Mr. Ramsay, William Bankes, and Augustus Carmichael also reveal the family-work tension, Woolf focuses primarily on the effect marriage has on female ambitions. Whereas the aspiring artist Lily Briscoe chooses to stay single, Mrs. Ramsay has repressed her dream of being a social worker so that she can embody the Victorian ideal of being a wife and mother. Nevertheless, I ask, do some aspects of Mrs. Ramsay's character model rebellion for her daughters? After all, Mrs. Ramsay does withhold part of herself from her husband. She seizes moments for herself, thinks angry thoughts ("she often felt she was nothing but a sponge sopped full of human emotions" [32]), questions the wisdom of having children (since life was "terrible, hostile, and quick to pounce on you" [60]), and refuses to let go of her ambitions completely (she longed to be "an investigator, elucidating the social problem" [9]).

As Sigmund Freud has suggested, human beings need both work and erotic love ("Fifth Lecture" 54–55). Forced to suppress her sexuality to be an artist, Lily denies herself the satisfaction that comes from intimacy. Like William Bankes, she feels "dried and shrunk" (21), yet she perceives that intimacy might be possible with men different from the extremely patriarchal Mr. Ramsay. Exploring how William Bankes differs from Mr. Ramsay (23–25), Lily dares to discuss her painting with him; she knows they have shared "something profoundly intimate" (53). With him she discovers "a power which she had not suspected—that one could walk away down that long gallery not alone any more but arm in arm with somebody—the strangest feeling in the world, and the most exhilarating" (54). Some students are relieved to note that Woolf's opposition is not to marriage but to patriarchal ones. Others wonder what effect Woolf's lesbianism (and her partial suppression of it) had on her view of marriage.

Many students are also fascinated by Woolf's intense desire for children and with her grief at not having any. Concerned for her mental stability and her art, her husband, Leonard, prompted doctors to tell Virginia that she should not have children because of her periods of mental illness (Q. Bell 2: 8). She envied her sister Vanessa, who was an artist and yet had children. Down deep, Woolf felt herself a failure for not being a mother; but, worse yet, when she completed her books, she feared failure in her primary area of commitment—her work. As she was writing *To the Lighthouse*, for example, she wrote in her diary: "Is it nonsense, is it brilliance?" (3: 76). Her fear of failure (which she shared with her father and Mr. Ramsay) caused deep depressions. After completing *To the Lighthouse*, she described in her diary one of these spells: "Oh [. . .] the horror—physically like a painful wave swelling about the heart—tossing me up. I'm unhappy unhappy! Down—God, I wish I were dead. [. . .] I watch. Vanessa. Children. Failure. Yes; I detect that. Failure failure" (3: 110). If she could not succeed at being both the "Angel in the House" and the artist, she *had* to succeed as the artist. Thus, her breakdowns occurred or threatened to occur after nearly every novel.

This additional reading is done not for its own sake but to enhance the students' interest in and understanding of *To the Lighthouse*. I place the relevant volumes of Woolf's diary (1 and 3) and her letters (3), the collection of her autobiographical writing (*Moments of Being*), and several biographies on reserve, and I suggest that students read as much of them as possible before we discuss the novel. At the beginning of the semester, students choose among these readings (as well as others) for their reports, and they select and reproduce relevant quotations to share with the rest of the class, always with this primary goal in mind—to illuminate the text of the novel.

Many conclude, for example, that by December 1927, Woolf could, at least intellectually, shed her envy of her mother's gift for nurturing men and children and her sister Vanessa's ability to be both mother and artist. After a party for Vanessa's children, Woolf could finally say, "[O]ddly enough I scarcely want children of my own now. This insatiable desire to write something before I die [. . .] make[s] me cling [. . .] to my one anchor" (*Diary* 3: 167). Writing *To the*

Lighthouse evidently reduced the tensions between devotion to family and commitment to work. She now saw her mother less as a promoter of marriage and motherhood and more as an artist and rebel (like herself). She saw her scholarly, self-centered father less as a domestic tyrant, demanding female attention, and more as a hero (like herself), boldly and hopelessly trying to capture "Z," the truth about human existence. We discuss how the changes in Cam's and James's feelings toward Mr. Ramsay in part 3 might represent Woolf's ambivalent feelings about her father and her similar progression from less hatred to more love, from less anger to more admiration as she worked on the novel. Older students frequently share with younger ones their growing tolerance for parental attitudes and flaws they once could not abide. Most are still struggling, however, to harmonize their ambition with their role as primary caretaker. Like Lily Briscoe, Woolf resolved the tensions she felt between her roles as woman and artist; she discovered just how intensely committed she was to her art. In conjunction with this discussion, I use material from Tillie Olsen's essay "Silences" about how few women writers married, that if they married they married late and had few (if any) children, and that all had household help (16–17).

To the Lighthouse illustrates how choices about family interact with those about the type or the quality of work a person does and how both relate to one's spiritual life. Many students care about these issues but often find them difficult to articulate. In the process of writing in their journals, outlining their responses to their parents, reading the autobiographical and biographical materials, and discussing *A Room of One's Own* and *To the Lighthouse*, however, most of them develop and express a greater understanding of their parents' sacrifices for family and work and begin to discuss structural solutions to the conflict between time for working and time for parenting. (They even begin to replace the word *mothering* with *parenting*, recognizing that gender should not determine roles or privileges!) Many realize, some for the first time, that they can make decisions consciously instead of automatically conforming to the norm. Despite social pressures to the contrary, for example, they can remain childless or choose not to marry. A close analysis of *To the Lighthouse* helps them ponder the questions they should ask ("Who am I? Why am I here? What is my place in the universe?"), how those questions interrelate, and to what extent gender may still determine their answers.

From the Dark House to the Lighthouse: The Ramsays as Dysfunctional Family

Gerald T. Cobb

In teaching *To the Lighthouse* to English majors and honors students at Seattle University, I have noted how frequently students describe the Ramsays as dysfunctional. They cringe at the philosopher-father's treatment of young James, perceive the Ramsay family atmosphere as threatening, and cherish what they see as Mrs. Ramsay's life-giving presence, first as she comforts her children and later as Lily Briscoe aesthetically resurrects her in a painting. Most students are aware, some painfully so, of family dysfunction and therefore can use a family systems approach to Woolf's novel. Such an approach gives students a manageable framework in which to place their diverse impressions and questions about the text.

Most students eagerly welcome this approach when they encounter Woolf's writing style, which they label unfamiliar, dense, abstract. To begin, students read the novel's first three sections and write two paragraphs, one describing the Ramsay family and another describing their experience of reading the text. Students consistently point out the opening scene's abrupt shift in tone from young James's bliss when his mother promises a journey to the lighthouse to his murderous thoughts about his father, prompted by Mr. Ramsay's brusque assertion that bad weather will surely cancel their trip (4). James's strong antipathy toward his father suggests that Mr. Ramsay's pronouncement is just the most recent sign of a long-standing patriarchal tyranny.

The scene arouses many students' suspicions about Mr. Ramsay, and they point to one sentence—"Such were the extremes of emotion that Mr. Ramsay excited in his children's breasts by his mere presence" (4)—as evidence that a few skeletons may reside in the Ramsay family closets. When I later ask if any actual skeletons appear in the novel, several enthusiastically discuss the ramifications of the skeletal boar's head hanging in the room where James and Cam sleep (114). The skull eerily suggests that the children are vulnerable to the brutal exercise of power, which they respond to either by "resist[ing] tyranny," as James and Cam phrase it (163, 168), or by accommodating and fleeing, as Nancy does when she retires to the attic "to escape the horror of family life" (73).

We talk about how this novel requires a reader's intense focus; younger students inevitably express some impatience for "something to happen," while older students counter by saying that they enjoy Woolf's subtle accuracy. One fifty-year-old student wrote, "Woolf knows how to capture the significance of those small experiences that add up to a family life; she knows where the real dramas in a family take place—often they are played out in small gestures at the dinner table." All students, regardless of age, feel they must read parts of the text two or three times, and I invite them to arrange small-group oral readings of selected passages to identify shifts in point of view. This tracking of narrative shifts is quite difficult; one student observed, "Woolf continually uses 'he' and 'she' instead of a name, which confused me until I could define the pronoun." To have pronoun meaning remain clear even when scenes shift, readers must dwell entirely within the text's (and the Ramsays') assumptive world. Woolf's pronoun use makes students members of the family: her usage assumes the consciousness of a family member who thinks and feels in terms of "he" and "she" and not in terms of formal names. Paradoxically, then, *To the Lighthouse* seems most unfamiliar to students precisely when most familiar, conveying awareness of a family's presuppositions and the internal consciousness patterns reflecting those presuppositions.

To dramatize this point during our discussion of the first three sections, I ask students to compare the proportion of external dialogue to internal reflection. They circle all spoken dialogue, and we then enact an oral reading of it, with students taking the roles of Mrs. Ramsay, Mr. Ramsay, and Charles Tansley. By omitting the extensive passages of internal consciousness, students can hear the give and take of a single, short conversation; moreover, they note Woolf's recurring use of a brief spoken statement to launch extended interior reflection.

This exercise lays the groundwork for what I consider the most important pedagogical moment in teaching the novel: after students have read "The Window," I ask them to speculate about why the novel so frequently dives beneath the surface of ordinary actions to flow with the subtle currents of interior life. Some students inevitably suggest that Woolf's style reflects how interior consciousness provides the only safe, secure refuge from the above-surface Ramsay world containing so many painful, unpredictable perils. In other words, the novel's stream of consciousness reflects the characters' defensive strategy to avoid or buffer the Ramsay family's dysfunction.

When these students see Woolf's style as a coping strategy, they realize why the novel radically understates many crucial events that they would expect to be extensively reported, such as the deaths of Mrs. Ramsay, Prudence, and Andrew in bracketed paragraphs that abruptly illuminate the characters' interior worlds (128, 132, 133). The narrative refuses to dwell on these latest painful blows to an already battered family. Recoiling from such realities, the narrative returns to the safety of interior realms, lovingly portraying the curve of a thought or the warmth of a sunbeam on a wall. The key student insight, then, comes in seeing that Woolf's bifurcation of external action and internal consciousness reveals a deep fissure in the Ramsay family.

At this moment, many students eagerly pursue research showing that Woolf experienced a similar fissure. Louise DeSalvo's *Virginia Woolf: The Impact of Childhood Sexual Abuse on Her Life and Work* provides extensive background on Woolf's troubled family life. I summarize some of this material in a mini-lecture, and I ask students to read Kennedy Fraser's excellent, deeply moving essay-review of DeSalvo's book in the *New Yorker*. They learn about striking instances of dysfunction in the Stephen household, such as the virtual imprisonment of Woolf's half-sister, Laura, in an isolated part of the house and the sexual abuse of her other half-sister, Stella, by her cousin, J. K. Stephen. These examples show how sexual abuse can create within a single household two overlapping worlds conflicting with one another. While on the surface the family may appear to provide children with a safe environment, in reality, violence may break in at any moment. Thus even the most ordinary moment becomes deeply ambiguous, fraught with fear and danger.

DeSalvo shows how such fear—stemming from sexual abuse by her half-brothers, Gerald and George Duckworth, that DeSalvo argues took place over a period of nearly sixteen years—filled Woolf's childhood. The abuse began when she was six years old, on a holiday with her family at St. Ives (*Moments* 68–69); *To the Lighthouse* opens in a similar locale and focuses at first on the six-year-old James. Because students need to steer clear of what Su Reid calls a "naïve method of relating fiction and biography" (65), I point out Eudora Welty's image from the novel's foreword, which likens Woolf's use of personal experience to the effect of lightning transforming one's vision of a landscape (vii). We should read *To the Lighthouse*, Welty implies, not as thinly veiled autobiography but as an imaginative text illuminated by biography.

One such flash occurred in May 1895, when the thirteen-year-old Virginia Stephen suffered her mother's death at forty-nine; the following summer she experienced her first emotional breakdown. After her father's death nine years later, she felt she might be even more vulnerable to the unwanted sexual advances of her half-brother, George, and she wrote to Violet Dickinson, "I begin to dread our joint household, but it cant [sic] be helped" (*Letters* 1: 132). Within three months of her father's death, Woolf experienced her second emotional breakdown, culminating in her first suicide attempt. DeSalvo believes that Woolf's emotional breakdowns and suicide attempts resulted from the sexual abuse she suffered.

Once students know something of Woolf's painful family background, many grow even more sensitive to the novel's images of violence and threat. We discuss how Mrs. Ramsay deplores her husband's tendency to "pursue truth with such astonishing lack of consideration for other people's feelings, to rend the thin veils of civilisation so wantonly, so brutally" (32). Images of tearing, cutting, and stabbing recur frequently in the novel, such as when James perceives his mother as having been slashed by his father's incisive philosophizing: "Standing between her knees, very stiff, James felt all her strength flaring up to be drunk and quenched by the beak of brass, the arid scimitar of the male, which smote mercilessly, again and again, demanding sympathy" (38). Much later, the sixteen-year-old James recalls the influence of his father's keenly honed rationality on his childhood: "something arid and sharp descended even there, like a blade, a scimitar, smiting through the leaves and flowers even of that happy world and making it shrivel and fall" (186). Woolf also uses the image of Macalister's boy cutting a square out of the side of a mackerel and throwing the lacerated but still-living fish back into the ocean to stress that although wounds may not always kill, they do cause lasting pain (180).

Throughout our two-week unit (in a quarter system), I focus attention on the novel's tripartite structure and the way it conveys Woolf's sense of the Ramsays' painful deterioration and the Victorian family's decay in the larger society. The novel's first part offers a window on the family and its divided consciousness. We first see Mr. Ramsay "stopping in front of the drawing-room window" (4), an obstacle or barricade between his children and their desires. While Mrs. Ramsay repeatedly urges that the house's windows be opened, Mr. Ramsay blocks the view from those windows. One student wrote that the window "represents the problem of interpretation in the family, how family life is to be seen," implying that Mr. Ramsay distorts his children's interpretation of family and world. This window image frames the entire novel, recurring at the end when Lily adds the last brush stroke to the painting she began at the novel's outset, a painting of Mrs. Ramsay sitting in the window with James.

The novel's second part, "Time Passes," hauntingly portrays the literal and symbolic decay of the Ramsay summerhouse, followed by its recuperation in anticipation of their return. Here we ponder the gruesome boar's head hanging in James and Cam's bedroom. DeSalvo notes that Woolf often referred to her sexually abusive half-brothers, George and Gerald, as "pigs" (*Woolf* 178), intensifying the connotation of threat and danger inherent in the image. This "horrid skull" provokes Cam and James to argue, since Cam fears the multiplied shadows of the skull's horns, while James fears sleeping without a light. Mrs. Ramsay accommodates the skull by saying, "Well then, [. . .] we will cover it up" (114). In draping her shawl over the skull, she has covered up the threat, not removed it. Gradually the folds of her shawl loosen and fall away, suggesting that concealment of violence within the family cannot be sustained indefinitely. In fact, the domestic violence portrayed in the children's bedroom has become global: people walking on the beach have seen oil slicks from sunken warships, Prue has died in childbirth, and Andrew has perished in an artillery shell explosion.

In the novel's third part, "The Lighthouse," Lily paints an imaginative healing and reconstitution of the family, benefiting from ten years' reflection and distance. At first, Lily strikes many students as just another eccentric Ramsay summer guest, but they eventually talk about her as an astute, caring observer standing outside the Ramsays' dysfunction and Victorian moral strictures. Lily's refusal to marry frees her from many conventional restraints, and she repositions family members as geometric forms on her canvas. Just as Mrs. Ramsay has been a domestic, parental arranger of the Ramsay family, so Lily is the aesthetic arranger of colored shapes standing for family members without realistically representing them. While Mrs. Ramsay considered Lily unfortunate for not having married, Lily exposes Mrs. Ramsay's matchmaking as supporting a false, oppressive system: the marriage Mrs. Ramsay orchestrated between Minta Doyle and Paul Rayley collapses (173–74), while Lily's painting endures.

As students read and discuss *To the Lighthouse*, we also discuss and come to appreciate Woolf's description of it as elegy, because Mrs. Ramsay's demise dissolves not only a particular family but also larger cultural assumptions about family life. I lecture briefly on late Victorian upper-middle-class families, showing how rigid gender roles made the wife and mother a domestic manager overburdened by an exhausting number of tasks, including visits to the sick such as Mrs. Ramsay undertakes. As Carol Dyhouse notes, such work was at least a break from domestic confinement (186–87); upper-middle-class women had little control over money and saw their children, who were relegated to the nursery, only during token visiting hours. Hearing about this enforced confinement, separation, and silence helps students understand why James never speaks aloud in the novel's opening pages, even though those pages focus on him.

Ultimately, students must, like Lily Briscoe, piece together and arrange clues to the family and the cultural forces coursing through its members' veins. Thus, if time allows, I ask students to reread pages 1–17, "Time Passes," and "The Lighthouse," because invariably they *have* put clues together and become better informed. More fully engaged readers of Woolf's text now, most find this second reading far easier and more meaningful.

Many of my students tell me they feel proud of their insights, won through investigating the Ramsay family dynamics, and they notice similar family issues in other texts. In a course for sophomore honors students, I have scheduled Toni Morrison's *Beloved* immediately after *To the Lighthouse*, so that students may use the family focus questions from Woolf's novel to analyze Morrison's powerful evocation of an African American household haunted by the obscene pains and ghostly memories of slave times. In another course, upper-division English majors moved from Woolf's novel to William Faulkner's *Absalom, Absalom!*, which raises similar issues regarding family ruptures and secrets. In the novels of Woolf, Morrison, and Faulkner, many students see a recurring theme: a family under pressure from past injuries produces terrible consequences for children.

Woolf wrote to Margaret Llewelyn Davies on 2 January 1918, "I believe the only hope for the world is to put all children of all countries together on an island and let them start fresh without knowing what a hideous system we have invented here" (*Letters* 2: 208). This "hideous system" surely refers to family life in a Victorian-Edwardian household, and the island journey represents an escape from the dark household of a dysfunctional family. We now know that Woolf experienced some of the worst such a family system had to offer, and yet her novel offers hope for a recovery of meaning, a hope fulfilled when James and Cam finally arrive at the lighthouse and Lily adds the finishing touch to her painting. Students also experience deep satisfaction at having completed a work of art—their own reading and response to this challenging, complex text.

Transformations: Teaching *To the Lighthouse* with Autobiographies and Family Chronicles

Marcia McClintock Folsom

I placed *To the Lighthouse* with autobiographies and family chronicles in an evening lecture series in literature that I taught at the Radcliffe Seminars. Of the ten books I used in that course, eight were written by American women (four were African American, two were Jewish, one was Irish American, and one was Chinese American), and two were by English women. I proposed in the course description to consider ways that autobiography and fiction tell the story of a life or transform lives into literature. Seminar participants were adult women reading for interest, conversation, and reflection. In a noncredit evening course full of women therapists, lawyers, librarians, homemakers, teachers, and artists reading to enrich their lives, the teacher can always rely on participants to read attentively. They always bring the richness of their prior reading, knowledge of the world, and their own lives into the conversation. Reading autobiographies, autobiographical novels, and family chronicles with such psychologically astute people thus insistently inspired reflection about readers' own lives and about what happens when a life is turned into a story.

Although I certainly counted on seminar participants to generate insights in every discussion, I still structured the whole series carefully. A complicated purpose of this series, which I expressed through the design of the two semesters (rather than in my lectures), was to suggest commonalities of human experience while never forgetting the tenacious hold of race, ethnicity, and class in shaping women's lives. Another purpose was implied in my course description: "Immense literary and psychological rewards may come from the transformation of lives into literature."

We read and discussed ten books in ten sessions over a year's time. In the fall series, which I called Telling My Life: The Autobiographical Self, we read Mary McCarthy's *Memories of a Catholic Girlhood*, Zora Neale Hurston's *Dust Tracks on a Road*, Dorothy Bussy's *Olivia*, Kate Simon's *Bronx Primitive*, and Ann Petry's *"Miss Muriel" and Other Stories*. The two African American writers in this group, second and fifth, came from opposite experiences of American racial segregation, and each wrote about childhood after time spent in New York had shaped her consciousness. Cities and schools were scenes of liberation in these autobiographies, places of relief from family.

The spring series, called Telling Our Lives: Conversations and Collaborations, included Pauli Murray's *Proud Shoes: The Story of an American Family*, Sara Lawrence Lightfoot's *Balm in Gilead: The Journey of a Healer*, Maxine Hong Kingston's *The Woman Warrior: Memoirs of a Girlhood among Ghosts*, Virginia Woolf's *To the Lighthouse*, and Kim Chernin's *In My Mother's House: A Daughter's Story*. This series thus began with two African American family chronicles with conflicting implications about skin color (as opposed to race), and an autobiographical novel by a Chinese American writer grappling with ghosts from the Chinese past and the American present. Woolf's novel, fourth in the series, stood not as the finale or last word but as another attempt to sort out the emotions of childhood, the relation of parents to children, and the relation of family to culture. Chernin's book, recent and American, came last in honor of its structural innovation, global perspective, and painstaking effort to convey opposing views.

To begin each two-hour session, I gave a thirty-minute background lecture on the evening's book. I then set up questions that invited multiple responses so that seminar participants would carry the conversation for the next hour. I always planned several new points to make in the last half hour, though I tried at the end of each class to build on that evening's discussion. I also tried in the last few minutes to work backward and forward to books already read and still to be read.

In my opening fall lecture, for example, I first described the genesis of McCarthy's book, a group of autobiographical sketches begun in 1944 and collected in a single volume in 1957. I argued that this book was the perfect one to open the lecture series because in it McCarthy explicitly confronts the question of truthfulness in memoirs. Is autobiography fiction or is it history? In her introduction, "To the Reader," McCarthy makes a claim for her account as historical, and in italicized sections at the end of each chapter, McCarthy interrogates her own memory, her sources, and the very writing just read. I explained that McCarthy's meditations on memory and autobiography would frame analysis of all the books in the series. I highlighted the defining event of McCarthy's childhood: her parents both died when she was six years old, and that loss was both obstacle to and motive for writing the memoirs.

To begin the first evening's discussion, I asked participants to comment on McCarthy's first chapter and to speculate about how an autobiography might be "an allegory" on "human indifference" (49). I asked them to contrast that chapter (written in 1948) with the second (written in 1957) to identify different motives for writing about the past. I asked participants to judge what part being Irish American and what part being Catholic played in McCarthy's story. I asked them to compare parochial and public schools in the memoir, and cultural differences between Minneapolis and Seattle. I invited speculation about the significance of the Jewish grandmother and Protestant grandfather in a "Catholic family" and asked why McCarthy claims that religion is only good for good people. As participants spoke, I continually sought specific passages in the book for them or for me to read aloud, verifying (or challenging) their observations. I kept suggesting that participants' comments about the motives for autobiography, the meanings of ethnic and religious identity, the effect of locale, and questions about the reliability of memory would resound across all ten sessions of the course.

The five books in the fall series are autobiographical memoirs and a collection of short stories, four of them American. The writers reveal varied motives for autobiography. McCarthy, a Catholic orphan growing up among incomprehensible adults, sought to write a historical record of a puzzling past. Hurston, an African American who grew up in an all-black Florida town and went to Columbia University, apparently wanted both to reveal and to conceal the origins of her self-confidence. Bussy, writing late in life about herself as an English schoolgirl, wanted to preserve but not profane a "rare and beautiful memory" of first passion (11). Simon, a Jewish immigrant child in New York City, sought a writer's revenge for her father's casual abuse of his children, incidentally revealing the source of the attention to streets, buildings, and place that made her a distinguished travel writer. Petry, an African American woman who grew up in a (nearly) all-white Connecticut town, celebrates the hidden strength of her family, whose vitality was "like having a concealed weapon to use against your enemy" (62).

In the spring series, we read five family chronicles centered on a mother or a mother-daughter relationship, and all but *To the Lighthouse* are American books. Each one renders a portrait of a real family changing over time, and each implies a complex connection between family and a larger world. The spring course's subtitle, Conversations and Collaborations, highlighted a difference between Woolf's method of composition and the method of writers who constructed collaborative autobiographies. To write *Proud Shoes*, Murray repeatedly interviewed her three elderly aunts, recovering the history of a family that included both slaves and slave owners. Kingston's five-part memoir, *The Woman Warrior*, although not written in collaboration, has as its most characteristic mode talk-story and implied conversation. The Chinese American daughter defies chronology as she recounts, puzzles over, and argues with her Chinese mother's enigmatic pronouncements, stories, and silences.

Two of the books in the spring series were created by purposeful collaboration between the writer and her mother: Lightfoot's *Balm in Gilead* and Chernin's *In My Mother's House*. Tape-recording their conversations, arranging visits across distance to recover together a story distant in time, these two mothers and daughters had the stimulation of each other's living presence to inspire, motivate, and enable the writing. *In My Mother's House*, in fact, dramatizes the conversations and the collaboration itself, its submerged angers and resistances, and its hard-won moments of forgiveness and shared understanding. The process of telling and hearing and writing the story *is* the story. In the seminar, people's talk about these two collaborations focused on the writers' strategies, partly because some participants were considering undertaking such projects themselves. Did the two collaborators proceed chronologically or thematically? What did they do when their memories conflicted? Did they transcribe every conversation? Are the books oral history, autobiography, or biography? How long did it take them?

In this context, Woolf's solitary creative act in writing *To the Lighthouse* emerged as an amazing achievement of memory, imagination, and emotional commitment. Her sister Vanessa's tone of wonder when she read the novel indicates that she had not collaborated in remembering their mother while Virginia wrote. Vanessa wrote to Virginia

> Anyhow it seemed to me that in the first part of the book you have given a portrait of mother which is more like her to me than anything I could ever have conceived of as possible. It is almost painful to have her so raised from the dead. [. . .] It was like meeting her again with oneself grown up and on equal terms and it seems to me the most astonishing feat of creation to have been able to see her in such a way.
>
> (*Letters* 3: 572)

Just how astonishing a feat of creation it was I tried to illustrate by reading aloud passages from the novel. Certain passages where Woolf imagines Mrs. Ramsay's thoughts startled us with their comic specificity. "Some creature anyhow was ruining her Evening Primroses," for example, or "Ah, but was that not Lily Briscoe strolling along with William Bankes?[. . .] Did that not mean that they would marry? Yes, it must! What an admirable idea! They must marry!" (71). In other passages I read aloud, Woolf captures Mrs. Ramsay's deep melancholy—"But what have I done with my life?" (82)—and her awareness of a secret center, a core of darkness. When I asked participants to compare these passages to the portrayal of character in the four other books, most participants felt that only Chernin, in characterizing her young mother, came close to Woolf's achievement in giving voice to another person's inner life. In general, we felt the superiority of the two novels to the other three books in rendering complex characters, which made some readers note the greater "truthfulness" of fiction than history.

Reading *To the Lighthouse* with autobiographies and family chronicles yielded other insights about the novel that were new to me. I briefly mention four here. I pointed out that for both McCarthy and Woolf, grappling with loss motivated the writing. I asked why the death of beloved parents is treated so differently in the memoir and the novel. Woolf expresses grief over her mother's death, while McCarthy represses and even denies it, and some participants argued that perhaps the difference in the writers' ages at the time of the parents' deaths—McCarthy six and Woolf thirteen—accounts for the difference.

A few seminar participants noted McCarthy's failure to give narrative room to emotion and her oddly affectless tone at moments of stark anguish. For example, on the afternoon when her grandmother's maid told the six-year-old McCarthy, "There is someone here to see you," she remembers, "My heart bounded; I felt almost sick (who else, after all, could it be?), and she had to push me forward" (39). I read this passage aloud and asked, "Why does McCarthy suppress mention of her dead parents and only allude to the dream of their return in a parenthesis?" Some participants speculated that the two deaths remained too devastating for McCarthy to explore fully. Others praised her determination not to exploit the pathos inherent in the literary stereotype of a child becoming an orphan. McCarthy herself mentions the Dickensian elements of her childhood as a deterrent to writing and an obstacle to credibility.

In contrast, Woolf boldly uses Lily to articulate both yearning and anguish. For example, I pointed to the passage where Lily experiences again the grief of Mrs. Ramsay's death: "'Mrs. Ramsay!' Lily cried, 'Mrs. Ramsay!' But nothing happened. The pain increased. That anguish could reduce one to such a pitch of imbecility, she thought!" (180). The self-mocking word "imbecility" marks Lily's (and Woolf's) resistance to bathos, but it does not undercut the intensifying pain of the exclamations and short sentences. The still-living mackerel thrown back into the sea with a piece of flesh cut out epitomizes Lily's (and Woolf's) agony—the emotional mutilation caused by a mother's death (180). One participant said, "There is nothing like this in all of McCarthy's memoir," and most considered the greater expression of deep feeling a strength of *To the Lighthouse*.

Second, reading *To the Lighthouse* with four American family chronicles made evident Woolf's comparatively oblique treatment of anger. Murray's book opens with the child's alarm at her grandmother's tremendous, raw rage; Lightfoot acknowledges anger at her busy, preoccupied mother but sublimates it out of respect; Kingston's whole book is a magnificent angry diatribe at her impossible mother; Chernin's book combines the greatest explicit anger with the greatest explicit resolution, achieved through the mutual book-writing project.

In comparison, Woolf seems not to acknowledge fully the anger she surely felt at a mother who was rarely available for uninterrupted attention, who allowed her husband's demands to absorb her energy, who failed to protect her daughter from abuse, and who disappeared irrevocably when Virginia was thirteen. Woolf disguises that anger, as Jane Lilienfeld suggests in "The Deceptiveness of Beauty," in Lily's self-deprecation (350, 354–55). Woolf also hints at it in Cam's dreaminess (182–83, 188–89), James's image of a foot being crushed (185), and his desire to kill his father (4, 186–87). A few participants noted that the rage is there but hidden or expressed indirectly.

Third, considering Woolf's novel with the four other books read in spring semester illuminated a quality it shares with them: in all five works, children of the writers' generation inherit psychic fractures caused by divisions within a parent, between parents, among grandparents, or between ancestors and culture. *Proud Shoes*, for example, constantly explores liminal terrain—north and south, slave and free, black and white—and the indistinct boundaries between these oppositions. Kingston's *Woman Warrior* opened dramatically to discussion when I asked how it reflects a divided heritage. A few participants mentioned, on the one hand, the mother's threat in the opening line—"you must never tell anyone what I am about to tell you" (3)—and, on the other, the wondrous power of the mother's talk-story about the woman warrior who saves her people.

Reading *To the Lighthouse* in this context made us notice Woolf's keen awareness of her own divided heritage. The Ramsay marriage unites people from two different worlds. Mr. and Mrs. Ramsay are constantly jarred by their differences, the incompatibility of their perceptions. Woolf explicitly contrasts them—"the folly of women's minds enraged him" versus "to pursue truth with such astonishing lack of consideration for other people's feelings" (31, 32)—to demonstrate her conviction that Victorians rigidly divided human qualities into feminine and masculine to the detriment of psychological wholeness. When asked if the notion of a divided heritage offered insights into their own lives, several seminar participants told stories ranging across generations, some including comments on their own marriages and children. "But perhaps," remarked one, "all marriages are cross-cultural, so children always inherit a divided past."

Fourth, Woolf's brilliant strategy in constructing her novel in three parts was illuminated by reading it with these other books. In "The Window," Woolf satisfies a desire to recapture the felt life of a family's past. Perhaps, I argued, recreating a day that the mother was attempting to shape as a memory for her children might stand as a conversation with that mother. Woolf's success at recovering it proves that the mother's intention was fulfilled; the memory *was* created, and finally the daughter does collaborate with the mother in "making of the moment something permanent" (161). In the novel itself, the past is immortalized, even though "it had become [. . .] already the past" (111).

Reading the second part, "Time Passes," with Chernin's and Lightfoot's books helped us see that in Mrs. McNab and Mrs. Bast, the two old women who clean up the deserted house, Woolf personifies the writer's impulse to clear away debris and undertake an autobiographical return to the past. And in the last part, "The Lighthouse," with its patient, languid movement back and forth from land to water, from Lily to James and Cam, from present to past and back again, we saw the family chronicler's urge to bring together the pieces of family past and personal present. Woolf's novel succeeds more completely than any other book in the series (except perhaps Chernin's) in proving that writing itself heals, bringing together individual and family history.

During the last seminar meeting, I read aloud several passages from *To the Lighthouse* where Woolf calls attention to the mind's capacity for existing on two levels at once, as when Mrs. Ramsay is "[r]aising her eyebrows at the discrepancy—that was what she was thinking, this was what she was doing" (83). Such scenes dramatize the double consciousness that often arises in conversations about autobiographical writing. Thoughts and feelings the teacher could never orchestrate enter the discussion in various forms: brief allusions to personal experience, fleeting comments, or sometimes, whole stories.

Talking about women's autobiographies with adult women who are thinking about their own life stories gives class time an intensity that cannot be fully acknowledged. The thirty or so people in the room are in the midst of lives that lend themselves to the same analysis or dramatization we found in the ten books. The public nature of the classroom and the distancing from the personal that comes from carefully reading a text have the paradoxical effect of intensifying one's consciousness of the inner world. The simple, stark outlines of one participant's situation, known to a few others in the class, or the reader's own situation, known to no one else, can make this parallel stream of thoughts absorbing indeed.

The diversity of experiences in the ten books and the multicultural range of the readings underline a point that does not have to be restated: writers transform all kinds of lives into literature. One's odd parents, distinctive racial identity, confusing ethnic roots, or unacceptable feelings do not disqualify a person from undertaking an autobiographical project. That project may be to write a book on the scale of one of these or only to write a plausible résumé or letter. It may also be simply to understand, name, and give shape to the life one is living at the moment or to construct a valid story about the stages of life and events that brought one to this point. I know from talking with seminar participants, from their letters and evaluations, and from my own experience that many autobiographical projects were carried on in this course, partly in silence, as we attempted to understand each writer's transformation of lives into literature.

Contextual Approaches

To the Lighthouse and Painting
Susan Yunis

When I taught *To the Lighthouse* as part of an upper-division, quarter-long undergraduate English seminar on E. M. Forster and Virginia Woolf, I placed the novel within its artistic context. Because I wanted to introduce students in a visual way to modernist (specifically Bloomsbury) writers' experimentation with form, I began the course with an art survey, showing an array of Romantic, impressionist, and postimpressionist paintings. Students in this course at an extension of a large state university vary widely in ability; some are literature majors, some not; some traditional age, some not. Though few have read modern British literature and many struggle with its experimental features, all have seen a van Gogh, a Degas, a Cézanne; they already understand, even if unconsciously, these artists' works and the existentialist mood the paintings anticipate. Unlike the audiences who first viewed these paintings, most contemporary students are comfortable with canvases whose centers are unoccupied and whose margins contain the only human activity. This mood is not new to them: they have heard the complaint of individuals struggling to create meaning in a world that scarcely seems to notice, much less reward, human effort.

The greater difficulties for students lie in articulating this mood so that they can apply it to other texts and in understanding the horror this mood first provoked in artists and audiences alike—such that it preoccupied most modernist artists and outraged most audiences. I find an art survey helpful because Romantic paintings help situate students in a culture confident that it was doing God's work in the world and that its prosperity was the mark of God's approval. This confidence, of course, was what modernism threatened, and impressionist and postimpressionist paintings provide the image of that threat. These paintings provide students with visual counterparts to Woolf's novel, helping them articulate concepts they can apply to the novel and deal more easily with its difficult prose.

An approach through painting suits *To the Lighthouse*. First, the novel reflects and responds to the artistic and philosophical impulses of its time. Second, Woolf situated herself among artists and increasingly saw the novel as a "cannibal" that devoured many art forms and would ultimately incorporate both "the power of music, the stimulus of sight" ("Narrow Bridge" 224–25, 229). Third, *To the Lighthouse* is about art, the position of the artist, the difficulties and frustrations of representation, and the artist's ability to find meaning through artistic form.

The idea for this approach grew out of my graduate studies at Case Western Reserve University in a seminar on the modern novel taught by Nancy Lampl. As part of her discussion of *To the Lighthouse*, Lampl assigned José Ortega y Gasset's essay "The Dehumanization of Art," which attributes the abstraction of the human form in modern art to the artist's focusing less on his or her subject than on the process of his or her vision, just as a distortion of the view from a window results from the viewer's focusing on some speck on the window. Intrigued and mystified by Ortega y Gasset's essay, I pored through modern art prints for a more concrete understanding of his ideas. As I *saw* what Ortega y Gasset's words meant, I realized the potential of paintings to provide insight into difficult literary and philosophical content. Years later, when preparing for my own seminar, I spent two days consulting with my university's specialist on impressionist art to identify artists and specific prints that would help me illustrate Woolf's aesthetic.

In my seminar, I spend two class sessions on background, one on the art survey and then one on the Bloomsbury artists, when I introduce Woolf's famous statement that "in or about December, 1910, human character changed" ("Mr. Bennett" 320). I link her statement to the first postimpressionist exhibition at the Grafton Galleries, where paintings by Cézanne, Gauguin, Manet, and van Gogh were shown, paintings that, according to Clive and Vanessa Bell and Roger Fry, replaced the human and narrative elements predominant in Romantic art with pure form. During this discussion, I refer often to J. K. Johnstone's *The Bloomsbury Group*, Richard Shone's *Bloomsbury Portraits*, and Diane Gillespie's *The Sisters' Arts*. After these introductory lectures, students read Forster's *A Room with a View* and *Passage to India* and then Woolf's *The Voyage Out, Mrs. Dalloway, To the Lighthouse*, and *Between the Acts*. Thus, by the time we discuss *To the Lighthouse*, students have already applied the postimpressionist aesthetic, the concepts they saw in the art survey, to several novels. To give some indication of how the process works in my seminar, this essay juxtaposes descriptions of my art survey with applications to Woolf's novel.

My survey of nineteenth-century Continental art puts the modernists in historical context and thus begins with the Romantic period: students can understand what the impressionist painters and modernist writers departed from when they see the conventional centering of the hero on the canvas, the conventional depiction of three-dimensional space, and the conventional disguising of technique by the Romantic artists. Then when we look at the impressionists and postimpressionists, they can see what that departure looked like before they encounter it in words and literary technique. As they look at and respond to prints, I try to relate their reactions to the philosophical attitudes toward humanity, God, and art that inspired the modernist departure. I emphasize Continental artists because most students immediately recognize their work and because large art texts of Continental artists are readily available, whereas reproductions of paintings by Bloomsbury artists are smaller and carry less impact. I use prints in art books rather than slides because they can be passed around and examined more closely. Most of the paintings I refer to here, for example, are in *Impressionism* (Clay et al.), *The Sisters' Arts*, and *Bloomsbury Portraits*; I take these books to all subsequent classes since I like to refer to the paintings again when some students struggle with the novels.

I begin the art survey with Romantic paintings that make the heroic act central to the canvas; powerful, heroic actors dominate David's *Oath of the Horatii*

(1784) and Goya's *Third of May* (1814), for example. In Goya's painting, a peasant, dressed in a luminous white tunic, standing cruciform and about to be executed by a firing squad, occupies the center of the canvas. His self-sacrifice dominates the emotional center of the dark canvas, and the artist clearly sees the heroic peasant participating in God's sacrifice for humanity.

Then I show Monet's *Boating on the Epte* (1877), Degas's *Ballet Dancers at the Old Opera House* (1877), van Gogh's *Montmartre* (1886), and Giacomo Balla's *The Staircase of Goodbyes* (1908). Empty space occupies these canvas centers, and the human subject moves to the canvas margins.

I like to walk slowly through the class with these prints as the students jot down their observations and then comment aloud on what they see. Their spoken reactions may range from "I have to search for the subject," "It's not flattering," and "I don't know what it's about" to (perhaps in response to Degas's *Ballet Dancers Climbing a Flight of Stairs*) "I feel like I'm seeing the rehearsal instead of the performance." At the conclusion of their remarks, I talk about their experience as a journey into the modernists' view of the world, where art has hollow centers, "hearts of darkness," through which artists seem to be meditating on the chaos that overwhelms and diminishes human efforts at order or meaning. No longer, I point out, does the canvas or, by extension, the world organize itself around acts of human courage. No longer do humans seem to be at the center of the world, nor do their struggles seem to be of central importance to their creator.

I like to ask students to apply our discussion of the Continental impressionist artists to the Bloomsbury artists Roger Fry, Duncan Grant, and Vanessa Bell, to look for parallels. They often point to the black square at the center of Fry's *The Barn* (1916), to the weeping black figure—her face hidden in her hands—at the center of Grant's *Le Crime et le Chatiment* (1909), to the empty expanse of the tub at the center of Bell's *The Tub* (1917) as hearts of darkness. And they notice the marginality of the artist in Grant's painting, *Interior* (1918), in which Vanessa Bell paints at one edge of the canvas and David Garnett writes at the other.

Later, when we discuss *To the Lighthouse* and particularly "Time Passes" and some students register their frustration and confusion with a story about an empty house as it succumbs to the disintegrating forces of nature, I remind them of the empty center of Monet's *Boating on the Epte*, in which a boatload of women seems to have moved from the center of the canvas to its edge before the artist can complete the painting. We examine parallels between the two works and student responses to them, especially their anger: their sense that both artists have deliberately betrayed them by failing to make "[l]ife stand still here" (161), by not exerting enough control over the actors or subjects. Some may decide that similar anger, directed toward all creators, Mrs. Ramsay as well as God, lies at the novel's center, perhaps *is* its subject. "Time Passes," then, is a "heart of darkness," a world from which God seems to have departed, taking compassion for humanity along, a world that marginalizes all human crises and all human struggles to make sense of these crises, treating them parenthetically.

Disorder takes center stage in "Time Passes": no human attempts at order—gardens, books, flower arrangements, painting—are immune to threat: "And so, nosing, rubbing, [the little airs] went to the window on the staircase, to the servants' bedrooms, to the boxes in the attics; descending, blanched the apples on the dining-room table, fumbled the petals of roses, tried the picture on the easel, brushed the mat and blew a little sand along the floor" (127). When I ask students to find the subject of the following sentence—"Nothing it seemed could break that image, corrupt that innocence, or disturb the swaying mantle of silence which, week after week, in the empty room, wove into itself the falling cries of birds, ships hooting, the drone and hum of the fields, a dog's bark, a man's shout, and folded them round the house in silence" (129–30)—they notice that even the sentence has been emptied of its actor. In fact, many sentences in this section have as their subject either the little airs or "nothing."

After showing the hero's decentering in the art survey, I cover the postimpressionist emphasis on form and note the modernist hallmark of moving from content to form. David's *Oath of the Horatii*, for instance, told a story, but postimpressionists, I say, struggled to replace stories with the form or shape of a more depersonalized experience. For writers, of course, diminishing the import of story, the centrality of character, presented an even more difficult problem. But Woolf took cues from modern painting's multiplication of points of view. I show students Bell's *The Tub*, and I demonstrate how within the painting the viewer's vantage point keeps changing: the nude at the painting's edge is seen from the front, while the tub is viewed from the top; the individual view surrenders to a more impersonal one. I also show Cézanne's *Three Bathers* (1879–82), in which the nude shapes mimic the curves and colors of the surrounding birch trees, and note that for the postimpressionists, nature's patterns transcend individual and even human experience.

When we discuss Lily in *To the Lighthouse*, then, I ask students to find evidence of her postimpressionism. Several point to her abstraction of Mrs. Ramsay into a wedge of darkness and to her insistence on the *shape* of her visions: "She could have done it differently of course; the colour could have been thinned and faded; the shapes etherealised; that was how Paunceforte would have seen it. But then she did not see it like that. She saw the colour burning on a framework of steel; the light of a butterfly's wing lying upon the arches of a cathedral" (48). When asked for evidence of Woolf's postimpressionism, other students point to the impersonality gained through shifting viewpoints in the novel, even though they feel frustrated by this narrative technique. We note that the narrator sometimes seems to know Mrs. Ramsay intimately, expressing her anger and frustrations, while at other times that same narrator doesn't know the reason for Mrs. Ramsay's profound sadness (28–29).

Several students find evidence of Woolf's postimpressionism, too, in her search for some overall shape or pattern in her characters' experiences, in her search for some transcendence of the personal through design. These students often observe that some characters, particularly Lily and Mrs. Ramsay, muse on impersonality, indeed seek it, but they need more help in seeing that most of the characters describe themselves and others as things that can be seen in terms of shape—triangles, scimitars, wheels, sails, deal tables, lighthouses—a sign of Woolf's attempt to transcend individuality and achieve an impersonal form. A student once pointed out in an essay that the Bloomsbury artists, when they painted each other, often obliterated or hid their faces, as if to erase personality: Grant's *Interior* (1918) and Bell's *Portrait of Lytton Strachey* (1913), *Virginia Woolf at Ashenham* (1912), and *Virginia Woolf* (1912) all efface their subjects in some way, either by angle of presentation or by simply blanking out the face.

In the art survey, I also show how the postimpressionists deliberately foregrounded the brush stroke, the flatness of the canvas, and the thickness of the paint (not apparent at all in Romantic paintings). Van Gogh's *Self-Portrait* (1886), *Starry Night* (1889), and *Sunflowers* (1887) and Monet's *Rue Montorgueil* (1878) all show the undisguised brush stroke. Paintings by Gauguin— *Siesta, Tahiti* (1893), *The Vision after the Sermon* (1888), *Eh quoi, es-tu jalouse?* (1892), *Bonjour, Monsieur Gauguin* (1889), and *Women in a Garden, Arles* (1888)—show the flattening of space, calling attention to the canvas and reminding the viewer of the artistic process and its limitations. Students can point to the same techniques in Grant's 1912 canvas *On the Roof at 34 Brunswick Square* and in his 1915 *At Eleanor: Vanessa Bell*. Paintings by Degas, *Miss Lola at the Fernando Circus* (1879) and *Singer with a Glove* (1878), and Edouard Vuillard's *The Game of Checkers at Amfreville* (1906) show that altered perspectives, either from below or above the subject, distort the human shape. All these techniques remind the viewer of the artist and of the limitations of his or her vision: vision itself becomes the subject. Thus, I conclude our discussion of pictorial art with the notion that the position of the hero, once assigned by the Romantics to the painting's subject, has now been assigned by the postimpressionists to the artist, whose perception and process, as well as the limitations of both, have been foregrounded.

Later, in our discussion of *To the Lighthouse*, most students feel comfortable with the idea that the novel is in many ways about perception and art, that the heroine is the artist, that the most significant action of the novel is the painting of a picture. I add that the smudged triangular shape in Lily's painting connects to both Mrs. Ramsay's shadow and the sail of Mr. Ramsay's boat and that Woolf thus meets one objective of the postimpressionistic artist: to find an overall shape or design that both represents people and transcends their personal differences.

We also examine the following passage:

> And this, Lily thought, taking the green paint on her brush, this making up scenes about them, is what we call "knowing" people, "thinking" of them, "being fond" of them! Not a word of it was true; she had made it up; but it was what she knew them by all the same. She went on tunnelling her way into her picture, into the past. [. . .]

So that was the story of the Rayleys, Lily thought. She imagined herself telling it to Mrs. Ramsay, who would be full of curiosity to know what had become of the Rayleys. She would feel a little triumphant, telling Mrs. Ramsay that the marriage had not been a success.

[. . .] Mockingly she seemed to see her there at the end of the corridor of years saying, of all incongruous things, "Marry, marry!" [. . .] And one would have to say to her, It has all gone against your wishes. They're happy like that; I'm happy like this.   (173–75)

I use this passage to show students that for Woolf, representation inevitably involves distortion and yet paradoxically reflects self-assertion; representation momentarily defines the self. Some students interpret Lily's final undisguised brush stroke at the conclusion of the novel as the letter *I*: by completing her painting, she has defined her self. Though she completes a painting whose "triangular purple shape" (52) refers to both Ramsays—the purple shadow Mrs. Ramsay casts as she read to James and Mr. Ramsay's triangular "greyish-brown sails" (170) as he takes James and Cam to the lighthouse—Lily's vision ultimately defines her as the artist. For she alone has perceived the connection between the Ramsays, has drawn the "line there, in the centre" (209) that will "connect this mass on the right hand with that on the left" (53).

One of our most provocative discussions centered on a student's question in class: "How could the modernists be foregrounding the artistic act at the same time that they were marginalizing it?" Several class members agreed; they, too, were confused. If there is no God who provides meaning, then isn't the heroic role of providing order centralized rather than marginalized? Though at the time we were unable to resolve this contradiction between the centrality and marginality of the artist, it seems to me now one of the most important tensions within *To the Lighthouse*. The artistic impulse to order the world, represented in Lily's painting, in some ways the central act of the text, nonetheless occurs at its margins. The literal center of the text is the house emptied of its human inhabitants, surrendering to nature's forces. Thus, the artistic act is always undercut or interrupted by the knowledge that the effort at order will never be enough. The distorting angle of the artist's personality will never be transcended in a work, nor will the limits of the medium, whether words or paint. As Lily complains, the "vision must be perpetually remade" (181).

Because *To the Lighthouse* focuses on the process of painting, the students' viewing of paintings enhances their understanding and appreciation of the novel. When asked to comment about their instructor's use of art on their anonymous class evaluations, one student wrote that she couldn't sleep after one day's discussion because she was so excited by what the Degas painting helped her understand about the novel and by how the novel helped her understand the painting, one she had seen many times before, in a new way. She had never dreamed that a painting could mean so much or say so much about the artist's attitude.

Another student wrote that he found the final section of the novel tedious and boring because so much attention was given to Lily's frustration as a painter. When he wrote his essays that way, saying things like "I can't find the right words to say what I mean" or "No words could do justice to my ideas" or "I really can't write very good essays," his writing teachers had filled the page with red scribbles and exclamation marks. But, he said, when we looked again at the Gauguins, he realized that Gauguin had been doing the same thing that Lily had done in the novel and as he had done in his essays—focusing on the process and the tools and the limitations of those tools. He gleefully concluded that he was a modernist and that none of his teachers had recognized how profound he was!

This student's comment underscores for me the rewards of teaching *To the Lighthouse* with impressionist and postimpressionist art. All these texts invite students into the artistic process by foregrounding the struggle to represent experience. The artists' frustrations with the limits of their media can be used to prompt students' reflections on their own processes as writers and thinkers. And when the text is as difficult as *To the Lighthouse* is, the students' processes as readers join the enterprises of writing and painting and thinking as heroic efforts at meaning, which are always, at best, approximations.

To the Lighthouse and the Publishing Practices of Virginia Woolf

Edward Bishop

Over the last few years, my teaching of *To the Lighthouse* in the senior modern British novel course at one of Canada's larger universities (30,000 students) has moved from a formalist to a materialist approach. I still do a close reading of the novel, often spending a fifty-minute class on the first three pages to introduce Virginia Woolf's syntax to students (many of whom tell me they don't do much textual analysis anymore). Increasingly, however, using the theories of Pierre Bourdieu and the resources of the university print shop, I have focused on how a given sentence gets produced: not how it gets written but how it gets printed, published, and promoted.

The Production of Culture

The Hogarth Press was more than a therapeutic hobby for Woolf, though she took enormous pleasure in setting type. It gave her control over the production of her works, which had implications for the writing of them. She could publish her work without the horrors of having it "pawed & snored over" (*Diary* 1: 129), as she put it, by Gerald Duckworth, the publisher of her first two novels and one of the half-brothers who had molested her. That Woolf's experimental style emerged only in her third novel, *Jacob's Room*, is not accidental, since it was the first one published by Hogarth. But Hogarth Press was also more than just a private press or a way to avoid the strictures of commercial publishing. Leonard Woolf declared proudly in his autobiography that the press made a profit from the very start (*Beginning* 54), and I use his statement to begin discussing the commodification of Woolf's work. We examine not the current Woolf industry, which began in the 1970s, but the process that took place during her lifetime, the way she negotiated that delicate balance between what Bourdieu calls "cultural capital" and "real capital," between literary status and hard cash (*Distinction* 228).

To the Lighthouse marked a pivotal point in Woolf's commercial writing career. As J. H. Willis, Jr., points out, advance sales were more than twice those for *Mrs. Dalloway*; Leonard Woolf ordered a first impression of three thousand copies (a thousand more than for *Mrs. Dalloway*) and the next month ordered another thousand. Harcourt Brace began with a first printing of four thousand, ordered another fifteen hundred in June, and then twenty-one hundred in August (132). Did these sales figures mean anything to Woolf? Yes. On the strength of the advance orders, she confided in her diary, "Now I think we are safe to get our motor car" (*Diary* 3: 134). As the first impression sold out, she rhapsodized on "the absorbing subject—the subject which has filled our thoughts to the exclusion of Clive & Mary & literature & death & life—motor cars." She continued, "We have decided on a Singer. [. . .] This is a great opening up in our lives. [. . .] With any luck The Lighthouse will reach 3,000 this week" (*Diary* 3: 146–47; see also *Diary* 3: 43).

Many students are a bit surprised, after struggling with the innovations of her indirect interior monologue, to learn that for Woolf, the book meant a new car; it doesn't sit well with their notion that the modernists, if not bohemians, lived in a kind of genteel poverty, different from the middle-class prosperity of the mid-Victorians. Here I point out that authors not only want to write, they want to be read, and they not only want to be read, they want to be bought. Bourdieu says the art business is "a trade in things that have no price," and the practices of this business only work by everybody "pretending not to be doing what they are doing," embodying a duality of disinterestedness and self-interest (*Field* 74). The pursuit of "symbolic capital" is deeply conflicted, for through accumulating symbolic or cultural capital, one acquires economic capital.

The artist renounces economic profit to reap cultural capital, a profit in "distinction." The publisher aims to acquire a name, for with "name" comes the power to "consecrate" cultural objects, to give them symbolic value and thus gain profits. If one "goes commercial," then one loses symbolic value, loses the power to consecrate, and eventually loses real capital. In other words, in publishing literature, if you try too hard to make a profit and trade reputation for dollars, you lose your reputation—and ultimately dollars. If Harcourt Brace started issuing Woolf's novels in bumpy Day-Glo covers, we'd be shocked—and they'd lose the university market. (One of my honors students refuses to read Anne Rice, because he will not "buy a book that looks like it was bought in Safeway.") The text's material embodiments help chart the way Woolf sought to preserve her distinction while pursuing the increased sales that could only come from moving beyond the coterie.

Promotion

At first, Hogarth Press publicized its efforts by sending circulars to friends and acquaintances, who signed up as subscribers on the "A" list, to whom all publications would automatically be sent, or the "B" list, to whom notifications would be sent. The first book, *Two Stories* ("Three Jews" and "The Mark on the Wall") had a total sale of 134 (L. Woolf, *Beginning* 236). By the 1920s, the Hogarth Press was advertising on a regular basis, but the ads were "visually unsophisticated" as befitted a no-nonsense publishing firm (Willis 375). In his study of the press, Willis includes examples of these ads and observes that "the type [is] heavy and black, the copy cramped, the list of titles and prices assaulting and dulling the eye. [. . .] The ads emphasized the author's name or the book's title and carried the publisher's name modestly at the bottom in smaller type, almost as an afterthought" (375). In 1927, Leonard declared, "My own belief is that books are, in general, not a commodity which, like patent medicines, cigarettes, or mustard, the consumer buys or can be induced to buy by the skill of the advertiser alone" (qtd. in Willis 374).

But Hogarth Press, as well as Virginia Woolf, had entered the commercial mainstream. By the end of 1928, prompted no doubt by the success of *To the Lighthouse* and the growth of the press—between 1927 and 1928, the profits jumped sixfold, from £64 to £380—Leonard could not ignore that the press itself sold books (Willis, app. B). To capitalize on this fact, he turned not to Vanessa Bell, whose work, significantly, was never used for advertising, but to E. McKnight Kauffer, a friend of Roger Fry's who had been associated with the Omega Workshop and the Vorticists (and so was ideologically sound) but who was famous for his London Underground posters (see Haworth-Booth).

Kauffer's device for the press was designed in and for type. With its sleek straight lines (basically an oblong on a triangle), it looked crisp regardless of type quality, and it looked like nothing else. It arrested the eye and, like the penguin in our own era, conferred instant brand-name recognition. Willis reproduces a 1931 ad for *The Waves* in which the device was inserted in the ruled border at the top (174). Six other Hogarth titles were arranged in descending order through two columns, leading the eye from the logo at the top to the Hogarth Press name in the ruled border at the bottom. *The Waves* was thus inscribed within the discourse of modernist advertising, and Virginia Woolf had become a Hogarth commodity.

In 1929 Hogarth published the uniform edition of Woolf's works, a decision that, as Willis says, served "to make a claim for the permanence and importance of the writer's work, to establish a canon, to suggest the classic." In issuing the uniform edition, "the Woolfs seem to have declared publicly the commercial value of Virginia's novels and their claim to artistic greatness" (156). Cultural capital and real capital came together. While the Vanessa Bell dust jacket, with the hand-drawn circle for the title and uneven roundels surrounding it, preserved the link with the avant-garde, the jade green cloth boards and gold lettering on the spine asserted Woolf's entry into the literary establishment. Significantly, however, the uniform edition sold for less than the regular edition: it marks a classic but makes a move toward the mass market.

That *Time* appropriated Woolf for its cover photo on 12 April 1937, then, is not so surprising. I show students a copy of the cover, briefly digressing on the politics of preservation: only public libraries preserve dust jackets and popular magazines. The cover is the famous Man Ray photograph (see Silver, "What's Woolf" 24–26) and the occasion the publication of *The Years*, ten years after *To the Lighthouse*. *The Years* sold thirteen thousand copies in the first six months in Britain and thirty thousand in the United States, where it outranked Steinbeck's *Of Mice and Men* and ranked sixth on a best-seller list led by *Gone with the Wind*. We discuss the significance of appearing on the cover of *Time*, and then look at the language of the review's opening:

> Last year Margaret Mitchell of Atlanta, Ga. wrote her first novel, *Gone with the Wind*. Last week Virginia Woolf of London England published her seventh, *The Years*. Margaret Mitchell's book has sold more copies

(1,300,000) than all Virginia Woolf's put together. But literary brokers who take a long view of the market are stocking up with Woolfs, unloading Mitchells (*Time* April 5). Their opinion is that Margaret Mitchell was a grand wildcat stock but Virginia Woolf a sound investment.   (93)

Literature has become an overt commodity; the "capital" of culture, always there, is now foregrounded. Notorious in the Woolf canon for being a commercial success and a critical failure, *The Years* perhaps obscures the move toward commodification that had already occurred. The exposure of her photographic portrait, the "vulgarization" of her books, and the association of her work with her personality (the review discusses her part in the Dreadnought hoax and runs the photograph of the entourage) did not just happen; these things occur, perhaps inevitably, in response to the dynamics of the field of cultural production.

Publication of *To the Lighthouse* marked the moment (with a motor car) when Woolf consolidated her position as a modernist, consolidated her cultural capital, and generated economic capital. At that moment, she effectively entered the American market (Willis 132), allowing the economic and cultural assertion of a uniform edition. By this point in a survey course, I will have already talked about how Lawrence Rainey and Michael Levenson see literary modernism entering the mainstream in 1922, Rainey with the selling, not the publishing, of *The Waste Land*, and Levenson with the founding of the *Criterion* (*Genealogy*). Students thus begin to see that the commodification of modernism is more complex than it has sometimes seemed, that we have tended to view modernists as heroically noncommercial, refusing to sell, and thus sell out, unlike the big Victorians. But the issue is not simply that all authors want money. Rather, the issue is that the author and his or her work are inseparable from what Bourdieu calls "cultural production." (If students want to further pursue Woolf in the American context, I suggest Janice Radway's work on the Book of the Month Club and Pamela L. Caughie's discussion of *Flush* [see *Postmodernism*].)

The Production of the Text

Next I take the class to the fine arts department for a lecture on printing and a chance to set type. Each student sets his or her name in one of six available typefaces, and we arrange the names for a single page. The inking is usually not quite even at first and has to be adjusted. Then a few letters prove to be worn and have to be replaced. Finally, a copy with solid black type comes through.

The students next print their own sheets, each one in turn giving a crank of the handle. They are delighted. They talk about the pleasure of handling the individual pieces of type and banter about how the typefaces chosen at random reflect the compositors' personalities. (My classic Garamond pleases me until the art professor explains it is an "old face" type; the extroverts inevitably find the italic, and someone always sets his or her name in full capitals.) When the art professor holds up one of the printed pages and a high-quality photocopy and challenges the students to identify which is which, several cheerfully scorn the copy: "It's not the same. Look at that deep black. *That's* the real thing." The tactile pleasure of the text, animating not only giddy sophomores but also hardened graduate students, makes Woolf's diary passages about printing come alive.

The Book and the Text

I show students the dust jacket of *Jacob's Room*, the first one for the Hogarth Press designed by Vanessa Bell (see Gillespie's *The Sisters' Arts* for illustrations and analysis of Bell's covers). Today the *Jacob's Room* jacket looks "cozy" (as one librarian put it), but in the early 1920s it was radical, declaring its allegiance to the handicrafts of Roger Fry's Omega Workshop. Leonard Woolf recorded that it was "almost universally condemned by the booksellers, and several of the buyers laughed at it." It violated the norm; it made no attempt at illustration; "it did not represent a desirable female or even Jacob or his room, and it was what in 1923 many people would have called reproachfully postimpressionist" (*Downhill* 76). It was, then, aggressively noncommercial. The Hogarth Press was a literary press, devoted not to fine printing as some small presses were but to fine literature that could not find an outlet elsewhere. The book itself embodies that ideology.

I next invite the students to discuss their editions of *To the Lighthouse*, to consider cover illustrations, jacket blurbs, paper quality, typefaces, and even type size. Compared with the first edition of *Jacob's Room*, I ask, to what extent has this book become a commercial product? Has Virginia Woolf achieved brand-name status? (On some editions, her name has a prominence similar to Stephen King's, whose name is often twice as large as the work's title.) What does such status mean in terms of a reader's expectations? How does reading a book already designated a masterpiece, a monument of modernism consecrated by the academy, differ from reading a new work by an author gaining a reputation, as Woolf was after *Mrs. Dalloway*?

Turning from the book to the text, I use both the American and British editions of the novel to discuss how bibliographic texts also affect our reading. I have a student read the final lines of "The Window" in the American Harcourt edition: "'Yes, you were right. It's going to be wet tomorrow. You won't be able to go.' And she looked at him smiling. For she had triumphed again. She had not said it: yet he knew" (124). And then I have a student read the same passage in the British Penguin edition: "'Yes, you were right. It's going to be wet tomorrow.' She had not said it, but he knew it. And she looked at him smiling. For she had triumphed again" (134).

Mrs. Ramsay sounds a bit smug, some students feel, in the British edition. Since both were published on 5 May 1927, which is the "real" one? I direct them to Susan Dick's discussion in the Shakespeare Head Press edition (xxx– xxxvii), pointing out that both editions were proofed at the same time and that Woolf could have incorporated the changes she made to the American edition in later British editions, but she never did. Thus both versions, in a sense, have the author's stamp of approval. Having read both versions, students can never again read one without the other being invoked, and their notion of text itself destabilizes, as well as their sense of *this* text and the relationship of the Ramsays.

Finally, I tell students that we have been using a sociology of the text or "history of the book" approach, which insists that a text is inseparable from the social matrix. Traditional bibliography concentrates on questions of establishing literary texts, but the French *histoire du livre* concerns itself with larger patterns of book production and consumption, and I direct them to studies by Roger Chartier, Robert Darnton, Peter Keating, Jerome McGann, and D. F. McKenzie, among others. Further, I exhort them to consider how typography, color, and paper texture create an impression. I ask them to reflect on how everything from printing to promoting to distributing to reviewing the book affects our reception of the text. And I encourage them to question how the mediating structures of presses, libraries, bookstores, and university classrooms themselves determine literary meaning. What I suspect they remember, however, is not Bourdieu and cultural theory but the smell of the ink.

Teaching *To the Lighthouse* as a Civilian War Novel

Karen L. Levenback

I taught *To the Lighthouse* in Virginia Woolf and the Years between the Wars, a mid- to upper-level undergraduate elective whose stated aim was to "develop an appreciation of Woolf's aesthetics, ethos, and times." The course covered over twenty years, when Woolf explored experiences and memories of the war in her fiction, indirectly acknowledging the changes war brought. This indirection may have led Great War scholars to exclude or minimize Woolf's contribution to literature of the war (Fussell; Wohl; Leed; Mosse; and Hynes, *War*). Only recently have scholars recognized what the noncombatant experience of the Great War contributes to our understanding of the war and the cultural changes it brought (Hanley; J. Marcus, "Asylums"; Gilbert; Hussey, *Woolf and War*; Levenback, *Woolf*; Allyson Booth).

Teaching *To the Lighthouse* in a course framed by the two world wars means showing that what Woolf wrote reflects her understanding that the Great War was neither confined to the trenches nor ended with the Treaty of Versailles in June 1919. Most students have never studied Woolf in a historical context, but none of them resists this approach, and they all seem to enjoy the challenge of discovering allusions to the war. Indeed, many become increasingly sensitive to these allusions as the course progresses. Their open-ended response sheets (two or more pages for each assigned work, due the day we begin discussion; sometimes, for *To the Lighthouse*, a response sheet for each part) focus more sharply on Woolf's civilian perspective and the tension between "historians' histories" and civilian experiences of the war ("War from the Street" 3).

As students become accustomed to seeing through Woolf's eyes, we also discuss the distinction between official history and individual memory. For example, in their first assigned reading, "A Sketch of the Past," Woolf acknowledges the subtle workings of memory and the chasm between what is remembered individually and what is deemed significant historically. In their responses, most students isolate the importance of memory, the inadequacy of existing forms (even autobiography) in exploring it, and the significance of the indefinite yet immense "influence"—"the War" (80-81). Their reading puts them in touch with two dislocations referenced by Woolf in "War in the Village" (1918) and "The War from the Street" (1919): loss of a secure, unchanging prewar world in the first and the distinction between "history as it is written" and "history as it is lived" in the second (3).

As students read works written by Woolf during and after the war, including the essays just mentioned, I help them recognize that she increasingly focused on civilian experiences and the exclusion of civilians from "what journalists call 'historic days'" ("War from the Street" 3). In "The Mark on the Wall" (1917) and "Kew Gardens" (1919), the war plays a decidedly minor role in civilians' lives, as when, in the first, a woman's train of thought is interrupted by an unidentified presence, leading several students to comment on the chasm between what happens on the front and how it is reported at home:

> "I'm going out to buy a newspaper."
> "Yes?"
> "Though it's no good buying newspapers. [. . .] Nothing ever happens. Curse this war; God damn this war!"   (89)

I indicate that they may also see war evidenced in "Kew Gardens" in the line "Widows! Women in black—" which resembles a newspaper headline, and in a reference to the "the dead" in Heaven, "known to the ancients as Thessaly," which is obliquely related to "this War" (92).

At this point, I offer students background on the Defence of the Realm Act and what Philip Knightly calls "the great conspiracy [. . .] to suppress the truth" (80). The suppression of war reportage had been largely the responsibility of Lord Northcliffe, who owned the *Times* (London) and the *Daily Mail* and who was director of propaganda, also known as "the Minister of Lying" (81). I may even bring in sample pages from the Defence of the Realm Act and London newspapers of the time, such as a copy of the *Times* article that Woolf mentions in her diary for 5 January 1915, an editorial saying that "the war has taught us a proper sense of proportion with respect to human life" (*Diary* 1: 7; note 18 misidentifies the date of the article, which appeared in the *Times* on 2 Jan. 1915). I may also ask students to examine London newspapers on their own, such as the *Times* for July and August 1914, available on microfilm, and sometimes I put photocopies on reserve of "For What Men Died" (pt. 8 in Philip Gibbs's *Now It Can Be Told*), "The Social Revolution in English Life" (ch. 6 in Gibbs's *More That Must Be Told*), and "The Last War" (ch. 5 from Knightly), all of which offer students examples and analysis of the constructions of the war in newspapers, along with historical background about the differences in the pre- and postwar worlds. Once alerted to the importance of newspapers, students can see their resonance in *Jacob's Room*, as Jacob Flanders returns to England to enlist with a copy of the *Daily Mail* in his hands, and in "Time Passes," where the bracketed sections resemble newspaper copy.

Those who have especial understanding of the Gulf War, in particular, have little difficulty in leaping from enforced and government-sanctioned ignorance to a civilian "illusion of immunity" from the war (Levenback, "Woolf's 'War'"). Many note the signals of the coming war throughout *Jacob's Room*, signals that prewar characters disregard. Similarly, Woolf juxtaposes the postwar life of civilians like Clarissa Dalloway, for whom "[t]he War was over" (5), with the "memories" of returning veteran Septimus Warren Smith.

By the time students read *To the Lighthouse*, then, they are used to seeking out references to the war and to fitting them into the historical and cultural context we've constructed. We discuss how the war changed not only the postwar lives of former servicemen but also the lives of those who experienced the war at home; in *To the Lighthouse*, they can hear the resonance of Woolf's 1926 comment in "The Cinema": "The war sprung its chasm at the feet of all this innocence and ignorance" (269). Among the metaphorical chasms in Woolf's writings and life, those related to the war itself become our class focus, especially the chasms existing between history and memory, between civilian and combatant experience, and between newspaper accounts and "reality." By our last session on *To the Lighthouse*, then, many students say that Woolf resembles Lily Briscoe, painting prewar pictures within postwar frames. Class discussions have helped them see that as consciousness of the war and its ongoing effects play an increasingly important role in Woolf's work, stylistic changes seem more and more to merge history and fiction.

As Woolf became aware of how the war affected her writing and what she called "life itself," she moved further from embodying the combatant experience or from presenting it as central to understanding the experience of the war. By the time she wrote *To the Lighthouse*, Woolf was taking into account the entire experience of the Great War from a wholly civilian perspective. Unlike *Jacob's Room*, in which Woolf divides attention between the self-conscious civilian narrator and Jacob Flanders, who perishes in the war, and unlike *Mrs. Dalloway*, in which she divides attention between the civilian Mrs. Dalloway and the former soldier Septimus Warren Smith, *To the Lighthouse* reflects only the civilian reaction—or lack of same—to the conditions that allowed the war to happen, to the war in progress, and to effects of the war. The sense of civilian immunity from the war, apparent in the first two postwar novels, takes on additional resonance in each section of *To the Lighthouse*, as Woolf's stylistic experiments serve as formal signals to it: civilian detachment from the war in "The Window," signaled by affirmative and definite syntax, positive hyperbolic diction, and repetition; civilian distance from the war in "Time Passes," signaled by bracketed reports of news in the outside world; and civilian recognition of the changes in the postwar world in "The Lighthouse," signaled by tentative diction and a preponderance of questions.

I devote three class meetings to the novel, each day covering one part, and collect and discuss responses to begin. On the first day this discussion inevitably leads to a consideration of how Woolf's personal memory and an absence of war-consciousness inform "The Window." We explore the atmosphere and character of England before the war, which brings us to a discussion of Mrs. Ramsay and narrative technique. Mrs. Ramsay's centrality to the family and guests may be seen as embodying her world. Lacking a first name (unlike Mrs. Dalloway), her identity is not individuated through personal memories of the past (as is Mrs. Dalloway's); rather, she doesn't distinguish between past and present and has only a conditional grasp of the future. She either avoids or smooths over external reality and maintains the stability of the prewar world. I help the students see how Woolf's syntax and diction reinforce this evasion and seeming security. For example, although "The Window" begins with Mrs.

Ramsay's conditional, incomplete, and in media res comment to her son about the projected trip to the lighthouse, her character is more commonly defined by her "habit of exaggeration" (6) and her sense of security and control, like the middle-class, prewar world in which the Ramsays live. However, I also indicate that Woolf's challenging syntax, long sentences, and limited dialogue reflect complexities hidden by the seeming stability of this prewar world.

In discussing "Time Passes," which includes the war years, we start with Mrs. Ramsay's death and how it deprives the house of centrality. A few students always respond strongly to this section, in part because of the single point of view, in part because they can see the war encroaching into the house. Structurally and thematically central to the novel, "Time Passes" opens with a sentence more tentative and more ominous than the one opening "The Window": "'Well, we must wait for the future to show,' said Mr. Bankes" (125). Some students recall the definite tone of "The Window" and the prewar/Victorian world, communicated through Mrs. Ramsay's and the narrator's definite pronouncements, and we examine the shift to hyperbolic nothingness in "Time Passes," suggesting the dissolution of prewar security and control:

> Nothing, it seemed, could survive the flood, the profusion of darkness [. . .]. [T]here was scarcely anything left of body or mind by which one could say, "This is he" or "This is she." Sometimes a hand was raised as if to clutch something or ward off something, or somebody groaned, or somebody laughed aloud as if sharing a joke with nothingness.
> Nothing stirred in the drawing-room or in the dining-room or on the staircase.   (125–26)

Consistent with what Paul Fussell calls "civilian incomprehension" of the war (87), the narrator can observe only when protected from external reality. Thus, in "Time Passes," the narrator figuratively (and the caretakers literally) follows Mrs. Ramsay's leitmotif: opening windows and closing doors. Unable to appreciate fully any reality apart from the house and its immediate environs, the narrator does not directly refer to the war or understand the proximate cause of the "empirical" dissonance (what Johnstone calls "the distant sounds of war" ["World War I" 535]): "Now and again some glass tinkled in the cupboard as if a giant voice had shrieked so loud in its agony that tumblers stood inside a cupboard vibrated too" (133). Offering only a mythical metaphor as explanation, the narrator cannot comprehend what is beyond her power to apprehend.

Students can thus see how "Time Passes" addresses the great chasm between civilian reality and combatant experience. The narrator, like the war-blind civilian population, is in a hiatus, enclosed by Mrs. Ramsay's shortsightedness on the one side and slanted newspaper reporting on the other, with Woolf rendering reality apart from the narrator's field of vision in bracketed reports resembling newspaper copy. While five of the six bracketed intrusions note civilian life and death, one "reports" combatant death: "[A shell exploded. Twenty or thirty young men were blown up in France, among them Andrew Ramsay, whose death, mercifully, was instantaneous.]" (133). The report depersonalizes the war, including Andrew Ramsay's death among the deaths of twenty or thirty men who, like so many balloons, are "blown up." Listening to Celia Johnson's twenty-minute lyrical recording of "Time Passes" (Mrs. Dalloway: Selections) gives students an even greater sense of the war's dreamlike quality to those at home. The only "report" of a home front effect of war involves the sudden popularity of the poet Augustus Carmichael: "The war, people said, had revived their interest in poetry" (134). To civilians like Mrs. McNab and Mrs. Bast, the war is what they read in the newspapers, a subject for gossip.

To end this session and provide a transition into the next, I suggest that before the war, external reality prevented the lighthouse trip: the weather was bad. After the war, reaching the lighthouse represents "mak[ing] contact with a truth outside oneself" (Daiches 86). Anticipating A Room of One's Own, assigned after To the Lighthouse, I refer to Woolf's comment that the war "destroyed illusion and put truth in its place" (Room 15): the illusion of stability replaced by the reality of instability, order replaced by chaos. In the final class on the novel, we discuss the way this transformation is suggested through Lily's recognition that not only the house but also life itself has "changed completely" (175) and in her movement out of the house, where she observes that "the whole world seemed to have dissolved in [. . .] a deep basin of reality" (179). Given the frequency of questions in the part, we discuss "The Lighthouse" as an interrogation of the postwar world and the lighthouse as an archetypal sign of the kind of personal epiphany that was not part of the prewar world with Mrs. Ramsay as its stable center.

We explore the implications of the postwar world by analyzing the survivors' responses to the death of the prewar world, both as represented by Mrs. Ramsay and as controlled and thought controllable by her. Of particular importance is the movement out of the house, where completion is achieved not only by the surviving Ramsays, who complete the trip to the lighthouse, but also by Lily Briscoe, who completes the picture, both tasks planned before the war. Through this completion, Lily approaches an answer to her question at the beginning of "The Lighthouse": "What does it mean then, what can it all mean?" (145). What she discovers is the "razor edge of balance between two opposite forces" (193), which many students identify as prewar security and postwar insecurity.

Lily, sharing with Woolf a desire "to be on a level with ordinary experience" (202), must complete the prewar painting of Mrs. Ramsay and child and thus establish a link between the ordinary life therein represented and the empirical circumstances operating at its completion: she must render prewar reality within a postwar frame. Coincident with the actual completion of the trip to the lighthouse, the artist's vision represents a new hope replacing the certitude negated when, as Woolf said, "suddenly, like a chasm in a smooth road, the war came" ("Leaning Tower" 167). Like a bridge over the chasm, art connects the prewar past and the postwar present; facing the bridge, the artist herself becomes a lighthouse.

By this point in the semester, many students see art as a vehicle for understanding the reality of the seemingly unreal war and what Lily Briscoe calls the "extraordinary unreality" it left behind (147). I remind them that in *Mrs. Dalloway*, Septimus feels nothing when he witnesses Evans's death: the effect of war's reality on a combatant; in *To the Lighthouse*, Lily feels nothing when she thinks of Andrew's death: the effect of war's unreality on a civilian (146). Lily's art, like the novelist's, depends on a merging of external reality and inner consciousness. It is a "strange life," Woolf wrote on 19 December 1920, "to believe in [the] division between reality & unreality" (*Diary* 2: 81). The artist must render her perception of the real within a framed nonreality, a task complicated for Lily by postwar longing for prewar security. What Woolf calls "the narrow bridge of art" links the past and present, allowing Lily to find a middle distance, to answer her question, and to have her vision.

In summarizing our reading of the novel, we discuss the tension between the prewar past and the postwar present and try to come to terms with the way Lily sees her role as an artist in what Samuel Hynes calls the "valueless post-war world" (*Auden Generation* 37). As the artist adjusts to new circumstances surrounding her art, she must develop, as Woolf says in "The Narrow Bridge of Art," "an attitude toward life" and "see things [. . .] four square, in proportion." As Lily completes her painting and has her vision, she anticipates Woolf's hope for artists who, "when they come into action [. . .] cut real ice" (220). Not until we consider *The Years* (1937), Woolf's "novel of fact," will we discover her realistic confrontation with the effects of the Great War in housing, for example, or in employment (Levenback, "Returning Soldiers").

Woolf's postwar perspective was not back-looking, not like Mr. Ramsay's despairing refrain, "We perished [. . .] each alone" (165, 167, 191, 207). While acknowledging the past, Woolf looked ahead clearly and decisively, proclaiming in 1924, "But enough of death—its [sic] life that matters" (*Diary* 2: 301). The experience of the Great War is central to understanding not only *To the Lighthouse* but Virginia Woolf and the world in which she lived. As students finish the novel, many have come to realize not only how the war affected life itself but also how one needed individual vision in the face of it.

"I Have Had My Vision":
Teaching *To the Lighthouse* as *Künstlerroman*
Bonnie Braendlin

In a fifteen-week semester course on literature written by women, cross-listed in English and women's studies for both upper-level undergraduate and graduate students, I teach *To the Lighthouse* as a salient example in a series of nineteenth- and twentieth-century quest novels (Abel, Hirsch, and Langland; DuPlessis, *Writing*) that depict life choices being made by a woman interacting with socially constructed and disseminated ideologies. As a *Künstlerroman* or artist novel, *To the Lighthouse* is in a subgenre of the *Bildungsroman* or self-development novel, a genre originating in Europe in the late eighteenth century, migrating to England and United States in the nineteenth, becoming important in United States 1970s feminism, and appealing still to contemporary women authors. Although often considered a "male" genre, the *Bildungsroman* has a "female" history as well (Abel, Hirsch, and Langland; Fraiman), one that begins with Jane Austen's novels (Moretti) and continues into contemporary fiction. My class first reads Charlotte Brontë's *Jane Eyre*—though one might start with *Pride and Prejudice* or *Emma*—Kate Chopin's *The Awakening*, and Woolf's *To the Lighthouse* as three early examples of the genre, setting the stage for their later-twentieth-century descendants, from which students select four: Jean Rhys's *Wide Sargasso Sea* (a pastiche of *Jane Eyre*), Rita Mae Brown's *Rubyfruit Jungle*, Maya Angelou's *I Know Why the Caged Bird Sings* (autobiography patterned on the *Bildungsroman*), Maxine Hong Kingston's *The Woman Warrior*, Margaret Atwood's *Lady Oracle*, Sandra Cisneros's *The House on Mango Street*, Jeanette Winterson's *Oranges Are Not the Only Fruit*, any of Alice Walker's novels, and a host of others. *To the Lighthouse* represents the era just after World War I, when professional opportunities for women increased, allowing or perhaps coercing women to choose between the private and public spheres separated during the rise of the middle class in nineteenth-century Britain. As a *Künstlerroman* or artist's development novel, it provides a pivotal link between earlier quest narratives, where marriage seems to be woman's only viable option, and later ones that overtly challenge or subvert traditional endings of marriage or death (DuPlessis, *Writing*).

Genre is usually defined as a cluster of characteristics that polices and regulates our reading of texts, but as Susan Fraiman notes, it should also be viewed as "constructed [by critics] and ideologically laden" (2). Thus open to possibilities for definitional change, genre study lends itself well to a pedagogy that combines instructor and student expertise in the making of meaning. To encourage—or perhaps convince—students to make meaning with me, I devote the first fifteen minutes of each seventy-five-minute class period to small-group work. Each week, students bring two copies of a question based on the assigned reading or current discussion topic; as they talk among themselves, I write words or phrases from their questions on the board to prompt later class discussion. My commitment to a feminist pedagogy, a mode of teaching that "must be collaborative, cooperative and interactive" because it conceptualizes "knowledge as a comparison of multiple perspectives leading towards a complex and evolving view of reality" (Maher 30, 33), thus encourages students to engage in dialogues and debates about literary texts and sociocultural contexts. To that end, class meetings combine small- and large-group discussions with minilectures and student reports to convey information and to share and debate interpretations.

In the cooperative classroom, as "a major contributor, a creator of structure and a delineator of issues, but not the sole authority" (Maher 30), I establish the basic premises of the course, in this case, tenets of discourse theory as they relate to the *Bildungsroman* genre. To move students toward such understanding, I discuss how conflicting ideologies function in cultural discourses or language fields, articulated through the various texts of social institutions (education, law, medicine, the media, literature, and the arts). Discourses operate through dialogue, with meaning constructed as people interact; when consensus is achieved, some discourses predominate over others, and the dominant ideologies often function to guide or even coerce people into socially acceptable roles (Weedon; Henriques et al.).

Early in the course, to help students understand how social discourses construct female subjectivity, I ask them to think and talk about how they learned what it means to be "male" or "female" in our society, what types of behavior they were permitted or forbidden, and how the kinds of choices they have made in their lives and will be expected to make have been influenced by parents, friends, teachers, and others. Together we analyze texts that define women in our culture—newspaper and magazine articles, legal documents, medical books, columns such as "Ann Landers" or "Miss Manners," MTV, rock music lyrics, television sitcoms, and the like. We identify various social positions available to women today—wife, mother, career woman, prostitute, politician, social worker, creative artist, and so on—and we debate the degree to which women are coerced into socially acceptable roles, disciplined by mentors and the media, and offered ways to transgress and hence to modify dictated positions. We note how various discourses often come into conflict and how ideologies may contradict one another. Of particular interest to many contemporary students are the conflicts embedded in the superwoman image, which combines, but not without contradictions, choices of career, marriage, and motherhood.

Out of our discussions emerges recognition of the ways dominant discourses condition the developing subject and direct the exercise of individual choice and yet, as sites of disunity and conflict, also allow transgression of dominant prescriptions of identity. In this way, ideologies, such as those that define gender, change, even if only imperceptibly (Weedon 22). From this perspective, students can acknowledge the choices available in previous eras, represented in decisions confronted by fictional protagonists, especially in the *Bildungsroman* and the *Künstlerroman*. Studying these genres helps students understand how individual choice in experiential reality and as represented in novels both perpetuates society's ideologies and effects change, often by transgressing or even transvaluing social conditioning.

I initiate genre discussions by explaining that as the *Bildungsroman* developed during the nineteenth century in Germany, France, and England, it expressed the values, mores, and goals of the rising European middle class. Protagonists of novels such as Goethe's *Wilhelm Meisters Lehrjahre*, Thomas Carlyle's *Sartor Resartus*, Charles Dickens's *David Copperfield*, and Somerset Maugham's *Of Human Bondage* embodied this ideology in a male protagonist, with women in secondary roles as tempting sexual distractions or as supportive, maternal, potential wife-mothers. Fraiman argues that novels by Frances Burney, Jane Austen, Charlotte Brontë, and George Eliot, while "reproducing many orthodoxies about middle-class female formation," also complicated the genre by constructing "the 'feminine' as a site of ideological confusion, struggle, and possibility" (31). As these nineteenth-century protagonists journey from childhood to maturity, innocence to experience, ignorance to knowledge of themselves and of their place in the world, they are mentored by representatives of their social class—parents and teachers predominantly—who teach the cultural expectations governing their self-development. Rebellious protagonists are ultimately tamed into preordained roles represented by the "choice" of a "proper" (i.e., socially sanctioned) vocation and spouse; through this narrative process, bourgeois society perpetuates itself and its values through its literary texts (Buckley; Moretti). Identity for male characters is inscribed in vocations solidly positioned in the business world, while female characters are generally guided into marriage. For Jane Eyre, even the possibility of a "career" as a missionary necessitates a wedded partnership with St. John Rivers, and her simple comment about Rochester, "Reader, I married him" (452) proclaims the triumph of the wife-mother script in the Victorian female *Bildungsroman*.

Early in the course, I assign several student reports on each novel; students exploring Jane Eyre's vocational options suggest that her desire for a vocation confronts only a socially inferior position as governess and a socially unacceptable role as Rochester's mistress, alternatives that reinforce marriage as a more desirable goal. The mid–nineteenth century, we conclude, permitted few opportunities for middle-class women outside the home, but the new professionalism around the turn of the century, reflected in *The Awakening*, offers more options, including that of artist, although Kate Chopin rejects that as an alternative to marriage for her rebellious protagonist, Edna Pontellier. Small-group discussions explore Edna's failure as an artist: Why is the Creole motherhood ideology, articulated by the "mother-woman" Adèle Ratignolle, so compelling and yet so offensive to Edna and to contemporary readers? Why can't Edna be content with her newfound independence, especially since she seems to be selling her paintings? How does the unflattering portrait of the artist Mademoiselle Reisz complicate Edna's choices? What conflicting ideologies confuse and ultimately defeat this potential artist?

When I introduce *To the Lighthouse*, I explain that in the early modern *Bildungsroman*, escape and exile began to replace social integration as the resolution of many maturation journeys, and the traditional roles of marriage and vocation were called into question by more open-ended texts. D. H. Lawrence in *Sons and Lovers* and James Joyce in *A Portrait of the Artist as a Young Man* adopted the *Künstlerroman* genre to depict the self-development journey as one guided by artistic ideologies often diametrically opposed to the ideologies of the bourgeoisie. Their novels inscribe the quest for selfhood as an exile into art, a resolution expressed not as acquiescence but as refusal, particularly of marriage and a business profession, and hence as a transgression of bourgeois ideology. A decade after Lawrence and Joyce, when Woolf in *To the Lighthouse* depicted the artist as a young woman, she situated female self-development in a modernist genre that offered art as an alternative vocational choice for men and also amid cultural issues fueled by the cataclysmic changes occasioned by World War I, by political activities of the suffragette movement, and by increased vocational opportunities for women (all possible topics for student reports). In an era when traditional marriage and motherhood were challenged by new roles in male-defined spheres and portrayed in cultural texts by images of the "new woman," Lily Briscoe has greater potential for transgressions and alternative female development than did her predecessors.

Using this context of female self-development as a choice among roles or as a positioning of self in the sociocultural discourses into which a woman is placed, my class reads *To the Lighthouse* as a *Bildungsroman* or *Künstlerroman*, foregrounding Lily as a developing artist and as the Ramsays' surrogate daughter rather than Cam, the actual daughter. (Instructors interested in Cam and the *Bildungsroman* should see Elizabeth Abel's essay "Cam the Wicked.") Through student reports (assisted by scholarly studies of Woolf on reserve), class discussions, and occasional minilectures, we first focus on generational conflicts central to maturation. Through James, Woolf delineates male individuation in a miniature version of the traditional journey wherein the son successfully makes the oedipal transition from symbiosis with the mother to identification with the father, thus assuming his "rightful place" in society (Minow-Pinkney, *Woolf* 91; Fullbrook 98). But she repositions the traditional male search for and choice of a suitable calling in the female quest for self-discovery, played out in Lily's ten-year inward struggle between the socially acceptable position of wife-mother, represented by Mrs. Ramsay, and an artistic calling that eschews marriage and motherhood.

Our class discussions and reports on the nineteenth-century *Bildungsroman* inform our understanding of Mrs. Ramsay as a reincarnation of the Victorian "Angel in the House" (whom Woolf insists must be killed for modern women to thrive ["Professions for Women"]): essentially passive, but powerful as a repository of moral and spiritual virtues, of selfless and sympathetic devotion to others' needs (Gilbert and Gubar, *Madwoman*; N. Auerbach; Ruddick). An "artist" whose medium is human emotions but who remains confined to the private sphere of home and family, Mrs. Ramsay achieves a momentary harmony among disparate and difficult individuals at her dinner party; this harmony anticipates the unity Lily hopes to accomplish in her painting. The surrogate mother offers the daughter a seductive ideal of femininity, especially as a refuge from an increasingly hostile and alienating world; later, when Mr. Ramsay reaches out to Lily for sympathy, she has the opportunity to replicate the wife-mother role, to recapture the lost maternal love and empathy she desires, and to avoid the social stigma of spinsterhood. Here, students debate issues central to the literary representation of female self-development: mother-daughter conflicts, female desire, professions for women, relationships with men and with other women, and particularly the obligatory either-or choice of marriage and motherhood or art. While Lily rejects traditional marriage, with its rigidly demarcated gender roles that insist on female dependency on the male, her character retains some of Mrs. Ramsay's sympathetic nature. However, her praise of Mr. Ramsay's boots as an act of honest compassion redefines (s)mothering love as camaraderie and friendship, leaving both individuals separate and unenslaved (DuPlessis, *Writing* 97); her gesture revises the time-honored relationship between men and women in that it rejects manipulative lying and the subordination of female sympathy to male demand and thus "microscopically alter[s]" gender relations (Fullbrook 102). Moreover, her rejection of marriage and her decision to be an artist are transgressive acts contributing to an ongoing transformation, in the spaces opened by conflicts among discourses, of social ideologies governing female self-development.

Lily's final expression of artistic success—"I have had my vision" (209), coupled with her decisive brush stroke in the center of her painting—occasions much discussion both in the scholarship and in the classroom. Questions that students debate include the following: What combination of personality traits traditionally designated as "masculine" (e.g., ambition, intellect, egoism) and as "feminine" (e.g., sympathy, unity, wholeness) does Lily now embody? What has Lily lost and gained in her decision to be an artist, especially if, as she fears, her paintings may be "hung in the attics" rather than in museums (208)? What has modern woman gained and lost by rejecting traditional roles in her decision to be a "new woman" artist? Perhaps, as Makiko Minow-Pinkney argues, Lily's vision expresses a "bleak loss of the possibility of total meaning" but also the possibility of liberation from her mother fixation that will allow Lily to exercise her talents as an artist (*Woolf* 8-9, 22, 116). Or perhaps, as Patricia Waugh suggests, Lily's final stance is one of "both separateness and relatedness, the connection of the symbolic [art] to the realm of human emotion and the foundation of both upon loss and acceptance of its pain" (*Feminine Fictions* 115). Some students are especially intrigued by Pamela L. Caughie's provocative suggestion that Lily is not only an artist who negotiates between art and life through the process of painting but also a narrator of the minijourney undertaken by Mr. Ramsay, James, and Cam in part 3 (*Postmodernism* 36). This linking of artist to narrator, and hence of art to literature, occasions stimulating discussion on possible relation between painting and writing fiction, between art and life.

Creating a course from a feminist pedagogical standpoint involves cooperative rather than competitive assignments (Maher 32), so in addition to some assigned readings on reserve, graduate students seek out scholarly articles on their own, and, along with individual short reports to the class, they work together to generate an annotated bibliography for each novel. Undergraduates work together to present examples of how discourses work in other disciplines they have studied; in this way, the class benefits from insights gleaned, for example, from sociology, psychology, and art history. Students who relate their own experiences to the fictional representations we study can construct their own definitions of the genre and their own particular outlooks on self, choice, and development either on the final exam or in term papers.

Although this feminist pedagogical model of the production of knowledge in a classroom encourages students to cooperate and interact with respect for one another's views, discussions of the novels and the issues they arouse are not always tranquil. Locked in their own ideological patterns yet also fearful of their own ideas and hence defensive, students often argue vehemently. As Frances Maher says, however, the feminist "stance does not, and should not, minimize conflict or disagreement: it clarifies it and seeks to put it in a larger context" (44). In my class on the *Bildungsroman* and *Künstlerroman*, student disagreements work both to clarify and to change inherited definitions of the genres; they also demonstrate to students a basic premise of the course, namely, that change comes about through the conflict of ideologies.

Intertextual Approaches

Portraits of Artists by Woolf and Joyce

Susan Currier

If women are to write fiction, concludes Virginia Woolf's narrator in *A Room of One's Own*, they need, besides privacy and independent income, a psychology of their own. Though she celebrates the legislative reforms that by 1928 had expanded women's rights and opportunities, at least two impediments remained: the demoralizing effect of male-authored scholarship claiming the mental, moral, and physical inferiority of women and the incompatibility between women writers and the literary forms bequeathed them by patriarchy. To release women from authority's investment in their inferiority and to discover the literary forms appropriate to women, she appeals for a female psychology from a female perspective: "Where shall I find that elaborate study of the psychology of women by a woman?" (78).

In my modern novel classes, where I purposely pair Woolf's *To the Lighthouse* with Joyce's *A Portrait of the Artist as a Young Man*, I have suggested a corollary to Woolf's premise: that if a new psychology of women by women can benefit women writers, it can also aid their readers. My students, capable juniors and seniors at a polytechnic university where men outnumber women and where far more students major in engineering, computer science, business, architecture, or agriculture than in any of the liberal arts, generally seek utilitarian benefits from their courses. Many are more attuned to conservative than to liberal values, institutions, and forms. For these reasons and more, the majority of students in this general education course do not readily discover shape, meaning, or value in Woolf's "portrait of the artist." Since Joyce's and Woolf's novels are both *Künstlerromane* and since, as Woolf argues in *A Room of One's Own*, traditional Western literary forms grow out of male experience, then female development novels must have forms of their own, and readers must learn to discern them.

Though I refer to research in female psychology by Jean Baker Miller, Nancy Chodorow, Alice Miller, and in more specialized advanced classes, Jessica Benjamin, I borrow most from Carol Gilligan's *In a Different Voice* for our discussions of *To the Lighthouse*. I justify applying Gilligan to Woolf's autobiographical novel of the woman artist by underscoring the similarity between her concerns and Woolf's in *A Room of One's Own*: Gilligan also sees "recurrent problems in interpreting women's development" and "repeated exclusion of women from the critical theory-building studies of psychological research" (1). I note Gilligan's attention to fictional and real voices in her studies and observe that the argument of *A Room of One's Own*, with its appeal for a psychology of women, probably grew out of *To the Lighthouse*, written only two years earlier. I also acknowledge differences between Gilligan's findings and the findings of other researchers, as well as the perils of generalizing about women or men across time, class, and ethnicity. Finally, I suggest that Gilligan's explications of patterns of difference between the male and female voices in her studies can help us find meaning in *To the Lighthouse* and appreciate both these modernist novels of development.

We read *To the Lighthouse* just after *Portrait of the Artist*, launching discussion by comparing Lily Briscoe with the now familiar figure of Stephen Dedalus. Usually students remark on Lily's physical deficiencies and outsider status, connecting her puckered face with Stephen's nearsightedness and her spinsterhood with his declining family. Nevertheless, she pales beside Stephen whether they like him or not. When I probe, asking why Lily seems less worthy as a protagonist, some students, in one way or another, end up contrasting Stephen's developing independence from his family and friends with Lily's apparent dependence on the Ramsays. That's when I introduce Gilligan's distinction from *In a Different Voice*: "male and female voices typically speak of the importance of different truths, the former of the role of separation as it defines and empowers the self, the latter of the ongoing process of attachment that creates and sustains the human community" (156). I also share her observation that the imagery men and women use to express their respective "truths" reflects their distinct emphases: men speak more commonly of individual achievement, drawing their metaphors from the arenas of hierarchy, victory, and defeat, while women refer more frequently to connection, using metaphors of webs, nets, and so on (62). Before we analyze the characteristic voice with which Lily interprets experience, we review, in the light of Gilligan's distinctions, what students already know about Stephen's voice.

In our reading of *Portrait of the Artist*, we have already explored Stephen's aspiration to mythic flight. Now we revisit some of his most well-known expressions of that aspiration: Stephen's incantations to the original Dedalus and his lament about the "nets" or false claims of nationality, language, and religion that fetter his soul (203). Many students easily associate "the hawklike man [. . .] soaring out of his captivity on osierwoven wings" (225) with the separation so important to the men in Gilligan's studies. When I invite them to elaborate on Stephen's separation, some call his escape an accomplishment, while at least a few judge it a dereliction of responsibility; many find it a combination of the two. We also discuss how Stephen's preoccupation with performance in schoolboy competitions, his humiliation at believing the souls of "[f]rowsy girls" to be more blessed than his own (140), and his intensity in ranking prose writers and poets reveal the centrality of hierarchy in this developing artist's "truths."

As we turn to Lily, I remind students of Gilligan's distinction between separation and connection and read them a passage in which she describes the different imageries of men and women in her studies and their implications for relationships:

> Thus the images of hierarchy and web inform different modes of assertion and response: the wish to be alone at the top and the consequent fear that others will get too close; the wish to be at the center of connection and the consequent fear of being too far out on the edge. These dis-

parate fears of being stranded and being caught give rise to different por-
trayals of achievement and affiliation, leading to different modes of
action and different ways of assessing the consequences of choice.   (62)

Some students, often women, remain suspicious, but now Lily's dependence
on the Ramsays at least elicits a little more interest and a little less disparage-
ment.

Together, we then turn to passages expressing Lily's interpretations of experience and her aspirations. I point to a somewhat obscure one in which Lily
ponders the relative merits of William Bankes and Mr. Ramsay. She first won-
ders, "How did one judge people, think of them?" (24). Then she resolves her
hypothetical contest between the two men not into a winner and a loser but
into an image of a tightly knit web including both: "All of this danced up and
down, like a company of gnats, each separate, but all marvellously controlled
in an invisible elastic net" (25). Though an odd and frustratingly obtuse image
for some students, we note the reappearance of "net" here, this time with positive connotations of connection rather than with negative connotations of
imprisonment. Next, when I ask about Lily's aspirations, some students direct
us to the passage where Lily, at thirty-four and much older than Stephen is
when he flees his family for his vocation, yearns to merge with Mrs. Ramsay:

> What device for becoming, like waters poured into one jar, inextricably
> the same, one with the object one adored? [. . .] Could loving, as people
> called it, make her and Mrs. Ramsay one? for it was not knowledge but
> unity that she desired [. . .], nothing that could be written in any language
> known to men, but intimacy itself, which is knowledge, she had thought
> [. . .].   (51)

These lines are easier for students, in some respects, though they inevitably
prompt questions about the role of sexuality in Lily's desire and the orientation
of that sexuality. We discuss these issues, but I suggest that students leave them
open until they have completed the novel. The contrast with Stephen is compelling enough, however, that we stop to posit a tentative hypothesis—that
Lily, unlike Stephen who embraces hierarchy and defines meaning in his life in
terms of separation and achievement, prefers inclusion and measures meaning
in her life by the presence or absence of connection.

As students read for expressions of Lily's aspirations, several often find
another key passage in part 3 where, on the morning of her return to the Ramsays' summer home after World War I has decimated Europe and three Ramsays have died, Lily sits "stupefied" (146) at the breakfast table, unable to feel
or act. She feels no emotion for the dead—Mrs. Ramsay, Andrew, and Prue—
and can prepare no provisions for the lighthouse. "Sitting alone, [. . .] [s]he had
no attachment here, she felt, no relations with it, [. . .] as if the link that usually
bound things together had been cut [. . .]" (146). Words become fragmented

symbols that Lily wishes to connect: "If only she could put them together, she felt, write them out in some sentence, then she would have got at the truth of things. [. . .] Such were some of the parts, but how bring them together?" (147).

Then we move back to Lily's formulation of her artistic goals in part 1, where Lily explains her painting to William Bankes: "It was a question [. . . of] how to connect this mass on the right hand with that on the left. She might do it by bringing the line of the branch across so; or break the vacancy in the foreground by an object [. . .]. But the danger was that [. . .] the unity of the whole might be broken" (53). This sequence of passages helps students conceive of Lily's aesthetic challenge as part and parcel of her personal quest. The specific issue here anticipates the precise problem at the breakfast table ten years later—how to generate new connections, integrate them into old relationships, and yet maintain unity. This formulation also helps those students who find more confusion than coherence in Lily's personal and aesthetic quests as well as in Woolf's tripartite structure.

Having expanded our discussion of Lily's relationships to include discussion of her art, we revisit Stephen's metaphor for himself as artist—going forth to "forge in the smithy of [his] soul the uncreated conscience of [his] race" (253)—and set it beside Lily's implicit metaphor for herself as artist: "There might be lovers whose gift it was to choose out the elements of things and place them together and so, giving them a wholeness not theirs in life, make of some scene, or meeting of people (all now gone and separate), one of those globed compacted things over which thought lingers, and love plays" (192). Some students appreciate Stephen's passion and conviction. Occasionally, a student points out that Stephen's disdain for the ordinary Irish would probably extend to us as well. Other students have suggested that Lily seems more ordinary, like us, or that Lily has more feeling for ordinary people like us. Lily seems tentative, incapable of influencing others. Stephen seems grandiose and detached from others. Often we devote some time to stereotypes of, attitudes about, and expectations of artists in our own culture(s). By the end of this discussion, we have contrasted the judgmental, corrective vision intended by Stephen with the loving divination of connection sought by Lily.

Having now listened closely to Lily's and Stephen's voices for several class discussions, we return to the task of explicating patterns of development in these two *Künstlerromane*. Even though both Lily and Stephen contend with false claims against their freedom and art, Lily's progress toward her vision's fulfillment and her painting's completion still resonates less boldly with most students in my classes than does Stephen Dedalus's "*Non Serviam*" (239). So I ask why and suggest that they consider the role and function of the myths we have already explored in *Portrait of the Artist*. If, as Woolf observes in *A Room of One's Own*, women "think back through [their] mothers" (76), Stephen thinks back through a series of surrogate fathers including Saint Stephen, Dedalus, and Satan, all of whom authorize his right not to serve that which he does not believe. Students can identify Stephen's grand rebellion as his patrimony and his isolation as its price. By the end of *Portrait of the Artist*, Stephen's development carries him toward exile, intimacy looms only as a threat, and separation serves vocation.

How does Lily's developmental dilemma differ from Stephen's? Thinking back through surrogate mothers has so profoundly imbued Lily with the value of connection that she can't counter subversion of her art with a sequence of separation into isolation; that pattern simply doesn't promise Lily the same rewards that it does Stephen (one of the few times I can predict that the women will almost all agree). To claim her vocation and still preserve connection with others, Lily must balance responsibilities to both in a way that damages neither. Some students consider such a balance impossible. So we look at two frequently discussed scenes that crystallize the conflict and identify possible resolutions (see, e.g., Brett 51–55; Heilbrun, *Recognition* 162).

Early in *To the Lighthouse*, Woolf presents Lily as an independent artist who rejects fashionable Pauncefortian pastels in favor of brighter colors. At Mrs. Ramsay's dinner party, when Lily sacrifices her self by petitioning Charles to take her to the lighthouse despite his insistence that "[w]omen can't paint, women can't write" (48), her complicity in her own "abasement" (86) discomfits male and female students alike. In her defense, some point to Lily's oft-quoted but imagined resistance to the seventh article of her culture's gender code: "But how would it be, she thought, if neither of us did either of these things?" (91), referring, of course, to men's rescue of women in physical danger and women's rescue of men from feelings of inadequacy. Others point to the pressure Lily feels emanating from Mrs. Ramsay, which forces Lily to choose between her integrity and her most important connection: "'I am drowning, my dear, in seas of fire. Unless you apply some balm to the anguish of this hour and say something nice to that young man there, life will run upon the rocks" (92).

Then we observe the same conflict reenacted ten years later. But first, as a transition, I ask students to summarize the human events from "Time Passes," reminding them that Lily is as conscious of these events as they are. They list the deaths of Mrs. Ramsay, Prue, and Andrew, easily recognizing them as sacrifices to the traditional gender roles dictated by the code Lily questioned. In the reenactment, then, Lily resumes painting and Mr. Ramsay demands solace for his desolation, just as Charles Tansley had sought salve for his ego. Most students acknowledge that Lily resists imitating "the self-surrender [. . .] she had seen on so many women's faces" (150), but many are confused about what happens next. Lily anticipates "annihilation" (153), compliments Mr. Ramsay on his boots, and discovers herself transported with him to a "sunny island where peace dwelt, sanity reigned and the sun for ever shone" (154). I suggest they think once again about myth, and we consider similarities between Lily's "sunny" isle and Eden, a new world achieved by "giving Mr. Ramsay something without forcing herself to say anything she doesn't want to," as one student put it.

Not all students are comfortable with Lily's momentary paradise—some insist Lily should abandon Mr. Ramsay; others suggest she ought to marry him—so we explore what Lily has accomplished and why the novel must continue. What, I ask them, will constitute closure for this novel? Usually several students agree that Lily must complete her painting, so I ask them what prevents her from doing so. Students often mention her earlier inability to feel or focus and her continuing grief.

Thus we turn from Lily's resolution of conflict with Mr. Ramsay to her unresolved need for Mrs. Ramsay. Lily's discovery that she needn't choose between sacrifice and separation in her relationship with Mr. Ramsay clears the way for another revelation. What is Lily doing, I ask them, sifting through all those memories of Mrs. Ramsay while she is ostensibly at work on her painting? In a variety of ways, they respond that she is still trying to merge with her surrogate mother. Then I ask what power allows Lily to transpose Mrs. Ramsay from the vale of death to the window where she read to James ten years before (202), and this question elicits lots of disagreement. Common responses include assertions that Lily's vision is a delusion and that writers can do what they want. I rephrase the question. Why does Woolf grant Lily a vision of Mrs. Ramsay at this point? What has changed? Some students remind us that Lily is stronger now, so we discuss how Lily's success with Mr. Ramsay has prepared her to connect with Mrs. Ramsay without having to sacrifice her self as she had at the dinner party years before. We also explore the possibility that by reclaiming her self in the encounter with Mr. Ramsay, Lily has become a mother to her self; the resurrected vision in the window simply confirms that she has discovered within her self the magic power and "inscriptions" that she once located in Mrs. Ramsay.

At the end of Woolf's novel, unlike the end of Joyce's, the protagonist's web of connections remains intact, though transformed. We discuss how that web has changed, returning to the notion that Lily has learned to connect to her self and to others simultaneously, maintaining both integrity and unity. And students generally relate her interpersonal successes to the completion of her painting—her drawing of the "line there, in the centre" (209) that connects masses and preserves the whole.

Returning, finally, to the issue of form in novels by women writers, I explain that critics who measure Lily against a modern male model of development can find her wanting and Woolf's novel problematic. To illustrate, I read a brief passage from Alex Zwerdling's chapter on *To the Lighthouse* from *Virginia Woolf and the Real World*, where he acknowledges the temptation to read this novel as a typical modern "liberation fable" (198) but discounts it because Lily's rebellious gestures in part 3 are so "compromised" (200). By this point, though, a few students are prepared to defend *To the Lighthouse*: "liberation isn't just separation; it means connection, too." Although students invariably close discussion by debating the two novels' relative power and profundity (thus betraying their proclivities for Stephen's mode of discourse), this time more of them measure the merits of each in more than one voice.

Pear Trees beyond Eden: Women's Knowing Reconfigured in Woolf's *To the Lighthouse* and Hurston's *Their Eyes Were Watching God*

Annette Oxindine

> For books continue each other, in spite of our habit of
> judging them separately.
> —Virginia Woolf, *A Room of One's Own*

The 1990 publication of *The Gender of Modernism: A Critical Anthology*, edited by Bonnie Kime Scott, brought together for the first time some of modernism's most disparate female voices. The anthology's introduction explores the way gender inflects modernist texts, ultimately expanding our definition of modernism beyond what Scott calls the "monological sort of phenomenon" evoked by the famous (male) manifestos (4). While my use of Scott's anthology is ancillary in the undergraduate-graduate course Gender and Modernism that I teach at Wright State University, its very presence suggests to many students the vast array of connections, both explored and unexplored, between canonical and noncanonical modernists as well as male and female modernists. In a dizzying diagram, appropriately entitled "A Tangled Mesh of Modernists," Scott links the names of fifty modernists (twenty-six of whom are anthologized in her book) by a series of lines. Scott explains that she drew a line "each time an important connection was made in an introduction or a primary work in the anthology" (9). Not surprisingly, many lines connect Virginia Woolf to other modernists—predictably to T. S. Eliot, less predictably to Willa Cather. But Scott's diagram, like the anthology itself, also fosters unmade connections.

"Modernism as we were taught it at midcentury," contends Scott, "was perhaps halfway to truth. It was unconsciously gendered masculine" (2). By consciously reading modernist texts for inscriptions of gender and sexuality —which, as Scott notes, "were not adequately decoded, if detected at all" in traditional studies of modernism (2)—students can participate in the ongoing process of defining modernism. To this end, I teach Woolf alongside a female writer to whom she is rarely connected, inviting students to draw their own lines in the increasingly "tangled web" of modernism (see McVicker; S. Friedman, "Geopolitical Literacy").

After I have my class read Woolf's *To the Lighthouse*, which has long held at least a peripheral place in the modernist canon, we read Zora Neale Hurston's *Their Eyes Were Watching God* (1937), whose rescue from decades of obscurity has itself become a famous narrative (Walker, *Search* 83–92, 93–116). I want students to read Woolf alongside Hurston rather than see her only alongside the European male modernists with whom she is usually grouped, because such a pairing forces students to forgo the literary paradigms made available by periodization and cultural similarity—paradigms that are "arguably the products of patriarchy" (Scott, *Gender* 5). This approach encourages students to explore the way gender inflects each novel's "modernism"; it also opens them up to the reading of ethnicity, class, nationality, and sexuality as categories that coexist and interact with the texts' inscriptions of gender. How is it, I want students to consider, that the most famous novel of an upper-middle-class British woman, whose name has become synonymous with modernism, shares so many concerns about the relation between gender and voice with the work of an African American woman, whose work is only recently being thought about within the context of modernism and who died in poverty and was buried in an unmarked grave?

My primary objective in reading the two novels together is to examine the way Woolf's and Hurston's depictions of the sensual inner lives of their female characters subvert the patriarchal word and world order represented by Mr. Ramsay's linear quest to get to "R" (34) and Joe Starks's desire to become a "big voice" (27)—the animus of which is suggestively conveyed by his oft-repeated, idiosyncratic "I god." Both Lily Briscoe and Janie Crawford, by contrast, seek self-definition through knowledge sensually rooted in female language: Janie wants to learn the "maiden language" (109), and Lily yearns for that which could not be "written in any language known to men" (51). Pedagogically, however, I don't find it effective to suggest this connection to students at the beginning of our discussion, mainly because most students respond to Janie's sensual inner life in a very direct way (they read *Their Eyes Were Watching God* as a love story culminating in a life-affirming heterosexual union between Janie and Tea Cake; see Hite), whereas they tend to read Lily as an asexual artist whose quest is predominantly intellectual and aesthetic (a conclusion they reach, I think, because Lily's most intense expressions of erotic longing are inspired by and directed at Mrs. Ramsay).

Therefore, I open up discussion of the two novels by asking students to consider two major parallels between the obstacles faced by Lily and Janie in their quests for self-expression. First, the matriarchal figures in each novel, Nanny and Mrs. Ramsay, value the security of marriage over the younger women's desire for deeper fulfillment: for Janie, it is the quest for true love, "de very prong all us black women gits hung on" (22); for Lily, it is the desire to capture her vision, "which a thousand forces did their best to pluck from her" (19). Not only do Lily and Janie lack foremothers to "think back through," as Woolf argues that women need in *A Room of One's Own* (76), but the maternal figures in their lives suffer from a limited vision that renders them incapable of seeing past patriarchally scripted narratives about women's life choices. On seeing Lily and William Bankes together, Mrs. Ramsay "focussed her short-sighted eyes upon the backs of a retreating couple. [. . .] They must marry!" (71); as for Lily's painting, thinks Mrs. Ramsay, "one could not take [it] very seriously" (17). Nanny is also short-sighted, unable to envision the expanse of the horizon Janie longs to explore: "Here Nanny had taken the biggest thing God ever made, the horizon [. . .] and pinched it in to such a little bit of a thing that she could tie it about her granddaughter's neck tight enough to choke her" (85).

Second, we explore the ways patriarchal figures insecure about their own stature thwart both Lily's and Janie's attempts at self-expression. The voice of Charles Tansley intoning "[w]omen can't paint, women can't write" (48) feeds Lily's self-doubt throughout the novel, contributing to her compulsion to hide her canvas from real and imagined critics. Tansley's social insecurity, "snubbed as he had been" by the Ramsay children, manifests itself in his overwhelming need for assertion, especially over women: during Mrs. Ramsay's dinner party, he resolves that "he is not going to be condescended to by these silly women" (10, 85). Ten years after Lily is "nice" to Charles Tansley at the dinner party and relieves him "of his egotism" (92), Mr. Ramsay's "greedy" need for sympathy and acknowledgment derail her brush, "the one dependable thing in a world of strife [. . .]. You shan't touch your canvas, he seemed to say, bearing down on her, till you've given me what I want of you" (150). In Janie's community on the porch in Eatonville, language, not paint, is the medium for artistic expression: they "passed around the pictures of their thoughts for others to look at and see" (48). Joe Starks wants to exclude his wife from this community to a large extent because his "big voice" is overshadowed by her gift to capture the vision of others: "Yo' wife is uh born orator, Starks [. . .]. She put jus' de right words tuh our thoughts" (55). But Joe insists that Janie "don't know nothin' 'bout no speechmakin'," and his silencing makes her dream of love under the pear tree recede: it "took the bloom off of things" (40–41). Even though Tea Cake returns the "bloom" to Janie's life and is himself a masterful storyteller, his inability to verbally confront Mrs. Turner, who thinks he is too black for Janie, leads him to beat Janie "tuh show dem Turners who is boss" (141; see Meisenhelder).

Once we explore these parallels between Janie's and Lily's obstacles to self-expression and self-fulfillment through the discussion of passages such as the ones I have included above, students express strong, and pedagogically important, resistance to making such connections. In essence, they argue that as black men, Tea Cake and Jody Starks struggle with insecurities that cannot easily be equated with those of the socially privileged and culturally elite Mr. Ramsay, whose major concerns are about his intellectual contribution to a world controlled by men just like himself, and Charles Tansley, who although of a lower social class than his host—"He had not got any dress clothes" (85)—is nonetheless entering the elite world of academia. Students are usually most adamant about the distinction between Nanny, a former slave, and Mrs. Ramsay, a middle-class Victorian wife. Nanny, "used for a work-ox and a brood-sow" (15) and pained by the rape of her daughter (18), wants Janie to marry for protection from cruelty and hardship, whereas Mrs. Ramsay, "up[held]" and "sustain[ed]" by the "admirable fabric of the masculine intelligence" (106), wants her daughters to experience the "worth" of protecting men (6). Once these crucial distinctions are made, and they do invariably surface (usually without any direct prompting), students can address the intersections of ethnicity, class, and gender and their bearing on the portrayal of power in both novels.

Although the portrayal of power is not my focus here, I mention two points for instructors who might like to pursue such connections in their classes. First, students have found it most illuminating to their understanding of power in *Their Eyes Were Watching God* not only to discuss Joe Starks's blatant emulation of white power systems and attainment of status symbols (whereby Janie becomes an ornament whom he "classes off") but also to explore the more subtle ways in which Tea Cake is inscribed by ethnic hierarchies that indirectly cost him his life. He is a victim of the flood because he decides to leave the muck too late, refusing to take as his cue the Native Americans' departure from the land: "Dey don't always know. Indians don't know much uh' nothin', tuh tell de truth. Else dey'd own dis country still. De white folks ain't gone nowhere. Dey oughta know if it's dangerous" (148). Second, in *To the Lighthouse*, we discuss how Mrs. Ramsay's desire for social change—"she ruminated the other problem, of rich and poor, and the things she saw with her own eyes [. . .] when she visited this widow, or that struggling wife" (9)—is incompatible with her desire for her daughters to continue her protection of the men who uphold capitalism and imperialism (6).

After we discuss some of the difficulties that arise from equating characters' external and internal struggles in both novels, students are more open to considering how Woolf's and Hurston's depictions of female consciousness challenge the more traditional ways of knowing and seeing also inscribed in the novels. Unlike Mr. Ramsay who wants to progress to "R" in his object-subject study of inanimate objects, Mrs. Ramsay approaches the mystery of phenomena by entering into inanimate objects: "It was odd, she thought, how if one was alone, one leant to inanimate things; trees, streams, flowers; felt they expressed one; felt they became one; felt they knew one, in a sense were one [. . .]" (63). Janie's consciousness is similarly drawn toward such communion with a pear tree—a communion "desecrated" (13) by Logan Killicks and later by Joe Starks because they, too, are confined by the subject-object nature of reality and hence make Janie another commodity among their possessions (see Davies). The pear tree's first bloom beckons Janie, calling her "to come and gaze on a mystery" (10). But Janie's gaze does not keep the bloom in the object position, for her identity, like Mrs. Ramsay's, merges with the thing she observes: the vision of the blossom, its "singing" and "breathing out smell [. . .] connected itself with other vaguely felt matters that had struck her outside observation and buried themselves in her flesh" (10). And like Mrs. Ramsay, Janie uses the metaphor of a growing tree to embody her own growth and pain: "Janie saw her life like a great tree in leaf with the things suffered, things enjoyed, things done and undone" (8). Mrs. Ramsay comes upon a similar image, which expresses "quite easily and naturally what had been in her mind the whole evening while she said different things": "And all the lives we ever lived and all the lives to be are full of trees and changing leaves" (111, 110).

Lily Briscoe uses the tree image to represent her artistic vision when confronted with self-doubt at Mrs. Ramsay's dinner party: "In a flash she saw her picture, and thought, Yes, I shall put the tree further in the middle [. . .]. She took up the salt cellar and put it down again on a flower in pattern in the table-cloth, so as to remind herself to move the tree" (84–85). Although Woolf does not name the kind of tree Lily envisions, it is likely the pear tree that engrossed Lily early in the novel. Ironically, both Lily and Janie are contemplating a pear tree when we first become aware of their vision-making or vision-absorbing consciousnesses. Perhaps Woolf and Hurston offer us an alternative narrative to the Garden of Eden's apple tree, in which a woman's quest for knowledge leads to damnation. (Another female modernist, Katherine Mansfield, also uses a pear tree in her short story "Bliss" as a symbol of a woman's quest for self-knowledge and self-articulation.) In Woolf's evocation of the pear tree as a tree of knowledge, patriarchal philosophy, not sensual knowledge, is doomed: "with a painful effort of concentration," Lily has to turn her mind from the "sil-ver-bossed bark" or "fish-shaped leaves" of a pear tree to contemplate the "scrubbed kitchen table" of Mr. Ramsay's philosophical mind, "hung in effigy" in the branches of the tree (23, 25). Thinking about the contrast between William Bankes's mind and Mr. Ramsay's, Lily "felt herself transfixed by the intensity of her perception" (24). The state of being "transfixed" seems height-ened by the tree itself:

> Standing now, apparently transfixed, by the pear tree, impressions poured in upon her of those two men, and to follow her thought was like follow-ing a voice which speaks too quickly to be taken down by one's pencil, and the voice was her own voice saying without prompting undeniable, ever-lasting, contradictory things, so that even the fissures and humps on the bark of the pear tree were irrevocably fixed there for eternity.   (24)

When we contrast this passage with Janie's lush and sensual musings on the pear tree, students quickly point out that Janie's experience is erotic, whereas Lily's is essentially cerebral. On the surface, this is certainly true.

I have found, however, that when we reread passages of *To the Lighthouse* after reading *Their Eyes Were Watching God*, students can locate a sensuality in Woolf, especially in Lily Briscoe, that they had not been open to before (they see sensuality more easily in Mrs. Ramsay). I ask students to compare, for example, the desire for knowledge in Lily's musing about Mrs. Ramsay as a "dome-shaped hive," which she approaches "like a bee, drawn by some sweet-ness or sharpness in the air" (51), to Janie's thoughts about "a dustbearing bee" that "sink[s] into the sanctum of a bloom" (10). Similarly, approaching passages of *Their Eyes Were Watching God* after having read *To the Lighthouse* makes it easier for students to see the more philosophical aspects of Janie's quest. Most students are, for example, more willing to address larger questions of identity—not just those related to love and sexuality—in Janie's post–pear tree ponderings: "She was seeking confirmation of the voice and vision, and every-where she found and acknowledged answers. A personal answer for all other creations except herself. She felt an answer seeking her, but where? When? How?" (11). In summary, most students can better locate and appreciate the intersections of sensuality and intellect in both novels. Doing so may also help students challenge the myth of the Garden of Eden: that women's sensuality combined with the quest for knowledge can only lead to doom—a myth held dear by many male modernists.

Hurston's and Woolf's explorations of language and gender result in some remarkably similar expressions of female consciousness, but still, major differences exist between what Lily and Janie seek to articulate within themselves. That Janie sustains her vision through the oral tradition of telling her story to Pheoby whereas Lily paints her vision onto a canvas can be used to suggest to students, for example, the differences between African American "modernism" and British "modernism" in their traditions of preserving culture and telling narratives (see McKay).

It is crucial, after all, that students not oversimplify the connections they find, that they recall James Ramsay's revelation that "nothing was simply one thing" (186). But exploring connections between Woolf and Hurston involves them in the ongoing process of defining modernism and allows them to draw their own lines in an increasingly tangled web that connects voices never before heard together.

Compulsory Heterosexuality and the Lesbian Continuum in *To the Lighthouse*: A Women's Studies Approach

Vara Neverow

I teach *To the Lighthouse* in conjunction with Adrienne Rich's controversial landmark essay "Compulsory Heterosexuality and Lesbian Existence" in both a combined graduate and upper-level-undergraduate course in feminist literary theory and a sophomore-level women's literature class that fulfills my university's general education requirement in literary studies. The student population that I work with in these classes is mostly female, partly because students self-select into these classes and partly because Southern Connecticut State University, located in New Haven, is a former all-female normal school for teachers and has over seventy percent women in the undergraduate programs and more than seventy-five percent women in the graduate programs. Almost half the students are nontraditional; many are the first women in their families to go to college; most are from strict, old-world, Catholic backgrounds; and quite a few are single mothers.

Demographics often determine how my students react to Rich and Woolf. Most of my nontraditional, advanced undergraduate, and graduate students, both female and male, tend to be politically aware and generally progressive; some are even actively feminist; but most are still subtly homophobic. Predictably, my traditional-age undergraduates of both sexes tend to be politically naive and socially sheltered and thus are comparatively conservative in their beliefs. They find feminist ideas intellectually and emotionally threatening yet exciting. And it is safe to say that the majority of my sophomore-level students are either inadvertently or overtly homophobic. Consequently, the topics covered in my women's studies courses generate a significant degree of anxiety at both the advanced and the sophomore levels.

Since both classes are relatively small, ranging from fifteen to a maximum of thirty-five students, I use an instructional style that relies heavily on student-led discussion to defuse some of this anxiety. This discussion process, from which I always derive fresh insights and perspectives, depends on students' response journal entries. They must complete an entry, which can be analytic, reflective, comparative, or even personal, for every class session. These written responses (250 words for undergraduates and 500 words for graduate students) serve several functions. First, they generate engaged discussion. Further, they ensure that students stay current with their assignments (the shame factor of peer pressure significantly enhances accountability). They also provide an intellectual history, tracing the students' evolution as literary critics. Finally, the responses strengthen students' writing skills, provide strong interpretive and writerly models for other students to emulate, and function as study notes for longer papers and exams. While I occasionally affirm an insight or remark on a detail, I usually do not comment extensively or give these responses letter grades.

I use a deliberately student-centered discussion format. Students sit in a circle so that they can make eye contact and address each other by name (during the first few classes, students put their names on their desks). In each session, I ask a student volunteer to be the first to read or summarize his or her response journal entry. If no one volunteers, I wait—on occasion as long as several minutes—until someone offers to contribute. Then, after sharing his or her own response, the first student calls on another student. In most sessions, all students—even the most tongue-tied or recalcitrant—thus have a structured opportunity to speak. On occasion, I change the format for the sake of variety and ask a few students to make formal statements and then open the discussion up to the class. In every class, I provide integrative commentary on student responses and offer relevant background information, including summaries of critical interpretations and biographical data. The discussion format is maintained, however; after making a statement or raising a question, each student must call on another student to respond.

Because this procedure creates an environment of mutual respect and trust, many students feel authorized to talk openly about difficult subject matter. They learn to tolerate dissonance and move beyond binary thinking. During a semester or even a summer session, my students routinely move from timid reluctance to speak in public to enthusiastic exchange of ideas. I admit that sometimes my classes sound a bit like a TV talk show; students occasionally divulge personal information, and they often get so excited that everyone starts to talk at once. But I also confess I prefer such moments of mayhem to the conventional teaching model in which the professor is situated as the locus of knowledge.

Because most students become acclimated to challenging each other's views, expressions of homophobia are generally addressed by other students who advocate more tolerant attitudes, offer anecdotes about relatives and friends who are gay, or even identify themselves as lesbian or gay, sparing me the dismal responsibility of the politically correct classroom dictator. Also, since I integrate lesbian-authored and lesbian-centered material into the entire course, students have already encountered lesbian reality or same-sex desire when they get to Rich and Woolf.

From years of experience, I have discovered that students unfamiliar with feminist issues—whether at the graduate or undergraduate level—need a theoretical grasp of women's lived realities. Rich's essay offers students definitions, an analysis of patriarchy, and a perspective on women's complex relations to other women. Further, Rich's essay brings the interdisciplinary methodologies of women's studies to bear on Woolf's novel. But because Rich directly indicts patriarchal practices, her argument is usually perceived as male bashing and provokes a strong reaction in most students. In "Compulsory Heterosexuality and Lesbian Existence," Rich unflinchingly attacks patriarchal control of female sexuality and creativity and corrects the heterosexist tendency to "treat lesbian existence as a marginal or less 'natural' phenomenon, as mere 'sexual preference,' or as the mirror image of either heterosexual or male homosexual relations" (140). (Rich's argument for a lesbian continuum has been criticized by both heterosexist critics and a number of lesbian critics, including Zimmerman and Ferguson, Zita, and Addelson. Additional resources on lesbian studies include Anzaldúa; Cruikshank; de Lauretis; Faderman; Jay and Glasgow; Meese; B. Smith; Smith-Rosenberg; Stimpson, "Zero Degree"; and Wittig.)

Challenging "the assumption that 'most women are innately heterosexual'" (156), Rich argues that lesbianism is women's natural tendency and that heterosexuality is a learned behavior. Further, she maintains that "heterosexuality [. . .] needs to be recognized and studied as a *political institution*" (145) and identifies how compulsory heterosexuality is enforced. As Rich establishes, sexual violence and sexist abuse of women, whether manifested as battery, rape, incest, exploitation, harassment, or intimidation, effectively ensures female compliance with male dominance and guarantees individual men what Judith Lewis Herman calls the "right to initiate and consummate sexual relations with subordinate women [. . .], a jealously guarded male prerogative, guaranteed by the explicit or tacit consent of all men" (qtd. in DeSalvo, *Woolf* 9; see also Barry; French; Griffin; Herman; and MacKinnon).

"Compulsory Heterosexuality and Lesbian Existence" gives my students a sophisticated if radical interpretive strategy for reading Woolf's representation of women's lives in *To the Lighthouse* (see also Swanson). Seeing the novel through the lens of Rich's argument, they independently trace the patterns of male dominance in it and recognize the homoerotic implications of what Woolf calls "those unrecorded gestures, those unsaid or half-said words, which form themselves [. . .] when women are alone" (*Room* 84).

Several students from my feminist literary theory class have documented both the violent enforcement of compulsory heterosexuality and the sweet camaraderie of the lesbian continuum in *To the Lighthouse*. Rather than see Mrs. Ramsay solely from the heterosexist perspective of matrimonial bliss and maternal triumph, they examine how she has been coerced into complying with the heterosexual mandate. For example, Rich's claim that the "idealization of heterosexual romance" is a manifestation of obligatory heterosexuality (148) radically alters the inflection of Mrs. Ramsay's obsessive matchmaking. As my former student Gail E. Gray has pointed out, Mrs. Ramsay both "enables" (in the codependent sense) and enforces compulsory heterosexuality when she manipulates Minta and Paul into marrying; when she defines true womanhood in terms of wifehood, motherhood, and physical beauty; and when she caters to the emotional neediness of men (see also Lilienfeld, "Like a Lion").

Donna Risolo, another former student, in "Mrs. Ramsay: Victim of Compulsory Heterosexuality," observes that Mrs. Ramsay is so ideologically committed to compulsory heterosexuality that she consciously refuses to scrutinize her own marriage: "But for her own part she would never for a single second regret her decision, evade difficulties, or slur over duties" (6; see also Risolo, "Outing"; Lilienfeld, "Flesh and Blood" 170). Risolo also notes the sinister overtones of the passage where Mrs. Ramsay, thinking of her marriage in the context of her matchmaking, reflects: "whatever she might feel about her own transaction, she had had experiences which need not happen to every one (she did not name them to herself); she was driven on, too quickly she knew, almost as if it were an escape for her too, to say that people must marry; people must have children" (60). This passage seems to allude to some severe but occluded psychological damage that Mrs. Ramsay has sustained. As Risolo indicates, the parenthetical repression of those unnamed "experiences which need not happen to every one" strongly suggests some secret horror, whether incest, sexual abuse, or marital rape, because survivors are often compulsively "driven on [. . .] as if it were an escape" in various compensatory activities (DeSalvo, *Woolf* 10).

As my former student Veronica Hendrick notes, Lily Briscoe's shame at her inability to respond to Mr. Ramsay's demands for sympathy is also linked to the ideology of compulsory heterosexuality. Lily regards herself as "not a woman, but a peevish, ill-tempered, dried-up old maid, presumably" (151) and, thus, a sexual failure, for she cannot solace Mr. Ramsay when he succumbs to "one of those moments when an enormous *need* urged him, without being conscious what it was, to approach any woman, to *force* them, he did not care how, his need was so great, to give him what he wanted: sympathy" (150–51; my emphasis).

Meeting this male demand for sympathy is debilitating for women, but Lily does not entirely recognize her right to deny that demand. Instead, she flagellates herself for what she has been trained to perceive as inadequacy. Gail E. Gray makes clear that Woolf views the sexual intensity of Mr. Ramsay's "need" as normative male behavior. Thus, Gray connects Charles Tansley's "urgently" desiring "a chance of asserting himself" (90) to Kathleen Barry's research about "the mystique of the overpowering, all-conquering male sex drive, the penis-with-a-life-of-its-own, [. . .] rooted in the law of male sex-right to women" (qtd. in Rich 153). In the novel, of course, Lily does "the usual trick" for Charles Tansley (92) and "help[s] him to relieve himself" (91) because she wants to please her beloved Mrs. Ramsay.

Rich observes that "the lie of compulsory female heterosexuality [. . .] keeps [. . .] women psychologically trapped, trying to fit mind, spirit, and sexuality into a prescribed script" that includes catering to male demands at the expense of their own needs and desires. This lie "pulls on the energy of such women" (165); it ultimately kills Mrs. Ramsay, who unstintingly satisfies Mr. Ramsay's demands but then is completely exhausted (38). As Lily Briscoe indicates, "Giving, giving, giving, she had died" (149). Similarly, Rich asserts that "the institutions of marriage and motherhood" are often a punishing form of "unpaid production" and exploited labor (147).

Compulsory heterosexuality not only forces women to sacrifice themselves, it also denies their creativity and thwarts their autonomy. Charles Tansley repeatedly asserts that women can neither write nor paint; thus he attempts to

"cramp [women's] creativeness," in Kathleen Gough's phrase, and ensure patriarchal dominance over women's desire to achieve self-realization independent
of men (qtd. in Rich 147–48). Rich refers to *A Room of One's Own* as an indict-
ment of this male tendency to obstruct women's creativity and dismiss their
achievements (148n19). Lily, occasionally seeing herself as a sexual failure, also
fears that she is an artistic failure. However, she is stubborn enough to perse-
vere and achieve her vision while Mrs. Ramsay is frustrated (and cruelly
mocked [103]) in her desire to "become what with her untrained mind she
greatly admired, an investigator, elucidating the social problem" (9). Many of
my students find this male ridicule of female achievement both frighteningly
familiar and infuriating.

Autonomy extends beyond social interaction to sexual self-determination. As
several students have noted, the novel illustrates not only same-sex desire but
also female autoeroticism. Mrs. Ramsay's meditative, self-absorbed reverie on
the dark wedge and the lighthouse stroke (65) verges on the solitary bliss of
masturbation and thus establishes her secret capacity for an autonomous sexual
life (see Bennett, "Female Sexual Imagery" 237–39; Koedt; McKenna). This
important episode counterbalances Mrs. Ramsay's draining encounter with her
husband when she dutifully endures the blows of "the arid scimitar of the male,
which smote mercilessly, again and again, demanding sympathy" (38).

In my sophomore literature class, I use an introductory women's studies text
in conjunction with the literary texts I assign because most of the students have
only limited theoretical knowledge of women's social and cultural circumstances
and have never been encouraged to think much about their own situations.
Feminist Frontiers IV, edited by Laurel Richardson, Verta Taylor, and Nancy
Whittier, includes Rich's essay on the lesbian continuum and is effective
because it alternates between essential but challenging scholarly material on
women's status in society and more accessible pieces (including poems, editori-
als, and interviews) that many students find stimulating and thought provoking.

For many of the sophomores, this class is their first and often only exposure
to literary and women's studies at the college level; as a result, their first
encounters with Rich and Woolf, authors difficult to read and interpret, are
frequently confusing. Students often resist Rich's essay because of her scholarly apparatus, her complexity, and her argument's radical implications (many
don't even get the point initially, but when they do, they are often outraged).
The response journal entries focus these ideas, ground the class discussion, and
provide an outlet for both emotional and intellectual reactions.

It is not easy for my students to assimilate Rich. Not only does Rich argue
disturbingly against the patriarchy's narrowly clinical definitions of "lesbian,"
she also contends that female friendship has been falsely divided from the
erotic realm. Rich states in a crucial passage:

> I mean the term lesbian continuum to include a range [. . .] of woman-
> identified experience; not simply the fact that a woman has had or con-

sciously desired genital sexual experience with another woman. If we expand it to embrace many more forms of primary intensity between and among women, [. . .] we begin to grasp breadths of female history and psychology which have lain out of reach as a consequence of limited, mostly clinical, definitions of "lesbianism."   (156–57)

Rich's argument verges on treating lesbianism as metaphor (see Stimpson, "Afterword" 380) since she extends the lesbian continuum far beyond erotic orientation to include all homosocial bonding among women. Thus, most of my female students at first recoil at being told they are innately lesbian and that all their women-to-women relationships are inherently lesbian. (Also, Rich's willingness to blame men for women's oppression angers them, and these issues have to be worked through in class discussion and the responses.)

Woolf is even more opaque than Rich is to most of my sophomore-level students. As we work to become comfortable with Woolf's indirect and associative style and her unannounced transitions from one center of consciousness to another, however, most recognize the complexity with which Woolf represents women's interactions with one another. Ideologically programmed to focus their attention primarily on men's relations to one another and on women's relations to men, these inexperienced readers have learned, thanks to Rich's article, to value women's connections with other women. Rich thus offsets the shock of the modern and gives Woolf's difficult experimental text a basis in reality.

Woolf herself knew that patriarchal society deliberately overlooks woman-to-woman intimacy, for, in *A Room of One's Own*, she notes that her auditors might be shocked to realize that "Chloe liked Olivia" (82), a relationship Rich explicitly locates in the lesbian continuum in her article (159; see also J. Marcus "Sapphistry" and "Sapphistory"). Indeed, all Woolf's novels depict intimate, potentially erotic relationships between female characters (see the works by Cramer and Olano for bibliographic information; see Barrett and Cramer, *Lesbian Readings*, for readings). When Woolf chides her listeners for their supposedly stunned reaction, her knowing tone suggests that they all clearly understand the issues at stake: "Do not start. Do not blush. Let us admit in the privacy of our own society that these things sometimes happen. Sometimes women do like women" (*Room* 82). Rich helps students reading *To the Lighthouse* to recognize, for example, that Lily Briscoe likes Mrs. Ramsay and Mrs. Ramsay reciprocates (see Risolo, "Outing").

Further, a few students who have read Rich see Mrs. Ramsay's daughters as innately protolesbian in their relations to other women and in their indifference to men: they have "sport[ed] with infidel ideas [. . .] of a life [. . .] in Paris, perhaps; a wilder life, not always taking care of some man or other" (6–7; see also Benstock). As my former student Mary Robicheau has noted, Nancy Ramsay is apparently drawn to Minta, while Cam, wild and fierce and free, will not give her *flowers* to Mr. Bankes (see Bennett's extensive work on clitoral imagery, especially flowers, in women's writing) and is terrified of the highly sexualized boar's skull. In the novel's final part, Nancy, an unwilling stand-in for her deceased mother, is responsible for packing the supplies for the trip; she asks "in a queer half dazed, half desperate way, 'What does one send to the Lighthouse?' as if she were forcing herself to do what she despaired of ever being able to do" (146). She is resisting, but will she succeed? Can she maintain her "queer" distance from male-dictated womanly duties? Cam, although she gets to go to the lighthouse, struggles desperately not to succumb to her father's seduction when he determines to "make her smile" and thus compel her to act as a surrogate for his dead wife (166–70).

Like Nancy and Cam, Minta rebels—and like Lily she may just possibly escape the obligations of heterosexuality. Mrs. Ramsay (who has been accused by at least one mother of "robbing her of her daughter's affections" [57]) describes Minta as "this incongruous daughter" and a "tomboy" (57), thus acknowledging that Minta only partially conforms to the doctrines of compulsory heterosexuality. Andrew intriguingly depicts Minta as an athletic young woman, "rather a good walker" who "wore more sensible clothes than most women" and "would jump straight into a stream and flounder across." As he observes, "She seemed to be afraid of nothing—except bulls" (74). According to Lily, Minta "never gave herself away. [. . .] She was far too conscious, far too wary" (174). Though seemingly lesbian-identified by her sensible clothing, her fear of bulls (!), her "business-like" way of handing her estranged husband the tools to repair the car, and her deep gratitude toward the woman that Paul "had taken up with" (174), Minta's sexuality remains indefinite but suggestive (Neverow-Turk).

Rich's "Compulsory Heterosexuality and Lesbian Existence" states explicitly what Woolf could refer to only obliquely. The article helps decode Woolf's deliberately cryptic discussion of women's intimate relationships and their resistance to male domination. Unlike Radclyffe Hall, whose novel *The Well of Loneliness* provoked a scandalous obscenity trial, Woolf chose to conceal her references to lesbian desire and, lest she be punished for being too strident, elected to "[t]ell all the Truth but tell it slant," understating her anger at male manipulation and intimidation. When linked together, "Compulsory Heterosexuality and Lesbian Existence" and *To the Lighthouse* powerfully endorse feminist and lesbian thought. These texts encourage homophobic students to rethink their positions, nonhomophobic students to be more outspoken, and lesbian and gay students to accept themselves and the validity of their sexuality, identity, and experiences. Even more important, however, students encounter the intensity of intertextual literary interpretation and realize how powerfully even radically disparate works can echo, inform, and redefine each other.

NOTES ON CONTRIBUTORS

Eileen Barrett is professor of English at California State University, Hayward. She has coedited *American Women Writers: Diverse Voices in Prose since 1845*, two volumes of *Selected Papers* for the Annual Conference on Virginia Woolf, and *Virginia Woolf: Lesbian Readings*.

Nancy Topping Bazin, Eminent Scholar and Professor Emeritus of English at Old Dominican University, is a coeditor of *Conversations with Nadine Gordimer*, the author of *Virginia Woolf and the Androgynous Vision*, a contributor on Woolf to volumes by Mark Hussey and Branimir M. Rieger, and the author of articles about Margaret Atwood, Anita Desai, Edith Wharton, Marge Piercy, Doris Lessing, Buchi Emecheta, Bessie Head, Athol Fugard, and Nadine Gordimer.

Edward Bishop, professor at the University of Alberta, has edited *Jacob's Room: The Holograph Draft* and compiled *A Virginia Woolf Chronology* and the Bloomsbury Group volume for the *Dictionary of Literary Biography*. His other publications include *Virginia Woolf* and essays on dust jackets, bookstores, and motorcycles. He is working on a book about the material production of modernism.

Bonnie Braendlin, associate professor of English at Florida State University, is writing a book about the 1970s American feminist *Bildungsroman*. She is the editor of *Cultural Power / Cultural Literacy* and the author of essays on Alice Walker, Mrs. Ramsay and menopause, *The Joy Luck Club*, and Jennie Kilpatrick Hoover, an 1893 student rebel in the West.

Pamela L. Caughie teaches at Loyola University, Chicago, where she is professor of English and director of women's studies. She is the author of *Virginia Woolf and Postmodernism* and *Passing and Pedagogy* and the editor of *Virginia Woolf in the Age of Mechanical Reproduction*. She has also contributed essays to several volumes, including *Rereading the New: A Backward Glance at Modernism* and *Approaches to Teaching the Works of D. H. Lawrence*.

Gerald T. Cobb is chair of the English department at Seattle University. Current projects include a book on integrating service learning into literature and composition courses and a book on sacred space in architecture (with the architect Steven Holl of New York City). As a Jesuit priest, he has done parish work with families in the Pacific Northwest.

Susan Currier, professor of English and associate dean of the College of Liberal Arts at California Polytechnic State University, San Luis Obispo, has contributed an essay on Virginia Woolf and Margaret Drabble to *Analyzing the Different Voice: Feminist Psychological Theory and Literary Texts* and has written essays on Maxine Hong Kingston, Pamela Hansford Johnson, Susan Cheever, Cynthia Ozick, and Fannie Hurst for the *Dictionary of Literary Biography*.

Beth Rigel Daugherty teaches English at Otterbein College and has served as chair of its general education core curriculum, integrative studies. She has written essays on

To the Lighthouse and *The Common Reader* and transcribed the draft of "How Should One Read a Book?" She is working on a book about Woolf's essays as education.

Laura Davis is associate provost for planning and academic resource management at Kent State University. With Jeanette McVicker, she edited two *Selected Papers* volumes, *Virginia Woolf and Her Influences* and *Virginia Woolf and Communities*. She is also the editor of *Conrad's Century: The Past and Future Splendour*.

Louise DeSalvo is professor of English and creative writing at Hunter College, City University of New York. She is the author of *Virginia Woolf's First Voyage: A Novel in the Making; Conceived with Malice; Virginia Woolf's Melymbrosia; Virginia Woolf: The Impact of Childhood Sexual Abuse on Her Life and Work*; three memoirs, *Vertigo, Breathless*, and *Adultery*; and a book about creativity, *Writing as a Way of Healing*.

Marcia McClintock Folsom, professor of literature at Wheelock College, has also served as chair of arts and sciences, vice president for academic affairs, and director of an NEH faculty development project. She edited *Approaches to Teaching Austen's* Pride and Prejudice and is editing *Approaches to Teaching Austen's* Emma.

Mark Hussey is professor of English at Pace University, New York, and founding editor of *Woolf Studies Annual*. He has written several articles and books on Virginia Woolf, including *Virginia Woolf A to Z* and *The Singing of the Real World*. He has also edited *Virginia Woolf and War* and *Major Authors on CD-ROM: Virginia Woolf*.

Patricia Laurence is professor of English at City College, City University of New York, and a research associate at the Center for the Study of Women and Society at the Graduate Center, City University of New York. Her publications include *The Reading of Silence: Virginia Woolf in the English Tradition*, several essays on Woolf, and the forthcoming *Conversations on a Scroll: Bloomsbury and China*.

Karen L. Levenback taught at George Washington University. She is the author of articles and reviews on Woolf and her circle in *English Literature in Transition, Modern Age, Virginia Woolf Miscellany*, and *Woolf Studies Annual*, and she has essays in *Anne Tyler as Novelist* and *Virginia Woolf and War*. She has also written *Virginia Woolf and the Great War*.

Toni A. H. McNaron, professor of English and women's studies at the University of Minnesota, Twin Cities, has written *Poisoned Ivy: Lesbian and Gay Academics Confronting Homophobia* and coedited *New Lesbian Studies: Into the Twenty-First Century*. She is also the author of several articles on Woolf, a memoir (*I Dwell in Possibility*), and two other books, *Voices in the Night: Women Speaking about Incest* and *The Sister Bond: A Feminist View of a Timeless Connection*.

Jeanette McVicker teaches at the State University College of New York, Fredonia, where she is associate professor of English and former director of women's studies. She is a coeditor, with Laura Davis, of the *Selected Papers* from the seventh and eighth Annual Conferences on Virginia Woolf. Her most recent work is on general education.

Vara Neverow teaches at Southern Connecticut State University, where she is professor of English and feminist theory and co-coordinator of women's studies. She has coedited three volumes of *Selected Papers* for the Annual Conference on Virginia

Woolf, and she has written about the sources for the footnotes in *Three Guineas* and about Woolf and composition pedagogy.

Annette Oxindine is associate professor of English at Wright State University, where she teaches courses in literature, women's studies, and disability studies. She is the author of essays on Woolf's short fiction, *The Waves*, and *Between the Acts*.

Janis M. Paul is the director of the English Assessment Program at the University of Oklahoma and is the author of *The Victorian Heritage of Virginia Woolf: The External World in Her Novels*.

Mary Pinkerton is associate professor of English and associate dean of the College of Letters and Sciences at the University of Wisconsin, Whitewater. She is the author of essays on E. M. Forster, modernism, and pedagogy. In 1992, she received the David Saunders Award for Excellence in Teaching in the Humanities.

Annis Pratt, retired professor of English at the University of Wisconsin, Madison, has written *Archetypal Patterns in Women's Fiction* and *Dancing with Goddesses: Archetypes, Poetry, and Empowerment*. She has also completed a novel trilogy, *The Marshlanders*, and a memoir, *The Peripatetic Papers: The Travel Diaries of a Commuting Professor*.

Mary Beth Pringle is professor of English at Wright State University, where she teaches courses in modern and contemporary literature, women's studies, and writing and has won awards for teaching and service. She has written essays on the Ramsay home, Woolf and memoir, and popular literature and is currently writing a travel memoir.

Susan Yunis is Rose Warner Professor of Literature at the College of Saint Scholastica and director of the WhiteWater Writers' Workshop for high school students. She is working on a book about the narcissistic family system as it shapes young women, with a chapter on Virginia Woolf. She is also the author of essays on William Faulkner and George Herbert.

SURVEY PARTICIPANTS

The editors would like to thank the following people for their assistance in preparing this volume. These participants were generous with their time and enthusiasm, responding to the survey of approaches to teaching *To the Lighthouse*, talking to us on the phone, submitting supplemental materials, or contributing to the volume in a variety of ways. We also extend a special thank you to Rachel Stevens; Cynthia Tucker, of Memphis State University; and Bernadette Vetter, of the Center for Learning in Rocky River, Ohio.

Christopher Ames, *Agnes Scott College*
Eileen Barrett, *California State University, Hayward*
Nancy Topping Bazin, Emeritus, *Old Dominion University*
Thomas C. Beattie, *Hartwick College*
Edward Bishop, *University of Alberta*
Bonnie Braendlin, *Florida State University*
Suzanne Bunkers, *Minnesota State University*
Elizabeth K. Cabot, *Boston University*
Pamela L. Caughie, *Loyola University, Chicago*
Mary Ann Caws, *Graduate Center, City University of New York*
Gerald T. Cobb, *Seattle University*
Patricia Cramer, *University of Connecticut, Stamford*
Sara E. Culver, *Grand Valley State University*
Susan Currier, *California Polytechnic State University, San Luis Obispo*
Elizabeth R. Curry, *Slippery Rock University of Pennsylvania*
Ulysses D'Aquila, *City College of San Francisco*
Laura Davis, *Kent State University, Kent*
Louise DeSalvo, *Hunter College, City University of New York*
Susan Dick, *Queen's University*
Linda Dittmar, *University of Massachusetts, Boston*
Sandra M. Donaldson, *University of North Dakota*
Terrence Doody, *Rice University*
Langdon Elsbree, *Claremont McKenna College*
Bonnie Blumenthal Finkelstein, *Montgomery County Community College, PA*
Marcia McClintock Folsom, *Wheelock College*
Ralph Freedman, Emeritus, *Princeton University*
Elaine Ginsberg, *West Virginia University, Morgantown*
James Hafley, Emeritus, *Saint John's University, Jamaica*
Evelyn Harris Haller, *Doane College*
Leslie Hankins, *Cornell College*
G. Held, *Queens College, City University of New York*
Katherine Hill-Miller, *Long Island University, C. W. Post Campus*
Edward A. Hungerford, Emeritus, *Southern Oregon University*
Mark Hussey, *Pace University, New York*
Sally Jacobsen, *Northern Kentucky University*

Edward T. Jones, *York College, PA*
Marty Knepper, *Morningside College*
Patricia Laurence, *City College, City University of New York*
Karen L. Levenback, *George Washington University*
Randy Malamud, *Georgia State University*
Thomas Matro, *Rutgers University, New Brunswick*
Pamela R. Matthews, *Texas A&M University, College Station*
James H. McGavran, Jr., *University of North Carolina, Charlotte*
Toni A. H. McNaron, *University of Minnesota, Twin Cities*
Jeanette McVicker, *State University College of New York, Fredonia*
Mark Muggli, *Luther College*
Gwen Neary, *Santa Rosa Junior College, CA*
Vara Neverow, *Southern Connecticut State University*
Luisanna Paggiaro, *Liceo Scientifico F. Buonarroti, Pisa, Italy*
Irene Papoulis, *Trinity College, CT*
Janis M. Paul, *University of Oklahoma*
Mary Pinkerton, *University of Wisconsin, Whitewater*
Annis Pratt, Emeritus, *University of Wisconsin, Madison*
Panthea Reid, *Louisiana State University, Baton Rouge*
Don Rice, *Feather River College, CA*
Harvena Richter, Emeritus, *University of New Mexico, Albuquerque*
Barbara Rigney, *Ohio State University, Columbus*
Ellen Rosenman, *University of Kentucky*
Lucio Ruotolo, Retired, *Stanford University*
Margaret K. Schramm, *Hartwick College*
Rita Shubb, *Tarzana, CA*
Elizabeth Steele, Emeritus, *University of Toledo*
Ruth Z. Temple, Emeritus, *Brooklyn College, City University of New York*
Gary Thompson, *Saginaw Valley State University*
Virginia Tiger, *Rutgers University, Newark*
Linda Ware, *University of Wisconsin, Marathon County*
Roberta White, *Centre College*
Lydia Reineck Wilburn, *Pepperdine University*
Susan Yunis, *College of Saint Scholastica*

WORKS CITED

Writings of Virginia Woolf

Please note: The edition of *To the Lighthouse* cited in contributors' essays is the 1989 Harvest-Harcourt paperback edition (from the 1927 first American edition), with a foreword by Eudora Welty.

Between the Acts. New York: Harcourt, 1941.

"The Cinema." *Collected Essays* 2: 268–72.

Collected Essays. 4 vols. New York: Harcourt, 1967.

The Common Reader. 1925. Ed. Andrew McNeillie. Annotated ed. San Diego: Harcourt, 1984.

The Complete Shorter Fiction of Virginia Woolf. Ed. Susan Dick. Rev. ed. New York: Harcourt, 1989.

The Diary of Virginia Woolf. Ed. Anne Olivier Bell. 5 vols. New York: Harcourt, 1977–84.

The Essays of Virginia Woolf. Ed. Andrew McNeillie. 4 vols. to date. Vols. 1–3: New York: Harcourt, 1986–88; Vol. 4: London: Hogarth, 1994.

"How Should One Read a Book?" *Second Common Reader* 258–70.

"Impassioned Prose." *Collected Essays* 1: 165–72.

Jacob's Room. 1922. New York: Harcourt, 1978.

"Kew Gardens." *Complete Shorter Fiction* 90–95.

"The Leaning Tower." *Collected Essays* 2: 162–81.

The Letters of Virginia Woolf. Ed. Nigel Nicolson and Joanne Trautmann. 6 vols. New York: Harcourt, 1975–80.

"The Mark on the Wall." *Complete Shorter Fiction* 83–89.

"Modern Fiction." *Collected Essays* 2: 103–10.

Moments of Being. Ed. Jeanne Schulkind. 2nd ed. New York: Harcourt, 1985.

"Mr. Bennett and Mrs. Brown." *Collected Essays* 1: 319–37.

Mrs. Dalloway. 1925. New York: Harcourt, 1990.

"The Narrow Bridge of Art." *Collected Essays* 2: 218–29.

Night and Day. 1920. New York: Harcourt, 1948.

Orlando. 1928. New York: Harcourt, 1956.

The Pargiters: The Novel-Essay Portion of The Years. Ed. Mitchell A. Leaska. New York: Harcourt, 1977.

A Passionate Apprentice: The Early Journals, 1897–1909. Ed. Mitchell A. Leaska. San Diego: Harcourt, 1990.

"Professions for Women." *Collected Essays* 2: 284–89.

A Room of One's Own. 1929. New York: Harcourt, 1989.

The Second Common Reader. 1932. Ed. Andrew McNeillie. Annotated ed. San Diego: Harcourt, 1986.

"A Sketch of the Past." *Moments* 61–159.

Three Guineas. 1938. New York: Harcourt, 1966.

To the Lighthouse. 1927. New York: Harcourt, 1955.

To the Lighthouse. 1927. Introd. Quentin Bell. London: Vintage, 1992.

To the Lighthouse. 1927. Ed. Julia Briggs. New York: Everyman-Knopf, 1991.

To the Lighthouse. 1927. Ed. Susan Dick. Shakespeare Head Press ed. Oxford: Black-well, 1992.

To the Lighthouse. 1927. Ed. Margaret Drabble. Oxford: Oxford UP, 1992.

To the Lighthouse. 1927. Ed. Sandra Kemp. English Texts. London: Routledge, 1994.

To the Lighthouse. 1927. Ed. Stella McNichol. London: Penguin, 1992.

To the Lighthouse. 1927. Foreword by Eudora Welty. New York: Harcourt, 1989.

To the Lighthouse: *The Original Holograph Draft*. Ed. Susan Dick. Toronto: U of Toronto P, 1982.

"An Unwritten Novel." *Complete Shorter Fiction* 112–21.

The Virginia Woolf Manuscripts: From the Henry W. and Albert A. Berg Collection at the New York Public Library. Microfilm. Woodbridge: Research Pubs. Intl., 1993.

The Virginia Woolf Reader. Ed. Mitchell A. Leaska. New York: Harcourt, 1984.

The Voyage Out. 1920. New York: Harcourt, 1948.

"The War from the Street." *Essays* 3: 3–4.

"War in the Village." *Essays* 2: 291–93.

The Waves. 1931. New York: Harcourt, 1978.

A Writer's Diary. Ed. Leonard Woolf. New York: Harvest, 1954.

The Years. 1937. New York: Harcourt, 1965.

Books and Articles

Abel, Elizabeth. "'Cam the Wicked': Woolf's Portrait of the Artist as Her Father's Daughter." J. Marcus, *Woolf and Bloomsbury* 170–94.

———. *Virginia Woolf and the Fictions of Psychoanalysis*. Chicago: U of Chicago P, 1989.

Abel, Elizabeth, and Emily K. Abel, eds. *The Signs Reader: Women, Gender, and Scholarship*. Chicago: U of Chicago P, 1983.

Abel, Elizabeth, Marianne Hirsch, and Elizabeth Langland, eds. *The Voyage In: Fictions of Female Development*. Hanover: UP of New England, 1983.

Abelove, Henry, Michèle Aina Barale, and David M. Halperin, eds. *The Lesbian and Gay Studies Reader*. New York: Routledge, 1993.

Abrams, M. H., gen. ed. *The Norton Anthology of English Literature*. 6th ed. Vol. 2. New York: Norton, 1993.

Albright, Daniel. *Personality and Impersonality: Lawrence, Woolf, and Mann*. Chicago: U of Chicago P, 1978.

Annan, Noel. *Leslie Stephen: The Godless Victorian*. New York: Random, 1984.

Anzaldúa, Gloria, ed. *Making Face, Making Soul*. San Francisco: Aunt Lute, 1991.

Ashcroft, Bill, Gareth Griffiths, and Helen Tiffin. *The Empire Writes Back: Theory and Practice in Post-colonial Literature*. London: Routledge, 1995.

———, eds. *The Post-colonial Studies Reader*. London: Routledge, 1995.

Auerbach, Erich. "The Brown Stocking." *Mimesis: The Representation of Reality in Western Literature*. Trans. Willard R. Trask. Princeton: Princeton UP, 1953. 525–53.

Auerbach, Nina. *Woman and the Demon: The Life of a Victorian Myth*. Cambridge: Harvard UP, 1982.

Bakhtin, Mikhail M. "Discourse in the Novel." *The Dialogic Imagination*. Ed. Michael Holquist. Trans. Caryl Emerson and Michael Holquist. Austin: U of Texas P, 1981. 259–422.

———. "Dostoevsky's Polyphonic Novel and Its Treatment in Critical Literature." *Problems of Dostoevsky's Poetics*. Trans. and ed. Caryl Emerson. Minneapolis: U of Minnesota P, 1984. 5–46.

Bal, Mieke. *Narratology: Introduction to the Theory of Narrative*. Trans. Christine van Boheemen. Toronto: U of Toronto P, 1985.

Barker, Francis, Peter Hulme, and Margaret Iverson, eds. *Postmodernism and the Rereading of Modernity*. Manchester: Manchester UP, 1992.

Barr, Tina. "Divine Politics: Virginia Woolf's Journey toward Eleusis in *To the Lighthouse*." *Boundary 2* 20.1 (1993): 125–45.

Barrett, Eileen, and Patricia Cramer, eds. *Re:Reading, Re:Writing, Re:Teaching Virginia Woolf: Selected Papers from the Fourth Annual Conference on Virginia Woolf*. New York: Pace UP, 1995.

———, eds. *Virginia Woolf: Lesbian Readings*. New York: New York UP, 1997.

Barry, Kathleen. *Female Sexual Slavery*. New York: New York UP, 1979.

Barzilai, Shuli. "The Politics of Quotation in *To the Lighthouse*: Mrs. Woolf Resites Mr. Tennyson and Mr. Cowper." *Literature and Psychology* 41.3 (1995): 22–43.

Batchelor, John. *Virginia Woolf: The Major Novels*. Cambridge: Cambridge UP, 1991.

Bateson, Mary Catherine. *Composing a Life*. New York: Plume-Penguin, 1990.

Bazin, Nancy Topping. *Virginia Woolf and the Androgynous Vision*. New Brunswick: Rutgers UP, 1973.

Beauvoir, Simone de. *The Second Sex*. 1949. Trans. H. M. Parshley. New York: Bantam, 1961.

Beebe, Maurice. "Criticism of Virginia Woolf: A Selected Checklist with an Index to Studies of Separate Works." *Modern Fiction Studies* 2 (1956): 36–45.

Beer, Gillian. "Hume, Stephen, and Elegy in *To the Lighthouse*." Beer, *Woolf* 29–47.

———. *Virginia Woolf: The Common Ground*. Edinburgh: Edinburgh UP, 1996.

Beja, Morris, ed. *Virginia Woolf: To the Lighthouse, A Casebook*. London: Macmillan, 1970.

Belenky, Mary Field, Blythe McVicker Clinchy, Nancy Rule Goldberger, and Jill Mattuck Tarule. *Women's Ways of Knowing: The Development of Self, Voice, and Mind*. New York: Basic, 1986.

Bell, Clive. *Art*. New York: Stokes, 1914.

Bell, Quentin. *Virginia Woolf: A Biography*. 2 vols. New York: Harcourt, 1972.

Beller, Thomas. "A Different Kind of Imperfection." *New Yorker* 11 Feb. 1991: 32–37.

Belsey, Catherine. *Critical Practice*. London: Methuen, 1980.

Benjamin, Jessica. *The Bonds of Love: Psychoanalysis, Feminism, and the Problem of Domination*. New York: Pantheon, 1988.

Bennett, Paula. "'Clitoral Clitoridectomy': Female Sexual Imagery and Feminist Psychoanalytical Theory." *Signs* 18 (1993): 235–59.

———. "The Mother's Part: Incest and Maternal Deprivation in Woolf and Morrison." *Narrating Mothers: Theorizing Maternal Subjectivities*. Ed. Brenda O. Daly and Maureen T. Reddy. Knoxville: U of Tennessee P, 1991. 123–38.

Benstock, Shari. *Women of the Left Bank: Paris, 1900–1940*. Austin: U of Texas P, 1986.

Bhabha, Homi K., ed. *Nation and Narration*. London: Routledge, 1990.

Bickman, Martin. "Active Learning in the University: An Inquiry into Inquiry." *On Teaching*. Ed. Mary Ann Shea. Boulder: Teaching Excellence Program, 1987. 31–66.

Bicknell, John. "Mr. Ramsay Was Young Once." J. Marcus, *Woolf and Bloomsbury* 52–67.

Blackstone, Bernard. *Virginia Woolf: A Commentary*. New York: Harcourt, 1949.

Bloom, Harold, ed. *Virginia Woolf's* To the Lighthouse. New York: Chelsea, 1988.

Blotner, Joseph. "Mythic Patterns in *To the Lighthouse*." *PMLA* 71 (1956): 547–62.

Bolen, Jean Shinoda. *Goddesses in Everywoman*. San Francisco: Harper, 1984.

Booth, Alison. *Greatness Engendered: George Eliot and Virginia Woolf*. Ithaca: Cornell UP, 1992.

Booth, Allyson. *Postcards from the Trenches: Negotiating the Space between Modernism and the First World War*. New York: Oxford UP, 1996.

Bourdieu, Pierre. *Distinction: A Social Critique of the Judgement of Taste*. Trans. Richard Nice. Cambridge: Harvard UP, 1984.

———. *The Field of Cultural Production: Essays on Art and Literature*. Ed. Randal Johnson. Cambridge, Eng.: Polity, 1993.

Bowlby, Rachel. *Feminist Destinations and Further Essays on Virginia Woolf*. Edinburgh: Edinburgh UP, 1997.

Bradbury, Malcolm, and James McFarlane, eds. *Modernism 1890–1930*. 1976. London: Penguin, 1991.

Branca, Patricia. *Women in Europe since 1750*. London: Croom, 1978.

Brantlinger, Patrick. "'The Bloomsbury Fraction' versus War and Empire." *Seeing Double: Revisioning Edwardian and Modernist Literature*. Ed. Carola M. Kaplan and Anne B. Simpson. New York: St. Martin's, 1996. 149–67.

Brett, Sally Alexander. "No, Mrs. Ramsay: Feminist Dilemma in *To the Lighthouse*." *Ball State University Forum* 19 (1978): 48–56.

Briggs, Julia. "Editing Woolf for the Nineties." *South Carolina Review* 29.1 (1996): 67–77.

———. "The Story So Far." *Virginia Woolf: Introductions to the Major Works*. Ed. Briggs. London: Virago, 1994. vii–xxxiii.

Brontë, Charlotte. *Jane Eyre*. Signet Classics ed. New York: NAL, 1960.

Buckley, Jerome Hamilton. *Season of Youth: The Bildungsroman from Dickens to Gold-ing*. Cambridge: Harvard UP, 1974.

Bussy, Dorothy. *Olivia*. 1949. New York: Arno, 1975.

Butler, Judith. "Contingent Foundations: Feminism and the Question of 'Postmod-ernism.'" *Feminists Theorize the Political*. Ed. Joan Scott and Butler. New York: Routledge, 1992. 3–21.

———. *Gender Trouble: Feminism and the Subversion of Identity*. New York: Rout-ledge, 1990.

Calinescu, Matei. *Five Faces of Modernity: Modernism, Avant-Garde, Decadence, Kitsch, Postmodernism*. Durham: Duke UP, 1987.

Cameron, Julia Margaret. *Victorian Photographs of Famous Men and Fair Women*. 1926. Introd. Virginia Woolf and Roger Fry. Ed. Tristram Powell. Boston: Godine, 1973.

Caramagno, Thomas C. *The Flight of the Mind: Virginia Woolf's Art and Manic-Depressive Illness*. Berkeley: U of California P, 1992.

Carter, Miranda. "A *Boeuf en Daube* for *To the Lighthouse*." *Charleston Magazine* 9 (1994): 50–53.

Caton, Hiram. *The Origin of Subjectivity: An Essay on Descartes*. New Haven: Yale UP, 1973.

Caughie, Pamela L. *Virginia Woolf and Postmodernism: Literature in Quest and Ques-tion of Itself*. Urbana: U of Illinois P, 1991.

———, ed. *Virginia Woolf in the Age of Mechanical Reproduction*. New York: Garland, 1999.

Caws, Mary Ann. *Women of Bloomsbury: Virginia, Vanessa, and Carrington*. New York: Routledge, 1990.

Chapman, Wayne K., ed. *Virginia Woolf International*. Spec. issue of *South Carolina Review* 29.1 (1996): 3–149.

Chapman, Wayne K., and Janet M. Manson, eds. *Women in the Milieu of Leonard and Virginia Woolf: Peace, Politics, and Education*. New York: Pace UP, 1998.

Chartier, Roger. "Texts, Printing, Readings." *The New Cultural History*. Ed. Lynn Hunt. Berkeley: U of California P, 1989. 154–75.

Chatman, Seymour. *Coming to Terms: The Rhetoric of Narrative in Fiction and Film*. Ithaca: Cornell UP, 1990.

———. "Narratological Empowerment." *Narrative* 1 (1993): 59–65.

———. *Reading Narrative Fiction*. New York: Macmillan, 1993.

———. *Story and Discourse: Narrative Structure in Fiction and Film*. Ithaca: Cornell UP, 1978.

Chernin, Kim. *In My Mother's House: A Daughter's Story*. New Haven: Ticknor, 1983.

Chipp, Herschel B., ed. *Theories of Modern Art: A Source Book by Artists and Critics*. Berkeley: U of California P, 1968.

Chodorow, Nancy. *The Reproduction of Mothering: Psychoanalysis and the Sociology of Gender*. Berkeley: U of California P, 1978.

Chopin, Kate. *The Awakening and Selected Stories*. Ed. and introd. Barbara H. Solomon. New York: Signet, 1976.

Christ, Carol P. *Diving Deep and Surfacing: Women Writers on Spiritual Quest*. Boston: Beacon, 1980.

Christian, Barbara. "Layered Rhythms: Virginia Woolf and Toni Morrison." *Modern Fiction Studies* 39 (1993): 483–500.

Clay, Jean, et al. *Impressionism*. Secaucus: Chartwell, 1973.

Cohan, Steven. "Why Mr. Ramsay Reads *The Antiquary*." *Women and Literature* 7.2 (1979): 14–24.

Cohn, Dorrit. "Narrated Monologue: Definition of a Fictional Style." *Comparative Literature* 28 (1966): 97–112.

———. *Transparent Minds: Narrative Modes for Presenting Consciousness in Fiction*. Princeton: Princeton UP, 1978.

Cohn, Ruby. "Art in *To the Lighthouse*." *Virginia Woolf: A Collection of Criticism*. Ed. Thomas S. W. Lewis. New York: McGraw, 1975. 63–72.

Cook, Blanche Weisen. "'Women Alone Stir My Imagination': Lesbianism and the Cultural Tradition." *Signs* 4 (1979): 718–39.

Copleston, Frederick. *Hobbes to Hume*. London: Burns, 1964. Vol. 5 of *A History of Philosophy*. 9 vols. 1961–75.

Cramer, Patricia. "Notes from Underground: Lesbian Ritual in the Writings of Virginia Woolf." Hussey and Neverow-Turk 187–88.

Cross, W. E. "The Thomas and Cross Models of Psychological Nigrescence: A Review." *Journal of Black Psychology* 5 (1978): 13–31.

Cruikshank, Margaret. *Lesbian Studies: Present and Future*. Old Westbury: Feminist, 1982.

Cuddy-Keane, Melba, Natasha Aleksiuto, Kay Li, Morgan Love, Chris Rose, and Andrea Williams. "The Heteroglossia of History, Part One: The Car." *Virginia Woolf: Texts and Contexts: Selected Papers from the Fifth Annual Conference on Virginia Woolf*. Ed. Beth Rigel Daugherty and Eileen Barrett. New York: Pace UP, 1996. 71–80.

Daiches, David. *Virginia Woolf*. 1942. New York: New Directions, 1963.

Daly, Mary. *Beyond God the Father: Toward a Philosophy of Women's Liberation*. Boston: Beacon, 1973.

Darnton, Robert. "What Is the History of Books?" *Books and Society in History: Papers of the Association of College and Research Libraries, Rare Books, and Manuscripts Preconference, 24–28 June, 1980, Boston, Massachusetts*. Ed. Kenneth E. Carpenter. New York: Bowker, 1983. 3–26.

Daugherty, Beth Rigel. "Teaching *Mrs. Dalloway* and *Praisesong for the Widow* as a Pair." *Virginia Woolf and the Arts: Selected Papers from the Sixth Annual Conference on Virginia Woolf*. Ed. Diane Filby Gillespie and Leslie K. Hankins. New York: Pace UP, 1997. 175–82.

———. "'There She Sat': The Power of the Feminist Imagination in *To the Lighthouse*." *Twentieth Century Literature* 37 (1991): 289–308.

———. "Virginia Woolf Teaching / Virginia Woolf Learning: Morley College and the Common Reader." Wussow, *New Essays* 61–77.

Davies, Sharon. "Free Mules, Talking Buzzards, and Cracked Plates: The Politics of Dislocation in *Their Eyes Were Watching God*." *PMLA* 108 (1993): 446–59.

Davis, Laura, and Jeanette McVicker, eds. *Virginia Woolf and Her Influences: Selected Papers from the Seventh Annual Conference on Virginia Woolf*. New York: Pace UP, 1998.

"Defence of the Realm Act." *Law Reports. The Public General Statutes*. Vols. 52–54, 56, 58. London: Eyre, 1915–16, 1919, 1921.

DeKoven, Marianne. "History as Suppressed Referent in Modernist Fiction." *ELH* 51 (1984): 137–52.

——. *Rich and Strange: Gender, History, Modernism*. Princeton: Princeton UP, 1991.

de Lauretis, Teresa. "Sexual Indifference and Lesbian Representation." *Theatre Journal* 40 (1988): 155–77.

DeSalvo, Louise. "Lighting the Cave: The Relationship between Vita Sackville-West and Virginia Woolf." *Signs* 8 (1982): 195–214.

——. *Virginia Woolf: The Impact of Childhood Sexual Abuse on Her Life and Work*. Boston: Beacon, 1989.

Dewey, John. *Democracy and Education*. New York: Macmillan, 1916.

DiBattista, Maria. *Virginia Woolf's Major Novels: The Fables of Anon*. New Haven: Yale UP, 1980.

Dobie, Kathleen. "This Is the Room That Class Built: The Structures of Sex and Class in *Jacob's Room*." J. Marcus, *Woolf and Bloomsbury* 195–207.

Doll, Mary Aswell. *To the Lighthouse and Back: Writings on Teaching and Living*. New York: Lang, 1995.

Donaldson, Sandra. "Where Does Q Leave Mr. Ramsay?" *Tulsa Studies in Women's Literature* 11 (1992): 329–36.

Downing, Christine. *The Goddess: Mythological Images of the Feminine*. New York: Crossroad, 1984.

Downing, Nancy E., and Kristin L. Roush. "From Passive Acceptance to Active Commitment: A Model of Feminist Development for Women." *Counseling Psychologist* 13 (1985): 695–708.

Doyle, Laura. "'These Emotions of the Body': Intercorporeal Narrative in *To the Lighthouse*." *Twentieth Century Literature* 40 (1994): 42–71.

Drabble, Margaret. "Virginia Woolf: A Personal Debt." *Virginia Woolf: A Collection of Critical Essays*. Ed. Margaret Homans. Englewood Cliffs: Prentice, 1993. 46–51.

Du Maurier, Daphne. *Vanishing Cornwall: The Spirit and History of Cornwall*. 1967. London: Penguin, 1972.

Dunn, Jane. *A Very Close Conspiracy: Vanessa Bell and Virginia Woolf*. Boston: Little, 1990.

DuPlessis, Rachel Blau. "Woolfenstein." *Breaking the Sequence: Women's Experimental Fiction*. Ed. Ellen G. Friedman and Miriam Fuchs. Princeton: Princeton UP, 1989. 99–114.

——. *Writing beyond the Ending: Narrative Strategies of Twentieth-Century Women Writers*. Bloomington: Indiana UP, 1985.

Dyhouse, Carol. *Feminism and the Family in England, 1880–1939*. New York: Blackwell, 1989.

Edel, Leon. *The Modern Psychological Novel, 1900-1950*. New York: Lippincott, 1955.

Eisenstein, Sergei. *Film Form: Essays in Film Theory*. 1949. Ed. and trans. Jay Leyda. San Diego: Harcourt, 1977.

Ellis, Sarah Stickney. "Characteristics of Husbands." *Strong-Minded Women and Other Lost Voices from Nineteenth-Century England*. Ed. Janet Horowitz Murray. New York: Pantheon, 1982. 124–27.

Ellmann, Richard, and Charles Feidelson, eds. *The Modern Tradition: Backgrounds of Modern Literature*. New York: Oxford UP, 1965.

Elton, Charles. "Luriana Lurilee." *Another World Than This*. Comp. Vita Sackville-West and Harold Nicolson. London: Joseph, 1946. 109.

Emery, Mary Lou. "'Robbed of Meaning': The Work at the Center of *To the Lighthouse*." *Modern Fiction Studies* 38 (1992): 217–34.

Ender, Evelyne. "Feminist Criticism in a Double Mirror: Reading Charlotte Brontë and Virginia Woolf." *Compar(a)ison: An International Journal of Comparative Literature* 1 (1993): 83–106.

Esch, Deborah. "'Think of a Kitchen Table': Hume, Woolf, and the Tradition of Example." *Literature as Philosophy / Philosophy as Literature*. Ed. Donald G. Marshall. Iowa City: U of Iowa P, 1987. 262–76.

Espinola, Judith. "Narrative Discourse in Virginia Woolf's *To the Lighthouse*." *Studies in Interpretation*. Ed. Esther M. Doyle and Virginia H. Floyd. Vol. 2. Amsterdam: Rodopi, 1977. 29–43.

Eysteinsson, Astradur. *The Concept of Modernism*. Ithaca: Cornell UP, 1990.

Faderman, Lillian. *Surpassing the Love of Men: Romantic Friendships and Love between Women from the Renaissance to the Present*. New York: Morrow, 1981.

Ferguson, Ann, Jacquelyn N. Zita, and Kathryn Pyne Addelson. "On 'Compulsory Heterosexuality and Lesbian Existence': Defining the Issues." *Feminist Theory: A Critique of Ideology*. Ed. Nannerl O. Keohane, Michelle Z. Rosaldo, and Barbara C. Gelpi. Chicago: U of Chicago P, 1982. 147–88.

Fisher, Jane. "The Seduction of the Father: Virginia Woolf and Leslie Stephen." *Women's Studies* 18 (1990): 31–48.

———. "'Silent as the Grave': Painting, Narrative, and the Reader in *Night and Day* and *To the Lighthouse*." Gillespie, *Muses* 90–109.

Fleishman, Avrom. "Woolf and McTaggart: An Interrogation of the Metaphysics in *To the Lighthouse*." *Fiction and the Ways of Knowing: Essays on British Novels*. Austin: U of Texas P, 1978. 163–78.

Flint, Kate. "Virginia Woolf and the General Strike." *Essays in Criticism* 36 (1986): 319–34.

Folsom, Marcia McClintock. "Gallant Red Brick and Plain China: Teaching *A Room of One's Own*." *College English* 45 (1983): 254–62.

Forster, E. M. *Aspects of the Novel*. New York: Harcourt, 1927.

Foucault, Michel. *The Foucault Reader*. Ed. Paul Rabinow. New York: Pantheon, 1984.

Fraiman, Susan. *Unbecoming Women: British Women Writers and the Novel of Development*. New York: Columbia UP, 1993.

Frank, Joseph. "Spatial Form in Modern Literature." *The Widening Gyre*. Bloomington: Indiana UP, 1963. 3–62.

Fraser, Kennedy. "Ornament and Silence." Rev. of *Virginia Woolf: The Impact of Childhood Sexual Abuse on Her Life and Work*, by Louise DeSalvo. *New Yorker* 6 Nov. 1989: 154–63.

Freedman, Ralph. *The Lyrical Novel: Studies in Hermann Hesse, André Gide, and Virginia Woolf*. Princeton: Princeton UP, 1963.

French, Marilyn. *The War against Women*. New York: Simon, 1992.

Freud, Sigmund. "Fifth Lecture." *Five Lectures on Psychoanalysis*. 1957. Trans. and ed. James Strachey. New York: Norton, 1977. 49–55.

———. "On Narcissism: An Introduction." *The Standard Edition of the Complete Psychological Works of Sigmund Freud*. Ed. James Strachey. Vol. 14. London: Hogarth, 1966. 73–102. 24 vols. 1966–74.

———. *The Psychopathology of Everyday Life*. 1901. New York: Mentor, 1951.

Friedman, Alan W., ed. *Forms of Modern British Fiction*. Austin: U of Texas P, 1975.

Friedman, Susan Stanford. "Geopolitical Literacy: Internationalizing Feminism at 'Home'—The Case of Virginia Woolf." *Mappings: Feminism and the Cultural Geographies of Encounter*. Princeton: Princeton UP, 1998. 108–31.

———. "Lyric Subversion of Narrative in Women's Writing: Virginia Woolf and the Tyranny of Plot." Phelan 162–85.

Fry, Roger. "An Essay in Aesthetics." Fry, *Vision* 16–38.

———. *Vision and Design*. 1920. Cleveland: Meridian, 1956.

Frye, Northrop. "The Four Forms of Fiction." *The Theory of the Novel*. Ed. Philip Stevick. New York: Macmillan, 1967. 31–43.

Fuderer, Laura Sue. "Criticism of Virginia Woolf from 1972 to December 1990: A Selected Checklist." *Modern Fiction Studies* 38 (1992): 303–42.

Fullbrook, Kate. *Free Women: Ethics and Aesthetics in Twentieth-Century Women's Fiction*. Philadelphia: Temple UP, 1990.

Fuss, Diana, ed. *Inside/Out: Lesbian Theories, Gay Theories*. New York: Routledge, 1991.

Fussell, Paul. *The Great War and Modern Memory*. New York: Oxford UP, 1975.

Gaggi, Silvio. *Modern/Postmodern: A Study in Twentieth-Century Art and Ideas*. Philadelphia: U of Pennsylvania P, 1989.

Gale, Matthew, and Chris Stephens. *Works in the Tate Gallery Collection and the Barbara Hepworth Museum, St. Ives*. London: Tate Gallery, 1999.

Genette, Gérard. *Narrative Discourse: An Essay in Method*. Ithaca: Cornell UP, 1980.

———. *Narrative Discourse Revisited*. Ithaca: Cornell UP, 1988.

Gibbs, Philip. *More That Must Be Told*. New York: Harper, 1921.

———. *Now It Can Be Told*. New York: Harper, 1920.

Gilbert, Sandra M. "Soldier's Heart: Literary Men, Literary Women, and the Great War." *Signs* 8 (1983): 422–50.

Gilbert, Sandra M., and Susan Gubar. *The Madwoman in the Attic: The Woman Writer and the Nineteenth-Century Literary Imagination*. New Haven: Yale UP, 1979.

———. *No Man's Land*. 3 vols. New Haven: Yale UP, 1987–94.

Gillespie, Diane F. "The Elusive Julia Stephen." J. Stephen 1–27.

———, ed. *Multiple Muses: Virginia Woolf and the Other Arts*. Columbia: U of Missouri P, 1993.

———. *The Sisters' Arts: The Writing and Painting of Virginia Woolf and Vanessa Bell*. Syracuse: Syracuse UP, 1988.

Gilligan, Carol. *In a Different Voice*. Cambridge: Harvard UP, 1982.

Ginsberg, Elaine, and Laura Moss Gottlieb, eds. *Virginia Woolf: Centennial Essays*. Troy: Whitston, 1983.

Goldman, Jane. *The Feminist Aesthetics of Virginia Woolf: Modernism, Post-impressionism, and the Politics of the Visual*. Cambridge: Cambridge UP, 1998.

———, ed. *Virginia Woolf:* To the Lighthouse; The Waves. Icon Critical Guides. Cambridge, Eng.: Icon, 1997.

Gordon, Lyndall. *Virginia Woolf: A Writer's Life*. New York: Norton, 1984.

Gorsky, Susan. *Virginia Woolf*. 1978. Rev. ed. Boston: Twayne, 1989.

Gottlieb, Laura Moss, comp. *Index to the Virginia Woolf Miscellany, 1973–1998: The First Fifty Issues*. Rohnert Park: Sonoma State UP, 1998.

Gough, Val. "The Mystical Copula: Rewriting the Phallus in *To the Lighthouse*." Hussey and Neverow 216–23.

Gray, Gail E. "Final Beginnings." Unpublished paper, 1990.

Greenwald, Elissa. "Casting Off from 'The Castaway': *To the Lighthouse* as Prose Elegy." *Genre* 19.1 (1986): 36–57.

Greg, W. W. "The Rationale of Copy-Text." *Studies in Bibliography* 3 (1950–51): 19–36.

Griffin, Susan. *Rape: The Power of Consciousness*. New York: Harper, 1979.

Guiguet, Jean. *Virginia Woolf and Her Works*. New York: Harcourt, 1965.

Hafley, James. *The Glass Roof: Virginia Woolf as Novelist*. Berkeley: U of California P, 1954.

Haller, Evelyn. "The Anti-Madonna in the Work and Thought of Virginia Woolf." Ginsberg and Gottlieb 93–109.

Handley, William R. "The Housemaid and the Kitchen Table: Incorporating the Frame in *To the Lighthouse*." *Twentieth Century Literature* 40 (1994): 15–41.

Hankins, Leslie Kathleen. "'Across the Screen of My Brain': Virginia Woolf's 'The Cinema' and Film Forums of the Twenties." Gillespie, *Muses* 148–79.

———. "A Splice of Reel Life in Virginia Woolf's 'Time Passes': Censorship, Cinema, and 'the Usual Battlefield of Emotions.'" *Criticism* 35 (1993): 91–114.

Hanley, Lynne. *Writing War: Fiction, Gender, and Memory*. Amherst: U of Massachusetts P, 1991.

Hanson, Clare. *Virginia Woolf*. New York: St. Martin's, 1994.

Haring-Smith, Tori. "Private and Public Consciousness in *Mrs. Dalloway* and *To the Lighthouse*." Ginsberg and Gottlieb 143–62.

Harrison, Jane Ellen. *Prolegomena to the Study of Greek Religion*. 1903. London: Merlin, 1980.

Harrison, Suzan. *Eudora Welty and Virginia Woolf: Gender, Genre, and Influence*. Baton Rouge: Louisiana State UP, 1997.

Hartman, Geoffrey. "Virginia's Web." Vogler 70–81.

Hauck, Christina. "'To Escape the Horror of Family Life': Virginia Woolf and the British Birth Control Debate." Wussow, *New Essays* 15–37.

Haule, James M. "'Le temps passe' and the Original Typescript: An Early Version of the 'Time Passes' Section of *To the Lighthouse*." *Twentieth Century Literature* 29 (1983): 267–311.

———. *To the Lighthouse* and the Great War: The Evidence of Virginia Woolf's Revisions of 'Time Passes.'" Hussey, *Woolf and War* 164–79.

Haule, James M., and Philip H. Smith, Jr., comps. and eds. *A Concordance to* To the Lighthouse. Microfilm. Oxford: Oxford Microform, 1983. 2nd ed. Ann Arbor: UMI, 1988.

Haworth-Booth, Mark. *E. McKnight Kauffer: A Designer and His Public*. London: Fraser, 1979.

Hedges, Elaine. "The Needle or the Pen: The Literary Rediscovery of Women's Textile Work." Howe, *Tradition* 338–64.

Heilbrun, Carolyn G. "*To the Lighthouse:* The New Story of Mother and Daughter." *ADE Bulletin* 87 (1987): 12–14.

———. *Toward a Recognition of Androgyny*. New York: Harper, 1973.

Hendrick, Veronica. "Male Power in *To the Lighthouse*." Unpublished paper, 1990.

Henriques, Julian, Wendy Hollway, Cathy Urwin, Couze Venn, and Valerie Walkerdine. *Changing the Subject: Psychology, Social Regulation and Subjectivity*. London: Methuen, 1984.

Herman, Dianne F. "The Rape Culture." *Women: A Feminist Perspective*. Ed. Jo Freeman. 4th ed. Mountain View: Mayfield, 1989. 20–44.

Hermann, Anne. *The Dialogic and Difference: "An/Other Woman" in Virginia Woolf and Christa Wolf*. New York: Columbia UP, 1989.

Highet, Gilbert. *The Art of Teaching*. New York: Knopf, 1951.

Hill, Katherine. "Virginia Woolf and Leslie Stephen: History and Literary Revolution." *PMLA* 96 (1981): 351–62.

Hirsch, Marianne. "The Darkest Plots: Narration and Compulsory Heterosexuality." *The Mother/Daughter Plot: Narrative, Psychoanalysis, Feminism*. Bloomington: Indiana UP, 1989. 91–121.

Hite, Molly. "Romance, Marginality, and Matrilineage: *The Color Purple* and *Their Eyes Were Watching God*." *Reading Black, Reading Feminist: A Critical Anthology*. Ed. Henry Louis Gates, Jr. New York: Meridian, 1990. 431–53.

Hoffman, A. C. "Subject and Object and the Nature of Reality: The Dialectic of *To the Lighthouse*." *Texas Studies in Literature and Language* 13 (1972): 691–703.

Hoffman, Anne. "Demeter and Poseidon: Fusion and Distance in *To the Lighthouse*." *Studies in the Novel* 16 (1984): 182–96.

Holtby, Winifred. *Virginia Woolf: A Critical Memoir*. 1932. Chicago: Cassandra, 1978.

Homans, Margaret. "Postscript: Mothers and Daughters in Virginia Woolf's Victorian Novel." *Bearing the Word: Language and Female Experience in Nineteenth-Century Women's Writing*. Chicago: U of Chicago P, 1986. 277–88.

Howe, Florence, ed. *Tradition and the Talents of Women*. Urbana: U of Illinois P, 1991.

———. "T. S. Eliot, Virginia Woolf, and the Future of 'Tradition.'" Howe, *Tradition* 1–33.

Hughes, Robert. *Shock of the New*. Rev. ed. New York: Knopf, 1991.

Humm, Maggie. *Practising Feminist Criticism: An Introduction*. New York: Prentice, 1995.

Humphrey, Robert. *Stream of Consciousness in the Modern Novel*. Berkeley: U of California P, 1954.

Hurston, Zora Neale. *Dust Tracks on a Road: An Autobiography*. 1942. Urbana: U of Illinois P, 1984.

———. *Their Eyes Were Watching God*. 1937. New York: Harper, 1990.

Hussey, Mark. *The Singing of the Real World: The Philosophy of Virginia Woolf's Fiction*. Columbus: Ohio State UP, 1986.

———. "*To the Lighthouse* and Physics: The Cosmology of David Bohm and Virginia Woolf." Wussow, *New Essays* 79–97.

———, ed. *Virginia Woolf and War: Fiction, Reality, and Myth*. Syracuse: Syracuse UP, 1991.

———. *Virginia Woolf A to Z: A Comprehensive Reference for Students, Teachers, and Common Readers to Her Life, Works, and Critical Reception*. New York: Facts on File, 1995.

Hussey, Mark, and Vara Neverow, eds. *Virginia Woolf: Emerging Perspectives: Selected Papers from the Third Annual Conference on Virginia Woolf*. New York: Pace UP, 1994.

Hussey, Mark, and Vara Neverow-Turk, eds. *Virginia Woolf Miscellanies: Selected Papers from the First Annual Conference on Virginia Woolf*. New York: Pace UP, 1992.

Hutcheon, Linda. *A Poetics of Postmodernism: History, Theory, Fiction*. New York: Routledge, 1988.

———. *The Politics of Postmodernism*. London: Routledge, 1989.

Huyssen, Andreas. *After the Great Divide: Modernism, Mass Culture, Postmodernism*. Bloomington: Indiana UP, 1986.

Hynes, Samuel. *The Auden Generation: Literature and Politics in the 1930s*. New York: Viking, 1977.

———. *A War Imagined: The First World War and English Culture*. New York: Atheneum, 1991.

Jacobus, Mary. "'The Third Stroke': Reading Woolf with Freud." *Grafts: Feminist Cultural Criticism*. Ed. Susan Sheridan. London: Verso, 1988. 93–100.

Jameson, Fredric. "Modernism and Imperialism." *Nationalism, Colonialism, and Literature*. Ed. Terry Eagleton, Jameson, and Edward Said. Minneapolis: U of Minnesota P, 1990. 43–66.

Jay, Karla, and Joanne Glasgow, eds. *Lesbian Texts and Contexts: Radical Revisions*. New York: New York UP, 1990.

Johnson, Barbara. *A World of Difference*. Baltimore: Johns Hopkins UP, 1987.

Johnson, Jeri. "Woolf Woman, Icon and Idol: The Canonization of a Sceptical Modernist." *Times Literary Supplement* 21 Feb. 1992: 5–6.

Johnstone, J. K. *The Bloomsbury Group: A Study of E. M. Forster, Lytton Strachey, Virginia Woolf, and Their Circle*. New York: Noonday, 1954.

———. "World War I and the Novels of Virginia Woolf." *Promise of Greatness: The War of 1914–1918*. Ed. George A. Panichas. New York: Day, 1968. 528–40.

Jones, Ellen Carol, ed. *Virginia Woolf*. Spec. issue of *Modern Fiction Studies* 38 (1992): 1–345.

Joyce, James. *A Portrait of the Artist as a Young Man*. 1916. New York: Penguin, 1985.

Jung, C. G. "The Psychological Aspects of the Kore." *The Archetypes and the Collective Unconscious*. Trans. R. F. C. Hull. New York: Bollingen, 1959. 182–203.

Jung, C. G., and C. Kerenyi. *Essays on a Science of Mythology: The Myth of the Divine Child and the Mysteries of Eleusis*. Trans. R. F. C. Hull. Princeton: Princeton UP, 1950.

Kahane, Claire. "The Nuptials of Metaphor: Self and Other in Virginia Woolf." *Literature and Psychology* 30 (1980): 72–82.

Kaivola, Karen. *All Contraries Confounded: The Lyrical Fiction of Virginia Woolf, Djuna Barnes, and Marguerite Duras*. Iowa City: U of Iowa P, 1991.

Kato, Megumi. "The Politics/Poetics of Motherhood in *To the Lighthouse*." *Virginia Woolf and Communities: Selected Papers from the Eighth Annual Conference on Virginia Woolf*. Ed. Jeanette McVicker and Laura Davis. New York: Pace UP, 1999. 102–09.

Keating, Peter. *The Haunted Study: A Social History of the English Novel, 1875–1914*. London: Secker, 1989.

Keeling, H. V. *Descartes*. London: Oxford UP, 1968.

Kern, Stephen. *The Culture of Time and Space, 1880–1918*. Cambridge: Harvard UP, 1983.

Kiely, Robert. *Beyond Egotism: The Fiction of James Joyce, Virginia Woolf, and D. H. Lawrence*. Cambridge: Harvard UP, 1980.

Kingston, Maxine Hong. *The Woman Warrior: Memoirs of a Girlhood among Ghosts*. New York: Random, 1975.

Kirkpatrick, B. J., and Stuart N. Clarke. *A Bibliography of Virginia Woolf*. 4th ed. Oxford: Clarendon, 1997.

Knightly, Philip. *The First Casualty: From Crimea to Vietnam: The War Correspondent as Hero, Propagandist, and Myth Maker*. New York: Harcourt, 1975.

Knox-Shaw, Peter. "*To the Lighthouse*: The Novel as Elegy." *English Studies in Africa* 29.1 (1986): 31–52.

Koedt, Anne. "The Myth of the Vaginal Orgasm." *Voices of Women's Liberation*. Comp. and ed. Leslie B. Tanner. New York: Signet, 1971. 158–66.

Lanser, Susan Sniader. *Fictions of Authority: Women Writers and Narrative Voice*. Ithaca: Cornell UP, 1992.

Laurence, Patricia Ondek. *The Reading of Silence: Virginia Woolf in the English Tradition*. Stanford: Stanford UP, 1991.

Leaska, Mitchell. *Virginia Woolf's Lighthouse: A Study in Critical Method*. New York: Columbia UP, 1970.

Lee, Hermione. *Virginia Woolf*. New York: Knopf, 1997.

Leed, Eric J. *No Man's Land: Combat and Identity in World War I*. Cambridge: Cambridge UP, 1979.

Lehmann, John. *Virginia Woolf and Her World*. New York: Harcourt, 1975.

Levenback, Karen L. "Virginia Woolf and Returning Soldiers: The Great War and the Reality of Survival in *Mrs. Dalloway* and *The Years.*" *Woolf Studies Annual* 2 (1996): 71–88.

———. *Virginia Woolf and the Great War.* Syracuse: Syracuse UP, 1999.

———. "Woolf's 'War in the Village.'" Hussey, *Woolf and War* 40–57.

Levenson, Michael H., ed. *The Cambridge Companion to Modernism.* Cambridge: Cambridge UP, 1999.

———. *The Genealogy of Modernism: A Study of English Literary Doctrine, 1908– 1922.* Cambridge: Cambridge UP, 1984.

———. *Modernism and the Fate of Individuality: Character and Novelistic Form from Conrad to Woolf.* Cambridge: Cambridge UP, 1991.

Levy, Eric. "Woolf's Metaphysics of Tragic Vision in *To the Lighthouse.*" *Philological Quarterly* 75 (1996): 109–32.

Libertin, Mary. "Speech Acts in *To the Lighthouse.*" Ginsberg and Gottlieb 163–85.

Lidoff, Joan. "Virginia Woolf's Feminine Sentence: The Mother-Daughter World of *To the Lighthouse.*" *Literature and Psychology* 32.3 (1986): 43–59.

Lightfoot, Sara Lawrence. *Balm in Gilead: The Journey of a Healer.* Reading: Addison, 1988.

Lilienfeld, Jane. "'The Deceptiveness of Beauty': Mother Love and Mother Hate in *To the Lighthouse.*" *Twentieth Century Literature* 23 (1977): 345–76.

———. "Flesh and Blood and Love and Words: Lily Briscoe, Stephen Dedalus, and the Aesthetics of Emotional Quest." *New Alliances in Joyce Studies.* Ed. Bonnie Kime Scott. Newark: U of Delaware P, 1988. 165–78.

———. "'Like a Lion Seeking Whom He Could Devour': Domestic Violence in *To the Lighthouse.*" Hussey and Neverow-Turk 154–64.

———. *Reading Alcoholisms: Theorizing Character and Narrative in Selected Novels of Thomas Hardy, James Joyce, and Virginia Woolf.* New York: St. Martin's, 1999.

———. "Where the Spear Plants Grew: The Ramsays' Marriage in *To the Lighthouse.*" J. Marcus, *New Feminist Essays* 148–69.

Lumsden, Robert. "Virginia Woolf's 'As If' in *To the Lighthouse*: The Modernist Philosophy of Meaning in Absentia." *The Silent Word: Textual Meaning and the Unwritten.* Ed. Ban Kah Choon et al. Singapore: Singapore UP, 1998. 119–33.

Lydon, Mary. *Skirting the Issue: Essays in Literary Theory.* Madison: U of Wisconsin P, 1995.

Lyon, George Ella. "Lighthouse." *Catalpa.* Lexington: Wind, 1993. 49–52.

Lyotard, Jean-François. *The Postmodern Condition: A Report on Knowledge.* Trans. Geoff Bennington and Brian Massumi. Minneapolis: U of Minnesota P, 1984.

MacKinnon, Catharine. *Sexual Harassment of Working Women: A Case of Sex Discrimination.* New Haven: Yale UP, 1979.

Maher, Frances. "Classroom Pedagogy and the New Scholarship on Women." *Gendered Subjects: The Dynamics of Feminist Teaching.* Ed. Margo Culley and Catherine Portuges. Boston: Routledge, 1985. 29–48.

Majumdar, Robin. *Virginia Woolf: An Annotated Bibliography of Criticism, 1915–1974.* New York: Garland, 1976.

Majumdar, Robin, and Allen McLaurin, eds. *Virginia Woolf: The Critical Heritage*. London: Routledge, 1975.

Marcus, Jane. *Art and Anger: Reading like a Woman*. Columbus: Ohio State UP, 1988.

———. "The Asylums of Antaeus: Women, War, and Madness: Is There a Feminist Fetishism?" *The Difference Within: Feminism and Critical Theory*. Ed. Elizabeth Meese and Alice Parker. Philadelphia: Benjamins, 1989. 49–83.

———. "Britannia Rules *The Waves*." *Decolonizing Tradition: New Views of Twentieth-Century "British" Literary Canons*. Ed. Karen R. Lawrence. Urbana: U of Illinois P, 1991. 136–62.

———. "An Embarrassment of Riches." *Women's Review of Books* Mar. 1994: 17–19.

———. "Invisible Mending." *Between Women: Biographers, Novelists, Critics, Teachers, and Artists Write about Their Work on Women*. Ed. Carol Ascher, Louise DeSalvo, and Sara Ruddick. Boston: Beacon, 1984. 381–95.

———, ed. *New Feminist Essays on Virginia Woolf*. London: Macmillan, 1981.

———. "Other People's I's (Eyes): The Reader, Gender, and Recursive Reading in *To the Lighthouse* and *The Waves*." *Reader* 22 (1989): 53–67.

———. "Pathographies: The Virginia Woolf Soap Operas." *Signs* 17 (1992): 806–19.

———. "Registering Objections: Grounding Feminist Alibis." *Reconfigured Spheres: Feminist Explorations of Literary Space*. Ed. Margaret R. Higonnet and Joan Templeton. Amherst: U of Massachusetts P, 1994. 171–93.

———. "Sapphistory: The Woolf and the Well." Jay and Glasgow 164–79.

———. "Sapphistry: Narration as Lesbian Seduction." J. Marcus, *Woolf and the Languages* 165–88.

———."Still Practice, A/Wrested Alphabet: Toward a Feminist Aesthetic." J. Marcus, *Art* 215–49.

———. "A Tale of Two Cultures." *Women's Review of Books* Jan. 1994: 11–13.

———."Tintinnabulations." J. Marcus, *Art* 157–81.

———, ed. *Virginia Woolf: A Feminist Slant*. Lincoln: U of Nebraska P, 1983.

———, ed. *Virginia Woolf and Bloomsbury: A Centenary Celebration*. Bloomington: Indiana UP, 1987.

———. "Virginia Woolf and Her Violin: Mothering, Madness, and Music." J. Marcus, *Woolf and the Languages* 96–114.

———. *Virginia Woolf and the Languages of Patriarchy*. Bloomington: Indiana UP, 1987.

Marcus, Laura. *Virginia Woolf*. Writers and Their Work. Plymouth, Eng.: Northcote, 1997.

Marder, Herbert. *Feminism and Art: A Study of Virginia Woolf*. Chicago: U of Chicago P, 1968.

Marks, Elaine, and Isabelle de Courtivron, eds. *New French Feminisms: An Anthology*. Amherst: U of Massachusetts P, 1980.

Marshall, Brenda K. *Teaching the Postmodern: Fiction and Theory*. New York: Routledge, 1992.

Martin, Bill. "*To the Lighthouse* and the Feminist Path to Postmodernity." *Philosophy and Literature* 13 (1989): 307–15.

Matro, Thomas. "Only Relations: Vision and Achievement in *To the Lighthouse*." *PMLA* 99 (1984): 212–24.

McCarthy, Mary. *Memories of a Catholic Girlhood*. 1946. New York: Harcourt, 1957.

McGann, Jerome. *Black Riders: The Visible Language of Modernism*. Princeton: Princeton UP, 1993.

McGavran, James Holt, Jr. "Teaching Virginia Woolf in the University: A First Dose for Unwilling Undergraduates." *CEA Forum* 15.2 (1985): 7–9.

McGee, Patrick. "The Politics of Modernist Form; or, Who Rules *The Waves*?" *Modern Fiction Studies* 38 (1992): 631–49.

McHale, Brian. *Postmodernist Fiction*. New York: Methuen, 1987.

McKay, Nellie. "'Crayon Enlargements of Life': Zora Neale Hurston's *Their Eyes Were Watching God* as Autobiography." *New Essays on* Their Eyes Were Watching God. Ed. Michael Awkward. Cambridge: Cambridge UP, 1990. 51–70.

McKenna, Kathleen. "The Language of Orgasm." Barrett and Cramer 29–38.

McKenzie, D. F. *Bibliography and the Sociology of Texts*. London: British Lib., 1985.

McNees, Eleanor, ed. *Virginia Woolf: Critical Assessments*. 4 vols. East Sussex: Helm, 1994.

McVicker, Jeanette. "Dislocating the Discourse of Modernism: The Examples of Woolf and Hurston." Hussey and Neverow 313–18.

Meese, Elizabeth. "Theorizing Lesbian: Writing—A Love Letter." Jay and Glasgow 70–87.

Meisel, Perry. *The Absent Father: Virginia Woolf and Walter Pater*. New Haven: Yale UP, 1980.

———. *The Myth of the Modern: British Literature and Criticism after 1850*. New Haven: Yale UP, 1987.

Meisenhelder, Susan. "Ethnic and Gender Identity in Zora Neale Hurston's *Their Eyes Were Watching God*." *Teaching American Ethnic Literatures: Nineteen Essays*. Ed. John Maitino and David R. Peck. Albuquerque: U of New Mexico P, 1996. 105–17.

Mellard, James M. *Using Lacan, Reading Fiction*. Urbana: U of Illinois P, 1991.

Mepham, John. *Criticism in Focus: Virginia Woolf*. New York: St. Martin's, 1992.

———. *Virginia Woolf: A Literary Life*. New York: St. Martin's, 1991.

Mezei, Kathy, ed. *Ambiguous Discourse: Feminist Narratology and British Women Writers*. Chapel Hill: U of North Carolina P, 1996.

Miller, Alice. *The Drama of the Gifted Child: The Search for the True Self*. Trans. Ruth Ward. New York: Basic, 1981.

Miller, J. Hillis. "Mr. Carmichael and Lily Briscoe: The Rhythm of Creativity in *To the Lighthouse*." *Modernism Reconsidered*. Ed. Robert Kiely. Cambridge: Harvard UP, 1983. 167–89.

Miller, Jean Baker. *Toward a New Psychology of Women*. 2nd ed. Boston: Beacon, 1986.

Minow-Pinkney, Makiko. "Reading Postmodernism in *To the Lighthouse*." Davis and McVicker 241–42.

———. *Virginia Woolf and the Problem of the Subject*. Brighton, Eng.: Harvester, 1987.

Moi, Toril. *Sexual/Textual Politics: Feminist Literary Theory*. London: Methuen, 1985.

Moore, G. E. *Principia Ethica*. Cambridge: Cambridge UP, 1903.

Moore, Madeline. *The Short Season between Two Silences: The Mystical and the Political in the Novels of Virginia Woolf*. Boston: Allen, 1984.

———, ed. *Virginia Woolf*. Spec. issue of *Women's Studies* 4 (1977): 149–300.

Moretti, Franco. *The Way of the World: The Bildungsroman in European Culture*. London: Verso, 1987.

Morrell, Ottoline Violet. *Lady Ottoline's Album*. Ed. Carolyn G. Heilbrun. New York: Knopf, 1976.

Mosse, George. *Fallen Soldiers: Reshaping the Memory of the World Wars*. New York: Oxford UP, 1990.

Murray, Pauli. *Proud Shoes: The Story of an American Family*. New York: Harper, 1987.

Naremore, James. *The World without a Self: Virginia Woolf and the Novel*. New Haven: Yale UP, 1973.

Naylor, Gillian. *Bloomsbury: Its Artists, Authors, and Designers*. Boston: Little, 1990.

Neverow-Turk, Vara. "'Mrs. Rayley Is Out, Sir': Re-reading That Hole in Minta's Stocking." *Virginia Woolf Miscellany* 39 (1992): 9.

Neverow-Turk, Vara, and Mark Hussey, eds. *Virginia Woolf: Themes and Variations: Selected Papers from the Second Annual Conference on Virginia Woolf*. New York: Pace UP, 1993.

Nicholls, Peter. *Modernisms: A Literary Guide*. Berkeley: U of California P, 1995.

Nicholson, Linda J., ed. *Feminism/Postmodernism*. New York: Routledge, 1990.

Noble, Joan Russell, ed. *Recollections of Virginia Woolf by Her Contemporaries*. Athens: Ohio UP, 1972.

Nussbaum, Martha A. "The Window: Knowledge of Other Minds in Virginia Woolf's *To the Lighthouse*." *Sex and Social Justice*. New York: Oxford UP, 1999. 355–73.

Olano, Pamela J. "'Women Alone Stir My Imagination': Reading Virginia Woolf as a Lesbian." Neverow-Turk and Hussey 158–71.

Olsen, Tillie. *Silences*. New York: Delacorte, 1978.

Ortega y Gasset, José. "The Dehumanization of Art." *"The Dehumanization of Art" and Other Essays on Art, Culture, and Literature*. Princeton: Princeton UP, 1968. 3–54.

Pankhurst, Christabel. *Unshackled: The Story of How We Won the Vote*. London: Hutchinson, 1959.

Pankhurst, Emmeline. *My Own Story*. 1914. New York: Kraus, 1971.

Parkes, Graham. "Imagining Reality in *To the Lighthouse*." *Philosophy and Literature* 6.1-2 (1982): 33–44.

Paul, Janis. *The Victorian Heritage of Virginia Woolf: The External World in Her Novels*. Norman: Pilgrim, 1985.

Pearce, Richard. *The Politics of Narration: James Joyce, William Faulkner, and Virginia Woolf*. New Brunswick: Rutgers UP, 1991.

Pedersen, Glenn. "Vision in *To the Lighthouse*." *PMLA* 73 (1958): 585–600.

Perry, William G., Jr. "Different Worlds in the Same Classroom: Students' Evolution in

Their Vision of Knowledge and Their Expectations of Teachers." *On Teaching and Learning: The Journal of the Harvard-Danforth Center* 1 (May 1985): 1–17.

———. *Forms of Intellectual and Ethical Development in the College Years: A Scheme*. New York: Holt, 1970.

Petry, Ann. *"Miss Muriel" and Other Stories*. 1971. Boston: Beacon, 1989.

Phelan, James, ed. *Reading Narrative: Form, Ethics, Ideology*. Columbus: Ohio State UP, 1989.

Phillips, Kathy J. *Virginia Woolf against Empire*. Knoxville: U of Tennessee P, 1994.

Poole, Roger. *The Unknown Virginia Woolf*. 4th ed. Cambridge: Cambridge UP, 1995.

Pratt, Annis. *Archetypal Patterns in Women's Fiction*. Bloomington: Indiana UP, 1981.

———. "Sexual Imagery in *To the Lighthouse*: A New Feminist Approach." *Modern Fiction Studies* 18 (1972): 417–31.

Rabinowitz, Peter J. *Before Reading: Narrative Conventions and the Politics of Interpretation*. Columbus: Ohio State UP, 1998.

Rado, Lisa, ed. *Rereading Modernism: New Directions in Feminist Criticism*. New York: Garland, 1994.

Radway, Janice. "The Book-of-the-Month Club and the General Reader: The Uses of 'Serious' Fiction." *Reading in America: Literature and Social History*. Ed. Cathy N. Davidson. Baltimore: Johns Hopkins UP, 1989. 259–84.

Rainey, Lawrence. "The Price of Modernism: Reconsidering the Publication of *The Waste Land*." *Critical Quarterly* 31 (1989): 21–47.

Raitt, Suzanne. *Virginia Woolf's* To the Lighthouse. Critical Studies of Key Texts. New York: St. Martin's, 1990.

———. *Vita and Virginia: The Work and Friendship of V. Sackville-West and Virginia Woolf*. Oxford: Oxford UP, 1993.

Reid, Panthea. *Art and Affection: A Life of Virginia Woolf*. Baton Rouge: Louisiana State UP, 1996.

Reid, Su. *To the Lighthouse*. Critics Debate. Basingstoke: Macmillan, 1991.

Rice, Thomas Jackson. *Virginia Woolf: A Guide to Research*. New York: Garland, 1984.

Rich, Adrienne. "Compulsory Heterosexuality and Lesbian Existence." Abel and Abel 139–68.

Richardson, Laurel, Verta Taylor, and Nancy Whittier, eds. *Feminist Frontiers IV*. New York: McGraw, 1997.

Richter, Harvena. *Virginia Woolf: The Inward Voyage*. Princeton: Princeton UP, 1970.

Rimmon-Kenan, Shlomith. *Narrative Fiction: Contemporary Poetics*. New York: Methuen, 1983.

Risolo, Donna. "Mrs. Ramsay: Victim of Compulsory Heterosexuality." Unpublished paper, 1990.

———. "Outing Mrs. Ramsay: Reading the Lesbian Subtext in Virginia Woolf's *To the Lighthouse*." Neverow-Turk and Hussey 238–48.

Robicheau, Mary. "Lesbianism in *To the Lighthouse*." Unpublished paper, 1990.

Rogat, Ellen Hawkes. "The Virgin in the Bell Biography." *Twentieth Century Literature* 20 (1974): 96–113.

Roof, Judith. *A Lure of Knowledge: Lesbian Sexuality and Theory*. New York: Columbia UP, 1991.

Rose, Phyllis. *Woman of Letters: A Life of Virginia Woolf*. New York: Oxford UP, 1978.

Rosenbaum, S. P., ed. *The Bloomsbury Group: A Collection of Memoirs, Commentary, and Criticism*. Toronto: U of Toronto P, 1975.

——, ed. *A Bloomsbury Group Reader*. Oxford: Blackwell, 1993.

——. *Edwardian Bloomsbury: The Early Literary History of the Bloomsbury Group*. Vol. 2. New York: St. Martin's, 1994.

——. *Victorian Bloomsbury: The Early Literary History of the Bloomsbury Group*. Vol. 1. New York: St. Martin's, 1986.

Rosenman, Ellen. *The Invisible Presence: Virginia Woolf and the Mother-Daughter Relationship*. Baton Rouge: Louisiana State UP, 1986.

Ruddick, Sara. "Learning to Live with the Angel in the House." *Women's Studies* 4 (1977): 181–200.

Ruotolo, Lucio P. *The Interrupted Moment: A View of Virginia Woolf's Novels*. Stanford: Stanford UP, 1986.

——, ed. *Virginia Woolf Issue*. Spec. issue of *Twentieth Century Literature* 25 (1979): i–v, 237–441.

Saunders, Rebecca. "Language, Subject, Self: Reading the Style of *To the Lighthouse*." *Novel* 26 (1993): 192–213.

Saxton, Ruth, and Jean Tobin, eds. *Woolf and Lessing: Breaking the Mold*. New York: St. Martin's, 1994.

Schaefer, Josephine O'Brien. *The Three-Fold Nature of Reality in the Novels of Virginia Woolf*. The Hague: Mouton, 1965.

Schlack, Beverly Ann. *Continuing Presences: Virginia Woolf's Use of Literary Allusion*. University Park: U of Pennsylvania P, 1979.

Schwartz, Sanford. "The Postmodernity of Modernism." *The Future of Modernism*. Ed. Hugh Witemeyer. Ann Arbor: U of Michigan P, 1997. 9–31.

Schwarz, Daniel R. *The Transformation of the English Novel, 1890–1930: Studies in Hardy, Conrad, Joyce, Lawrence, Forster, and Woolf*. 2nd ed. New York: St. Martin's, 1995.

Scott, Bonnie Kime, ed. *The Gender of Modernism: A Critical Anthology*. Bloomington: Indiana UP, 1990.

——. *Refiguring Modernism*. 2 vols. Bloomington: Indiana UP, 1995.

Shone, Richard. *Bloomsbury Portraits: Vanessa Bell, Duncan Grant, and Their Circle*. New York: Dutton, 1976.

Showalter, Elaine. *A Literature of Their Own*. Princeton: Princeton UP, 1977.

——. "Piecing and Writing." *The Poetics of Gender*. Ed. Nancy K. Miller. New York: Columbia UP, 1986. 222–47.

Silver, Brenda. "Retro-Anger and Baby-Boomer Nostalgia: A Polemical Talk." Davis and McVicker 221–33.

———. "Textual Criticism as Feminist Practice; or, Who's Afraid of Virginia Woolf, Part II." *Representing Modernist Texts: Editing as Interpretation*. Ed. George Bornstein. Ann Arbor: U of Michigan P, 1991. 193–222.

———. *Virginia Woolf's Reading Notebooks*. Princeton: Princeton UP, 1983.

———. "What's Woolf Got to Do with It? or, The Perils of Popularity." *Modern Fiction Studies* 38.1 (1992): 21–60.

Simon, Kate. *Bronx Primitive*. New York: Viking, 1982.

Smith, Angela. "Thresholds in 'Prelude' and *To the Lighthouse*." *Commonwealth Essays and Studies* 4 (1997): 39–49.

Smith, Barbara, ed. *Home Girls: A Black Feminist Anthology*. Latham: Kitchen Table, 1981.

Smith, Susan Bennett. "Reinventing Grief Work: Virginia Woolf's Feminist Representations of Mourning in *Mrs. Dalloway* and *To the Lighthouse*." *Twentieth Century Literature* 41 (1995): 310–27.

Smith-Rosenberg, Carol. "The Female World of Love and Ritual: Relations between Women in Nineteenth-Century America." Abel and Abel 27–56.

Smythe, Karen. "Virginia Woolf's Elegiac Enterprise." *Novel* 26 (1992): 64–79.

Spilka, Mark. *Virginia Woolf's Quarrel with Grieving*. Lincoln: U of Nebraska P, 1980.

Spivak, Gayatri C. "Unmaking and Making in *To the Lighthouse*." *Women and Language in Literature and Society*. Ed. Sally McConnell-Ginet, Ruth Borker, and Nelly Furman. New York: Praeger, 1980. 310–27.

Squier, Susan Merrill. *Virginia Woolf and London: The Sexual Politics of the City*. Chapel Hill: U of North Carolina P, 1985.

Stansky, Peter. *On or about December 1910: Early Bloomsbury and Its Intimate World*. Cambridge: Harvard UP, 1996.

Stape, J. H., ed. *Virginia Woolf: Interviews and Recollections*. Iowa City: U of Iowa P, 1995.

Stemerick, Martine. "Virginia Woolf and Julia Stephen: The Distaff Side of History." Ginsberg and Gottlieb 51–80.

Stephen, Julia Duckworth. *Julia Duckworth Stephen: Stories for Children and Essays for Adults*. Ed. Diane F. Gillespie and Elizabeth Steele. Syracuse: Syracuse UP, 1987.

Stephen, Leslie. *Hours in a Library*. New York: Scribner's, 1875.

———. *Mausoleum Book*. Ed. Alan Bell. Oxford: Clarendon, 1977.

Stephen, Leslie, and Sidney Lee, eds. *Dictionary of National Biography*. 1885–1901. 22 vols. London: Oxford UP, 1950.

Stevenson, Randall, and Jane Goldman. "'But What? Elegy?': Modernist Reading and the Death of Mrs. Ramsay." *Yearbook of English Studies: Strategies of Reading: Dickens and After (Special Number)*. Vol. 26. London: Mod. Humanities Research Assn., 1996. 173–86.

Stimpson, Catharine R. "Afterword: Lesbian Studies in the 1990s." Jay and Glasgow 377–82.

———. "Zero Degree Deviancy: The Lesbian Novel in English." *Where the Meanings Are: Feminism and Cultural Spaces*. New York: Routledge, 1989. 97–110.

Strachey, Ray. *The Cause*. 1928. Port Washington: Kennikat, 1969.

Swanson, Diana. "The Lesbian Feminism of Virginia Woolf's *To the Lighthouse*." Barrett and Cramer, *Re:Reading* 38–44.

Temple, Ruth. "Never Say 'I': *To the Lighthouse* as Vision and Confession." *Virginia Woolf: A Collection of Critical Essays*. Ed. Claire Sprague. Englewood Cliffs: Prentice, 1971. 90–100.

Tindall, William York. *The Literary Symbol*. Bloomington: Indiana UP, 1955.

Tratner, Michael. *Modernism and Mass Politics: Joyce, Woolf, Eliot, Yeats*. Stanford: Stanford UP, 1995.

Tremper, Ellen. "In Her Father's House: *To the Lighthouse* as a Record of Virginia Woolf's Literary Patrimony." *Texas Studies in Literature and Language* 34 (1992): 1–40.

Vanita, Ruth. "Bringing Buried Things to Life: Homoerotic Alliances in *To the Lighthouse*." Barrett and Cramer, *Lesbian Readings* 165–79.

Virginia Woolf. Spec. issue of *Modern Fiction Studies* 18 (1972–73): 331–488.

Virginia Woolf Issue. Spec. issue of *Bulletin of the New York Public Library* 80 (1977): 137–301.

Virginia Woolf Issue II. Spec. issue of *Bulletin of Research in the Humanities* 82 (1979): 269–366.

Vogler, Thomas, ed. *Twentieth Century Interpretations of* To the Lighthouse. Englewood Cliffs: Prentice, 1970.

Walker, Alice. "In Search of Our Mothers' Gardens." Walker, *Search* 231–43.

———. *In Search of Our Mothers' Gardens: Womanist Prose*. New York: Harcourt, 1983.

Waugh, Patricia. *Feminine Fictions: Revisiting the Postmodern*. London: Routledge, 1989.

———. *Metafiction: The Theory and Practice of Self-Conscious Fiction*. London: Methuen, 1984.

———. *Practising Postmodernism / Reading Modernism*. London: Arnold, 1992.

Weedon, Chris. *Feminist Practice and Poststructuralist Theory*. Oxford: Blackwell, 1987.

Weil, Lise. "Entering a Field of Vision: *To the Lighthouse* and *Between the Acts*." Barrett and Cramer, *Lesbian Readings* 241–58.

Weiser, Barbara. "Criticism of Virginia Woolf from 1956 to the Present: A Selected Checklist with an Index to Studies of Separate Works." *Modern Fiction Studies* 18 (1972): 477–86.

Welty, Eudora. Foreword. *To the Lighthouse*. By Virginia Woolf. New York: Harcourt, 1989. vii–xii.

White, E. B. "Once More to the Lake." *Essays of E. B. White*. New York: Harper, 1977. 197–202.

Williams, Raymond. *Marxism and Literature*. Oxford: Oxford UP, 1977.

Willis, J. H., Jr. *Leonard and Virginia Woolf as Publishers: The Hogarth Press, 1917–1941*. Charlottesville: UP of Virginia, 1992.

Wilson, Deborah. "Fishing for Woolf's Submerged Lesbian Text." Barrett and Cramer, *Re:Reading* 121–28.

Wilson, Jean Moorcroft. *Virginia Woolf: Life and London: A Biography of Place*. London: Woolf, 1987.

Winston, Janet. "'Something out of Harmony': *To the Lighthouse* and the Subject(s) of Empire." *Woolf Studies Annual* 2 (1996): 39–70.

Winterson, Jeanette. *Art Objects: Essays on Ecstasy and Effrontery*. New York: Vintage, 1995.

Wittig, Monique. "The Straight Mind." *Feminist Issues* 1.1 (1980): 102–10.

Wohl, Robert. *The Generation of 1914*. Cambridge: Harvard UP, 1979.

Woolf, Leonard. *Beginning Again: An Autobiography of the Years 1911–1918*. New York: Harcourt, 1964.

———. *Downhill All the Way: An Autobiography of the Years 1919-1939*. New York: Harcourt, 1967.

Wussow, Helen, ed. *New Essays on Virginia Woolf*. Dallas: Contemporary Research, 1995.

———. *The Nightmare of History: The Fictions of Virginia Woolf and D. H. Lawrence*. London: Associated UP, 1998.

Rev. of *The Years*, by Virginia Woolf. *Time* 12 Apr. 1937: 93–96.

Zimmerman, Bonnie. "What Has Never Been: An Overview of Lesbian Feminist Criticism." *The New Feminist Criticism: Essays on Women, Literature, and Theory*. Ed. Elaine Showalter. New York: Pantheon, 1985. 200–24.

Zwerdling, Alex. *Virginia Woolf and the Real World*. Berkeley: U of California P, 1986.

Audiovisual Materials

Major Authors on CD-ROM: Virginia Woolf: Works. Ed. Mark Hussey. Woodbridge: Primary Source, 1997.

Moments of Being. Read by Peggy Ashcroft. Audiocassette. Norton, 1980. Audio-Forum ECN 135/1135/3. 163 mins.

Mrs. Dalloway: Selections; To the Lighthouse: "Time Passes." Read by Celia Johnson. Audiocassette. 1958. Caedmon, 1977. CDL 51105. 58 mins.

A Room of One's Own. Adapt. and dir. Patrick Garland. Perf. Eileen Atkins. PBS. Insight, 1990. LO420. 55 mins.

Saliers, Emily, and Amy Ray (Indigo Girls). "Virginia Woolf." *Rites of Passage*. Sony, 1992.

Stevenson, James. Cartoon. *New Yorker* 12 Mar. 1979: 39.

To the Lighthouse. Read by Eileen Atkins. Abridged. Audiocassette. Penguin Audiobooks, 1995. PEN 69.

To the Lighthouse. Screenplay by Hugh Stoddart. Dir. Colin Gregg. Perf. Rosemary Harris, Michael Gough, Suzanne Bertish, and Lynsey Baxter. BBC. Magnum, 1983. E1303. 115 mins.

To the Lighthouse; The London Scene. Read by Wanda McCaddon. Special Library Edition. Audiocassette. Books on Tape, 1984. 1787.

Virginia Woolf. Conversation between Julie Rivkin and Christine Froula, with excerpts from *To the Lighthouse* and *A Room of One's Own.* Introduction to Modern English and American Literature. Audiocassette. Annenberg–CPB Project, 1989. 29 mins.

Virginia Woolf. Modern World: Ten Great Writers 8. Screenplay by Kim Evans and Gillian Greenwood. Dir. Kim Evans. Perf. Eileen Atkins, Susan Tracy, John Castle, Robert Daws, and Jenifer Landor. Films, 1988. 58 mins.

Virginia Woolf: A Portrait in Sound. Read by Irene Worth. Audiocassette. Listening Library, 1990. 425 mins. (Available from G. K. Hall Audio, ISBN 0-807-231274.)

Virginia Woolf: Novelist, 1882–1941. Famous Authors. Screenplay by Peter Hort. Dir. Hort. Landmark, 1995. 30 mins.

The War Within: A Portrait of Virginia Woolf. Dir. John Fuegi and Jo Francis. Narr. Ian Redford. Voices by Anna Massey and Juliet Nicolson. Interviews with Angelica Garnett, Quentin Bell, Dadie Rylands, Nigel Nicolson, Hermione Lee, Jane Marcus, Carolyn Heilbrun, Frances Partridge, and others. Flare, 1995. 52 mins. (800 237-3801)

Waves of Pure Lemon. Dir. Joseph Christopher Schaub. Narr. Muriel Heineman. Schaub, 1996. 15 mins. (Write to Schaub at Fort Lewis College, 1000 Rim Dr., Durango, CO 81301-3999.)

Woolf's To the Lighthouse. Lesson 7 of *The Twentieth Century: Modernism and Existentialism.* Taught by Victor Brombert. Superstar Teachers. 2 videocassettes. Teaching, 1993.

INDEX

Modern Language Association of America

Approaches to Teaching World Literature

Joseph Gibaldi, series editor

Achebe's Things Fall Apart. Ed. Bernth Lindfors. 1991.

Arthurian Tradition. Ed. Maureen Fries and Jeanie Watson. 1992.

Atwood's The Handmaid's Tale *and Other Works*. Ed. Sharon R. Wilson, Thomas B. Friedman, and Shannon Hengen. 1996.

Austen's Pride and Prejudice. Ed. Marcia McClintock Folsom. 1993.

Balzac's Old Goriot. Ed. Michal Peled Ginsburg. 2000.

Baudelaire's Flowers of Evil. Ed. Laurence M. Porter. 2000.

Beckett's Waiting for Godot. Ed. June Schlueter and Enoch Brater. 1991.

Beowulf. Ed. Jess B. Bessinger, Jr., and Robert F. Yeager. 1984.

Blake's Songs of Innocence and of Experience. Ed. Robert F. Gleckner and Mark L. Greenberg. 1989.

Boccaccio's Decameron. Ed. James H. McGregor. 2000.

British Women Poets of the Romantic Period. Ed. Stephen C. Behrendt and Harriet Kramer Linkin. 1997.

Brontë's Jane Eyre. Ed. Diane Long Hoeveler and Beth Lau. 1993.

Byron's Poetry. Ed. Frederick W. Shilstone. 1991.

Camus's The Plague. Ed. Steven G. Kellman. 1985.

Cather's My Ántonia. Ed. Susan J. Rosowski. 1989.

Cervantes' Don Quixote. Ed. Richard Bjornson. 1984.

Chaucer's Canterbury Tales. Ed. Joseph Gibaldi. 1980.

Chopin's The Awakening. Ed. Bernard Koloski. 1988.

Coleridge's Poetry and Prose. Ed. Richard E. Matlak. 1991.

Dante's Divine Comedy. Ed. Carole Slade. 1982.

Dickens' David Copperfield. Ed. Richard J. Dunn. 1984.

Dickinson's Poetry. Ed. Robin Riley Fast and Christine Mack Gordon. 1989.

Narrative of the Life of Frederick Douglass. Ed. James C. Hall. 1999.

Eliot's Middlemarch. Ed. Kathleen Blake. 1990.

Eliot's Poetry and Plays. Ed. Jewel Spears Brooker. 1988.

Ellison's Invisible Man. Ed. Susan Resneck Parr and Pancho Savery. 1989.

Faulkner's The Sound and the Fury. Ed. Stephen Hahn and Arthur F. Kinney. 1996.

Flaubert's Madame Bovary. Ed. Laurence M. Porter and Eugene F. Gray. 1995.

García Márquez's One Hundred Years of Solitude. Ed. María Elena de Valdés and Mario J. Valdés. 1990.

Goethe's Faust. Ed. Douglas J. McMillan. 1987.

Hebrew Bible as Literature in Translation. Ed. Barry N. Olshen and Yael S. Feldman. 1989.

Homer's Iliad *and* Odyssey. Ed. Kostas Myrsiades. 1987.

Ibsen's A Doll House. Ed. Yvonne Shafer. 1985.

Works of Samuel Johnson. Ed. David R. Anderson and Gwin J. Kolb. 1993.

Joyce's Ulysses. Ed. Kathleen McCormick and Erwin R. Steinberg. 1993.

Kafka's Short Fiction. Ed. Richard T. Gray. 1995.

Keats's Poetry. Ed. Walter H. Evert and Jack W. Rhodes. 1991.

Kingston's The Woman Warrior. Ed. Shirley Geok-lin Lim. 1991.

Lafayette's The Princess of Clèves. Ed. Faith E. Beasley and Katharine Ann Jensen. 1998.

Lessing's The Golden Notebook. Ed. Carey Kaplan and Ellen Cronan Rose. 1989.

Mann's Death in Venice *and Other Short Fiction*. Ed. Jeffrey B. Berlin. 1992.

Medieval English Drama. Ed. Richard K. Emmerson. 1990.

Melville's Moby-Dick. Ed. Martin Bickman. 1985.

Metaphysical Poets. Ed. Sidney Gottlieb. 1990.

Miller's Death of a Salesman. Ed. Matthew C. Roudané. 1995.

Milton's Paradise Lost. Ed. Galbraith M. Crump. 1986.

Molière's Tartuffe *and Other Plays*. Ed. James F. Gaines and Michael S. Koppisch. 1995.

Momaday's The Way to Rainy Mountain. Ed. Kenneth M. Roemer. 1988.

Montaigne's Essays. Ed. Patrick Henry. 1994.

Novels of Toni Morrison. Ed. Nellie Y. McKay and Kathryn Earle. 1997.

Murasaki Shikibu's The Tale of Genji. Ed. Edward Kamens. 1993.

Pope's Poetry. Ed. Wallace Jackson and R. Paul Yoder. 1993.

Shakespeare's King Lear. Ed. Robert H. Ray. 1986.

Shakespeare's Romeo and Juliet. Ed. Maurice Hunt. 2000.

Shakespeare's The Tempest *and Other Late Romances*. Ed. Maurice Hunt. 1992.

Shelley's Frankenstein. Ed. Stephen C. Behrendt. 1990.

Shelley's Poetry. Ed. Spencer Hall. 1990.

Shorter Elizabethan Poetry. Ed. Patrick Cheney and Anne Lake Prescott. 2000.

Sir Gawain and the Green Knight. Ed. Miriam Youngerman Miller and Jane Chance. 1986.

Spenser's Faerie Queene. Ed. David Lee Miller and Alexander Dunlop. 1994.

Stendhal's The Red and the Black. Ed. Dean de la Motte and Stirling Haig. 1999.

Sterne's Tristram Shandy. Ed. Melvyn New. 1989.

Stowe's Uncle Tom's Cabin. Ed. Elizabeth Ammons and Susan Belasco. 2000.

Swift's Gulliver's Travels. Ed. Edward J. Rielly. 1988.

Thoreau's Walden *and Other Works*. Ed. Richard J. Schneider. 1996.

Voltaire's Candide. Ed. Renée Waldinger. 1987.

Whitman's Leaves of Grass. Ed. Donald D. Kummings. 1990.

Woolf's To the Lighthouse. Ed. Beth Rigel Daugherty and Mary Beth Pringle. 2001.

Wordsworth's Poetry. Ed. Spencer Hall, with Jonathan Ramsey. 1986.

Wright's Native Son. Ed. James A. Miller. 1997.